Nonprint Cataloging
for
Multimedia Collections

Nonprint Cataloging
for
Multimedia Collections

A Guide Based on AACR 2

Second Edition

JoANN V. ROGERS
with
JERRY D. SAYE

1987
LIBRARIES UNLIMITED, INC.
Littleton, Colorado

LIBRARIES UNLIMITED, INC.
P.O. Box 263
Littleton, Colorado 80160-0263

Library of Congress Cataloging-in-Publication Data

Rogers, JoAnn V., 1940-
    Nonprint cataloging for multimedia collections.

    Includes index.
    1. Cataloging of non-book materials--Handbooks,
manuals, etc. 2. Descriptive cataloging--Rules--
Handbooks, manuals, etc. 3. Anglo-American cata-
loguing rules--Handbooks, manuals, etc. I. Saye,
Jerry D. II. Anglo-American cataloguing rules.
III. Title. IV. Series.
Z695.66.R63 1987   025.3'4   87-22589
ISBN 0-87287-523-7

Libraries Unlimited books are bound with Type II nonwoven material that meets
and exceeds National Association of State Textbook Administrators' Type II
nonwoven material specifications Class A through E.

Contents

Preface

When the first edition of *Nonprint Cataloging for Multimedia Collections* was published in 1982, the cataloging code for which it is a guide, the *Anglo-American Cataloguing Rules*, second edition, had only recently been published. The second edition of the rules appeared in 1978, and libraries were in the process of evaluating it for possible adoption in cataloging nonprint materials in their collections. Although most libraries readily and promptly began using the code for print materials, the decision to use it for nonprint was more complex. Most libraries used the first edition of the code for print, whereas many did not use it for nonprint. Bibliographic records for nonprint were seldom integrated with those for print, and nonprint usually received less thorough treatment than did print. With the rules for descriptive cataloging of both print and nonprint presented in one unified code, catalogers began to see impelling reasons for applying the same standard practices to print as to nonprint. Use of the code for nonprint, however, required a rather drastic departure from common practices prior to its publication and exacted a greater commitment from the organization in time involved in the process and the training of nonprint catalogers to achieve a level of expertise in use of the new tool.

The first chapter of the first edition of *Nonprint Cataloging* presented background information intended to provide a context in which to place the new rules. It compared characteristics of the rules and resulting bibliographic records using *AACR 2* with methods for cataloging nonprint used prior to its publication. The author recommended the use of *AACR 2* for most multimedia collections. Now that *AACR 2* has been in use for almost a decade, the vast majority of libraries which acknowledge the importance of adherence to international standards for bibliographic description on which the code is based are using it for both print and nonprint. This discussion is omitted, therefore, from the second edition of *Nonprint Cataloging*. Libraries which are still not using the code may wish to refer to chapter 1 of the first edition.

More catalogers are using *AACR 2* for nonprint, and the need for assistance in its application has increased. A second edition of this guide to using *AACR 2* for nonprint was considered necessary for several reasons. Neither the rules in *AACR 2* nor even the International Standard Bibliographic Description on which it is based is etched in stone. Since the 1978 publication of the code, many changes in the rules have occurred. This edition incorporates the revisions of the code published by the American Library Association in 1982 and 1985. Reference to these, cataloging aids, and other source material can be found in appendix A. Additional Rule Interpretations of the Library of Congress have also been published in the LC *Cataloging Service Bulletin*, a quarterly publication. The first edition of this text included information about the decisions LC had made prior to its publication, and this edition includes those which have been made since.

This edition, as did the first, selectively chooses those rules of *AACR 2* Chapter 1, "General Rules for Description" and rules from the chapters devoted to nonprint formats which are the most important for nonprint formats and which may raise a number of questions for catalogers. This edition includes an explanation of the application of more rules from *AACR 2* and additional examples, both throughout the text and in the form of full records grouped at the end of each of the chapters.

The limited number of examples included here cannot possibly deal with the infinite number of challenges which the cataloger will encounter. Those provided in this book are intended to illustrate points made in the narrative part of the text. They are not prescriptive and should not be used as templates for cataloging items which may have similar characteristics. The user of this book is urged to use the examples in conjunction with the explanation in the text.

Organized according to the mnemonic structure of the code, the text provides information and makes suggestions to aid the cataloger in making judgments and decisions in preparing bibliographic descriptions of nonprint materials. It begins with some background information and a general discussion of bibliographic control of nonprint. Chapter 2 deals with general rules for description. Although the introduction to *AACR 2* instructs the cataloger that a more specific rule in the chapters dealing with nonprint formats takes precedence over a general rule found in the "General Rules for Description," this chapter is important for nonprint as it is the basis for the more specific rules. Seldom can an item be cataloged without referring to this chapter. It also includes the general material designation terms and instructions about the level of description. A general policy decision about level of description used for nonprint is important for any library or information agency. The text provides some insight into why level is important and what factors should be considered when making the policy decision.

Following the structure and order of *AACR 2*, chapter 3 covers cartographic materials, chapter 4 sound recordings, both spoken word and musical, chapter 5 motion pictures and videorecordings, chapter 6 graphics, chapter 7 machine-readable data files or computer files, chapter 8 realia and three-dimensional materials, and chapter 9 microforms. All of these chapters relate to rules for description found in Part I of *AACR 2*. One chapter from Part II, Headings, Uniform Titles, and References, is also discussed in this text. Those rules from *AACR 2* Chapter 21, "Choice of Access Points" which are intended specifically for nonprint, and some rules which are also important for nonprint, are explained in chapter 10, "Access Points for Nonprint Materials." Users access nonprint formats differently from the way they search for print materials. Information in the body of a description as well as much information which the cataloger may put in notes give the cataloger the opportunity to provide access to the record in many ways useful to the searcher. The way in which the rules in this chapter are applied will determine the accessibility of the record and the item to the user. The cataloger will want to provide as many access points as the various types of users of nonprint may need to locate the record with perhaps only one piece of information about an item.

The first edition of this book did not include a chapter on machine-readable data files. Presented in Chapter 9 of *AACR 2*, the original rules were intended for files used with a mainframe computer, few of which were included in multimedia collections. Changes were later made in the rules to accommodate computer files for use with microcomputers. These were published as *AACR 2 Chapter 9: Computer Files, Draft Revision* (Chicago: American Library Association, 1987). The second edition of this book, therefore, includes a chapter (7) to help in the description of this material which is being collected in large amounts by all types of libraries.

Included in appendix A are references to print materials useful in the cataloging process. They include cataloging rules, *AACR 1* and *AACR 2* and their revisions; international standard bibliographic descriptions; Library of Congress catalogs as well as National Library of Medicine catalogs; NICEM catalogs; and some general as well as format-specific cataloging aids.

Dr. Jerry D. Saye of the School of Information and Library Studies at the University of North Carolina at Chapel Hill has collaborated with me in the preparation of the second edition of this book. A nationally recognized authority in the field of cataloging and classification, his expertise and experience in teaching a course which covers cataloging nonprint have proven invaluable. I wish to acknowledge his substantial contribution in adding much new material, in the revision of some sections which were retained, and in the preparation of the manuscript with computer equipment and software which was not available to me. I am gratified that his good opinion of the first edition warranted his acceptance of my invitation to collaborate in the preparation of this second edition. We hope that this guide will prove useful to experienced catalogers, those responsible for policy decisions about the cataloging of nonprint in multimedia collections, and the serious student interested in gaining an understanding of the context of current cataloging practices as well as of the application of the rules.

JoAnn V. Rogers

1
Bibliographic Control of Nonprint

The purpose of adopting and applying a cataloging code for print and nonprint materials in a library or media center is to provide effective bibliographic control of the collection for its users. Since the publication of the *Anglo-American Cataloguing Rules*, second edition, in 1978, most libraries have adopted this standard code for cataloging most of their materials. The major bibliographic utilities require its use for participation in their cooperative cataloging programs and other subsystems such as interlibrary loan. Many libraries which began using *AACR 2* and the cataloging programs of the utilities initially only for print or book material have added nonprint formats to the list of materials which they are cataloging using this standard code. Cataloging nonprint materials using the code and integrating standardized records for print and nonprint materials in a union catalog within a library greatly enhances the access to nonprint materials within that library and across the networks.

Providing bibliographic control of nonprint materials remains a challenge to the library and media professions. Some of the problems associated with cataloging nonprint materials have been solved, and some new ones have surfaced. They can be summarized under the following categories:

- the characteristics of the materials

- the diverse nature of nonprint collections

- the characteristics and needs of users

- cataloging practices and procedures

NONPRINT MEDIA MATERIALS

Cataloging nonprint necessitates an understanding of the physical characteristics of the materials, the way in which the individual formats reveal their physical characteristics, and the way in which these characteristics can be presented to the user of the bibliographic record. The cataloger must understand which elements are important for an adequate description, where and how these elements can be found on the item, and how the rules relate to their presentation in a catalog entry. The rules in *AACR 2* for nonprint formats are grouped into chapters representing format families having basic physical characteristics in common. Most of the rules in the chapters for nonprint description can be applied to most of the individual formats which the rules cover. When a specific individual format which is a part of the family requires specialized treatment, rules which apply only to that individual format within the family are included. Thus not all rules will apply to all members of the family.

Standardization of terminology related to format families, individual formats, and specific physical characteristics of individual formats has long been and continues to be a problem. Librarians, media specialists, information scientists, computer scientists, educators, and the general user may treat nonprint formats from different contexts with different vocabularies. Also, individuals and groups connected with the creation and dissemination of nonprint may speak yet another language. In cataloging nonprint using *AACR 2*, the cataloger must use its vocabulary. This includes format family names used as chapter titles, general material designation terms, specific material designation terms, and the definition of each of these found in the *AACR 2* glossary, appendix D. The use of the general material designation (GMD) is optional in the rules but will be used by most collections, particularly when print and nonprint bibliographic records are integrated in a catalog.

Another vocabulary which the cataloger must master is that of the hardware associated with the use of the nonprint item. The rules often stipulate that in the physical description of an item, if the item can be used with many different pieces of hardware manufactured by different companies, an indication of type of equipment needed is not necessary. If an item can be used uniquely with only one type of equipment, this information must be given. If use is conditional upon a specific rather than a generic piece of equipment, the name of the specific equipment is included in the extent of the item in the physical description. The cataloger, therefore, must be able to distinguish between the two and must know the vocabulary of the hardware manufacturers as well as their standards for physical characteristics of equipment.

It is a challenge for the cataloger of nonprint material to master all of the information about the software and the hardware of all of the nonprint formats. In a small multimedia collection, one cataloger may handle all formats. In larger collections, catalogers may specialize in format families. In many libraries, certain types of formats are housed and cataloged in special collections. This is most often true of film and sound recordings. In these collections specialists who have in-depth knowledge of the format and the terminology associated with the materials and equipment do the cataloging. A good example of this type of situation is that at the Library of Congress, where three divisions which process nonprint contribute records to an online Visual Materials file. The Special Materials Cataloging Division catalogs many different formats housed in its collection. The Prints and Photographs Division and the Motion Picture, Broadcasting and Recorded Sound Division contribute records from their special collections. The later two divisions have developed manuals to supplement the basic *AACR 2*. In an integrated catalog, the objective is to provide the user with needed information using terminology relevant to the materials without deviating from the standards for description represented by the basic rules.

In addition to the specialized terminology needed for different formats in the research collection, the cataloger of nonprint must be aware of developments related to new hardware and nonprint materials. New products spawn a vocabulary of new terms appropriate for bibliographic description. Compact discs for sound recording and software for the microcomputer are examples of two types of formats which, since the publication of *AACR 2* and the first edition of this guide, have begun to be collected in great numbers by libraries. In response to the development of these formats, rules have been revised. In the case of computer software, a new chapter of *AACR 2* was published in March 1987 to accommodate microcomputer software, partly because the terminology of the original chapter dealing with machine-readable data files was intended for use with software used with mainframe computers.

Cataloging rules and the terminology suggested for use in bibliographic description do change in response to developments in the field. By the very nature of the process of evolution of the rules, however, there is a lag between the time when new formats are collected and cataloged and when the rules are revised to provide adequate guidance to the cataloger. If the cataloger understands the intent of the general rules for description, the characteristics of the new format, and the family to which the new format belongs, a useful entry can be constructed. Until revised rules appear, however, standardization of terminology related to new formats remains a problem.

If a library uses a bibliographic utility to catalog nonprint, the cataloger must also deal with the terminology used with the utility's cataloging system and with the documentation related to use of the system for cataloging nonprint.

In addition to understanding and working with the physical and technical characteristics of the various nonprint formats, the cataloger needs to be able to locate and decifer from packaging, labeling, and documentation those pieces of information which are needed for a bibliographic description. Unlike the book publishing industry with a long tradition of fairly standard ways of presenting the bibliographic facts of a monograph, the media industry and the information industry publishing nonprint materials have few guidelines to follow in packaging and labeling. In fact, marketing considerations seem to play as great a role as any other in the way in which much nonprint is prepared for personal and library consumption.

One of the most important factors for the nonprint cataloger is to understand and pay careful attention to the rules identifying acceptable sources of information from the item being cataloged. *AACR 2* Chapter 1, "General Rules for Description," gives general guidelines. Recognizing that information needed for bibliographic description of nonprint formats is presented on the item very differently from information about print, specific rules for determining appropriate sources of information for format families are given in each separate chapter covering nonprint. Quite often pieces of bibliographic information are given in several different forms on, or within, a given item. For example, in order to determine the actual title proper, the cataloger may have to consider the title information given on the item in as many as four or five different forms. The purpose of the rules in each chapter for determining the correct source of information is to give the cataloger guidance in making the right choice among the four or five options so that the item will be described consistently by different catalogers. If the rules for sources of information for each area are not followed carefully, an item cannot be uniquely and accurately identified. Failure to follow these rules can and does result in many different unit records for nonprint items which cannot be identified as duplicate records because they are not exact matches. It is essential that the cataloger choose the right piece of information from the correct source to construct an entry according to the applicable rule.

The great diversity which one sees in nonprint formats collected by libraries is exceeded by an even greater diversity of individuals and groups associated with the creation, manufacture, publication, and distribution of nonprint. Nonprint materials which traditionally have been part of educational collections in school media centers are often referred to as audiovisual materials. In a sense, this term has become synonymous with the educational objectives of the material. As nonprint formats become increasingly accepted as legitimate carriers of information not necessarily designed to instruct, this emphasis on collecting audiovisual educational materials has broadened to include collection of nonprint information for purposes other than instruction. Librarians and media specialists familiar with the traditional audiovisual publishers and producers find that the media industry has broadened. Still helpful in understanding the patterns of publication of many formats is the R. R. Bowker annual publication *Audiovisual Market Place*, which lists organizations, firms, activities, and personnel of publishers and distributors of mostly educational audiovisual materials. The index series of the National Information Center for Educational Media also remains a valuable source of information on media materials and their publication. In spite of its name, the Center gathers and publishes information about nonprint materials not limited only to those which are instructional. It continues to have the most complete listing of published nonprint software. Although these tools provide information about the major nonprint publishers and their products, many publishers and their products are not included in these tools. While these publications can be helpful to the cataloger in understanding patterns of publication and in determining information for the description related to publication and distribution, the cataloger must be aware that information about publishers in these tools may not be accurately applied to the item in hand.

As computer files and other nonprint, nontraditional formats for storage of information are cataloged by the nonprint cataloger, a knowledge of what might be termed the information industry, as well as the audiovisual media industry, will be necessary for the cataloger. This is a world unto itself, characterized by as much diversity as the media industry. Reliable indexes and directories of computer software producers and publishers are just beginning to become available.

Other types of formats also have specialized guides and directories which can yield information about publication in that format. The *Schwann Catalog*, which lists information about sound recordings currently available, is an example of a specialized format guide. In cataloging nonprint formats, these sources can serve as useful reference tools providing information about publication facts.

Both the media industry and the information industry are extremely dynamic, changing name, location, imprints, etc., on a regular basis. In order to have the most accurate information possible, bibliographic tools for media should be acquired for cataloging use on a regular basis. Also, the cataloger should be aware that information in these sources may be out-of-date and inaccurate by the time the publication is available.

NONPRINT MEDIA COLLECTIONS

Two seemingly divergent trends can be identified in libraries and media centers which collect and catalog nonprint materials. Nonprint is becoming more integrated while at the same time it is being given more specialized and more complete bibliographic treatment. The application of the standard bibliographic description of the MARC format with the rules for its use in *AACR 2* has made this practical as well as possible.

Nonprint materials are found in libraries of all types, including public, academic, school, and special libraries. Each of these types of libraries may in turn handle nonprint in several different ways. Some materials may be integrated into a multimedia collection while some specialized types of formats such as sound recording collections or film collections within the same institution may be handled separately in special collections. Special collections with a subject focus may also contain a mixture of print and nonprint and may be handled separately from the general collection. Bibliographic records for those items in a multimedia collection will most likely be integrated into the general catalog. Records for materials in special collections are less likely to be bibliographically integrated.

Special collections present a somewhat different problem. Many institutions, prior to the development of the code, had developed sophisticated specialized methods for providing bibliographic and subject access to special collections of or containing nonprint. A large special collection will require a considerable amount of time and money to conform to the new code. In these libraries, *AACR 2* is less likely to be adopted.

School library media centers contain a large number of instructional nonprint materials. Microcomputer software and optical disc technology are the newest formats the library media specialist must catalog. Schools have been slow to adopt and rigorously apply standard cataloging practices to nonprint. This is true for many reasons. Preservice educational programs for library media specialists emphasize the service role of the library media program, sometimes providing inadequate preparation in the theory and practice of technical processes. Many school media specialists received their education prior to the publication of *AACR 2* and have not had access to continuing education to introduce them to the methods which have become standard in other types of libraries. As budgets for media programs have decreased and costs have risen, fewer and fewer school districts employ a district level supervisor who would be in a position to urge district-wide adoption of the standards and urge administrators to provide money for training and retrospective conversion of records.

Two trends in schools are affecting the quality of cataloging records. One promotes the use of international bibliographic standards and *AACR 2*, and the other often does not. Schools that are part of networks use the international standards and *AACR 2*. Other schools have begun to use microcomputers to handle online catalogs and circulation systems. Too often the decisions about "computerization" in the school library media center are based more on the requirements of a commercial turnkey system rather than on which computer-based system would provide the best cataloging and bibliographic control. Even when commercial programs allow MARC records, these are abbreviated and do not contain the more complete cataloging of the minimum level acceptable to the utilities. Schools which use a microcomputer-based system should realize that there is a trade-off here in terms of the future potential for their participation in networks.

There is one bright prospect for the future, however, which may solve the problem. The work being done in developing standards for the Open Systems Interconnection reference model by the International Standards Organization and in developing the Linked Systems Protocol for retrieval of bibliographic information by Committee D of the National Information Standards Organization will make possible linkages between dissimilar systems. These may include microcomputer systems used in schools and some other types of libraries for cataloging. The actual application of the Linked Systems Protocol (239.50) is only in the experimental stage. And even when linkage is possible and eventually economically feasible, the basic problem of inadequacy of nonstandard bibliographic records which the systems contain will remain. Abbreviated and simplified records may be adequate and easier for students to use for some purposes, but they severely limit the usefulness of the catalog for most other users. Schools have a great deal to gain as well as to contribute to a network of other types of libraries as well as other school libraries. Schools that want to be equal participants in networks need to consider the quality of the bibliographic information which they contribute and share. The best way to assure the level and quality acceptable to most libraries and to networks is to use *AACR 2* and follow the guidelines for the level two cataloging discussed in the next chapter.

Media collections in public libraries are of several different types. Small and medium-sized public libraries often integrate print and nonprint, at least in terms of bibliographic access in one catalog if not in a storage arrangement. These libraries which use *AACR 2* for print are beginning to use it for nonprint also in greater numbers. Many are part of public library systems, some of which participate in cooperative cataloging within the system. And the system itself is likely to use one of the bibliographic utilities for cataloging. Barriers to the adoption of the standard code in small independent public libraries, however, are similar to those which exist in schools. Some have not made the change.

Large public libraries follow somewhat the same pattern, although they are more likely to house large specialized research collections as well as an omnimedia collection for general circulation. General collections are usually cataloged in the same way for print and nonprint. Special collections are less likely to have adopted *AACR 2*, and their bibliographic access is separate and different from that in the general catalog.

Academic libraries represent the largest membership in the programs of bibliographic utilities. This being the case, nonprint is most likely to be cataloged using *AACR 2* in this type of library, including all postsecondary institutions. Two-year community colleges collect nonprint formats for general use in larger numbers than many four-year colleges and universities. The use of the standard code in an integrated catalog has greatly enhanced accessibility of their learning resources. In research institutions, instructional nonprint may be handled in the same way as print while research collections continue to be separate in terms of collection development, technical processing, and circulation.

Special libraries, particularly those which are part of commercial companies, often have developed methods to access material, both print and nonprint, which are different from libraries of other types. A recent report by the Special Libraries Association indicates that they perceive barriers to multitype networking and participation in cataloging programs of the utilities. They are more likely to network among themselves and see little benefit from using a library standard for cataloging. Until recently at least, one utility denied membership to special libraries which would not enter all of their bibliographic records into the shared cataloging system.

USER NEEDS

The purpose of bibliographic description is to accurately and uniquely identify an item in a collection with information which will be of use to the library or media center client or patron. The format for standard description makes certain assumptions about which information is important for unique identification. The standard format in itself is an aid to the user because it provides consistency and predictability related to all searches in a catalog.

If one uses *AACR 2*, one accepts certain assumptions about which bibliographic facts are needed by the user. Although these assumptions were originally based on cataloging of monographs, many accommodations have been made for nonprint. The most obvious one is the provision of extensive rules for the description of the physical format. These rules require that all of the information about the type of equipment needed for the use of the item be given in a standard way. Many of the suggested notes also enable the cataloger to expand the information about physical characteristics.

Other types of accommodation of the rules to nonprint include at least partial standardization of terminology in the general material designation and in describing multipart items. Generic names for categories of materials may not be universally understood by the library patron, but they do lend consistency. In several places in the code, rules are given for cataloging multipart items. Many nonprint materials are or can be considered multipart. Flexibility is allowed in constructing a description for the whole or the parts. When the description in the body of the entry is not sufficient for the user, notes associated with every area are suggested for use. Access points are possible for much of the information about nonprint presented in notes.

Beyond those general assumptions embodied in the code that certain pieces of information, such as the title, publisher, etc., are important for all items, this code asks of the cataloger and the cataloging agency to make certain decisions. These decisions should be based on the needs of the user in a given library or media center and users of the collection through network affiliation. When these two types of user needs coincide, policy decisions are less difficult than when the types of immediate and distant users may differ greatly. As mentioned above, for example, the level of description which might be viewed as sufficient for an elementary school library would not be adequate for users other than elementary school children. In making policy decisions the broadest possible potential audience should be considered.

Unfortunately, not a great deal is known about the patterns of use of the catalog for accessing nonprint specifically, and less is known about what the user of nonprint formats wants to know about the item. It is fortunate when the person who catalogs nonprint has firsthand experience using the media. Cataloging media is not an automatic exercise of rule application. It requires judgment based on an understanding of information and access points relevant to the user.

Many decisions will have to be made on an item-by-item basis, but some general guidelines for a library are useful and ultimately save time. An example for a school library media center or any collection used for mainly educational purposes would be to include information about the intended audience (e.g., grades 4-6). A public library collecting educational materials may purposely omit this information if it were thought that adult learners might avoid materials specified for a particular age level. Again, in schools, librarians know that teachers often search for materials by a certain publisher and would therefore provide an access point for these publishers, although another type of library may restrict the use of these access points. A library of recorded sound used for broadcast purposes might choose to catalog all multipart items according to the separate parts, whereas a public library that circulates multipart items as they are packaged will want to catalog the item as the packaged unit.

All of the factors which allow flexibility in the application of the rules should be considered by a cataloger or cataloging department in view of user needs. Those in public service positions can help in the decision-making process. A policy manual discussing the known or probable characteristics of the user as they relate to rule decisions is a good idea for every cataloging agency. Policy decisions such as the level of description, the number and types of added entries or access points, the inclusion or exclusion of note information about audience, the inclusion and the extent of summary notes for different format families, and the way in which accompanying material will be described can be useful to the cataloger. More important, however, it will aid the user of the catalog when these decisions are consistently applied. Decisions related to optional rules and other rules which may or may not be applied at the discretion of the cataloger should be recorded in a copy of the code itself.

CATALOGING PRACTICES AND PROCEDURES

The first edition of *Nonprint Cataloging for Multimedia Collections* contained in this section a lengthy discussion of cataloging practices prior to *AACR 2*. At the time of its publication, libraries and media centers were in the process of deciding upon the adoption of the new code. Those libraries that had been using the first edition of the *Anglo-American Cataloging Rules* (Chicago: American Library Association, 1967) for both print and nonprint readily adopted *AACR 2*. For reasons mostly associated with the inadequacy of the 1967 rules covering nonprint and the difficulty of their application, few libraries other than those which followed Library of Congress practice in using *AACR 1* used *AACR 1* for nonprint. During the 1970s, revised chapters of *AACR 1* providing better coverage of nonprint were issued. Some libraries did begin using these revised chapters. Revised Chapter 12 of *AACR 1*, covering several format families, was published in 1975, and Revised Chapter 14, covering sound recordings, was published in 1976. Prior to the publication of *AACR 2* in 1978, however, there was no standard code which adequately met the needs of the nonprint cataloger and the multimedia collection.

Catalogers, particularly in school collections, had become accustomed to using one of many different manuals which subscribed to few standard practices and often were lacking in a theoretical framework as a basis for their rules. At that time catalogers were considering the advantages and disadvantages of the new code.

Several studies of the adoption and use of *AACR 2* for cataloging nonprint were done within several years of its publication. In 1981 Nancy Olson discussed cataloging of nonprint in academic libraries in *Cataloging of Audiovisual Materials: A Manual Based on AACR 2* (Mankato, Minn.: Minnesota Scholarly Press). In 1984, JoAnn Rogers published the results of a survey of state school library media supervisors concerning the use of *AACR 2* and multitype library networks in schools within their states. "Progress in Access to Nonprint Materials" (*School Library Media Quarterly* [Winter 1984]: 127-35) reports that school library media specialists were beginning to use the new code. They were also becoming more interested in network participation. Based on a dissertation concerning technical processing of media in public libraries, Sheila Intner, in 1984, published *Access to Media: A Guide to Integrating and Computerizing Catalogs* (New York: Neal-Schuman). These studies demonstrate that *AACR 2* did not receive immediate acceptance by nonprint catalogers but that practices were gradually changing.

One impediment to the widespread availability of catalog records for nonprint based on *AACR 2* was the time lag associated with entry of those records into the shared cataloging databases of the bibliographic utilities. The formats for entry of records for nonprint appeared later than those for print and have in most cases been revised since their original edition. And some utilities were slow to enter records for nonprint into the databases. These problems have been solved, and the proportion of nonprint records available from the utilities is increasing.

Increased interest on the part of the profession in nonprint cataloging is evidenced by the formation of On-line Audiovisual Catalogers, an organization which publishes a quarterly newsletter. In addition, the meetings and programs of the Audiovisual Committee of the Resources and Technical Services Division of the American Library Association have been well attended. These two groups provide a forum for discussion of issues and practices related to the field.

Now, almost ten years after the publication of *AACR 2*, this code which standardizes practices has received widespread acceptance as the best tool available to use for multimedia collections. Many specialized collections are also using it because it is based on the international standard bibliographic description for machine-readable records.

Since original publication of *AACR 2* in 1978, two sets of revisions have been published; these are cited in appendix A. In 1987, the chapter which deals with computer files has been revised. Many of the rule interpretations of the Library of Congress also relate to nonprint formats. Revisions are published by the American Library Association, and rule interpretations are issued in the LC *Cataloging Service Bulletin*.

While librarians and media specialists are becoming more skilled in application of the rules, library users are becoming more accustomed to use of the bibliographic format and the cataloging record. Both manual and online catalogs are moving toward integration of print and nonprint. Increased bibliographic access to nonprint materials has caused an increased demand for these materials. The rather artificial distinction between technical services and public services as traditionally defined library functions is becoming blurred, as well it should be. The purpose of technical processes is to maximize accessibility of materials for the user. The use of *AACR 2* has done a great deal to bring together the user and nonprint.

2
AACR 2 and Nonprint Materials

0.21

The consideration in *AACR 2* of the bibliographic description of library materials reflects a change in emphasis from *AACR 1*, which considered entries and headings first. The expanded detail given to the description of library materials in *AACR 2* also reflects this change in emphasis. The introduction to Part I of *AACR 2* and the Chapter 1, "General Rules for Description," are directed toward the description of all types of materials, both print and nonprint. Selected general rules from Chapter 1 of *AACR 2* which are of particular importance in the description of nonprint materials will be discussed in this chapter.

0.22

The framework on which the rules in this code are based is noted in this section of the introduction. That framework, the General International Standard Bibliographic Description, ISBD(G), provides a standard format within which all materials can be described and is of prime importance to catalogers of nonprint materials. The adoption of this standard reflected the realization by the library profession that modifications were needed to the existing International Standard Bibliographic Description for Monographic Publications, ISBD(M), to allow it to accommodate other types of materials. It also reflected the realization that although specialized standards may be desirable for the description of specific materials formats, including nonprint materials, a general standard should be the basis for their development. The rules in *AACR 2* follow the general international standard in two important aspects: the order of elements and their prescribed punctuation. The outline in figure 2.1 represents a modification of the original ISBD(G) framework and illustrates the organization of the elements of description and their associated punctuation. This outline has been modified slightly to reflect the use and punctuation of the elements in *AACR 2*.

Area	Prescribed Preceding (or Enclosing) Punctuation for Elements		Element

Note: Each area, other than the first area in a paragraph, is preceded by a period, space, dash, space (. –).

1. Title and statement of responsibility area		.1B	Title proper
	[ ]	.1C	General material designation
	=	.1D	Parallel titles
	:	.1E	Other title information
		.1F	Statements of responsibility
	/		[First statement]
	;		[Each subsequent statement]
2. Edition area		.2B	Edition statement
	=	.2B5	[Parallel edition statement]
		.2C	Statement of responsibility relating to the edition
	/		[First statement]
	;		[Each subsequent statement]
	.	.2D	Subsequent edition statement
		.2E	Statements of responsibility relat- to each subsequent edition statement
	/		[First statement]
	;		[Each subsequent statement]
3. Material (or Type of Publication) Specific Details Area			
4. Publications, Distribution, etc. Area		.4C	Place of publication, distribution, etc.
			[First place]
	;		[Each subsequent place]
	:	.4D	Name of publisher, distributor, etc.
	[ ]	.4E	Statement of function of publisher, distributor, etc.
	,	.4F	Date of publication, distribution, etc.
		.4G	Place of manufacture, name of manufacturer, date of manufacture
	(		Place of manufacture
	:		Name of manufacture
	,)		Date of manufacture
5. Physical Description Area		.3B	Extent of item (including specific material designation)
	:	.3C	Other physical details
	;	.3D	Dimensions
	+	.3E	[Each] Accompanying material

Area	Prescribed Preceding (or Enclosing) Punctuation for Elements		Element
6. Series Area		.6B	Title proper of series
Note: A series statement is en-	=	.6C	Parallel title of series
closed by parentheses. When	:	.6D	Other title information of series
there are two or more series		.6E	Statements of responsibility relat-
statements, each is enclosed in			ing to the series
parentheses.	/		[First statement]
	;		[Each subsequent statement]
	,	.6F	ISSN of series
	;	.6G	Numbering within series
	.	.6H	Subseries
	=		[Parallel title of subseries]
	:		[Other title information of subseries]
			[Statements of responsibility relating to the subseries]
	/		[First statement]
	;		[Each subsequent statement]
			[ISSN of subseries]
	;		[Numbering within subseries]
7. Note Area			
Note: The punctuation used for			
date in the note area follows the			
ISBD style for the reporting of			
those data in the other areas of			
description except that a period			
ends each area rather than a			
period, space, dash, space (Rule			
1.7A3)			
8. Standard Number and Terms of		.8B	Standard number
Availability Area	=	.8C	Key title
	:	.8D	Terms of availability
	( )	.8E	Qualification

Adapted from: International Federation of Library Associations. Working Group on the General International Standard Bibliographic Description, *ISBD(G): General International Standard Bibliographic Description: Annotated Text* (London: IFLA International Office for UBC, 1977), pp. 2-3.

Figure 2.1. International Standard Bibliographic Description style used in *AACR 2*

0.23

This section explains the relationship of Chapter 1, "General Rules for Description" in *AACR 2* to the chapters for specific types of materials (Chapters 2-10) and the chapters of "partial generality" (Chapters 11-13). The creation of a chapter of general rules for description which can apply to the cataloging of all material formats is new to American cataloging rules. Rules which are not unique to a particular material format appear only in Chapter 1 and are not repeated in the later material specific chapters. Instead, in these chapters, the cataloger is referred to a general rule in Chapter 1 which addresses that particular situation for all forms of materials. Chapters 11 (microforms), 12 (serials), and 13 (analytics) are called chapters of "partial generality" in the rules because their characteristics are not unique to one form of material, that is, microproductions may be made for books, cartographic materials, music, or art works.

The rule numbering in *AACR 2* is also explained in this section. Whereas previous American cataloging codes used a form of sequential numbering (e.g., 136B1a), which carried no implicit meaning, *AACR 2* has introduced a mnemonic structure to the rule numbering of the chapters for description which facilitates the location of a specific rule within a chapter. It also aids in the location of that same rule in a chapter for another material format. The mnemonic structure of each rule consists of:

Chapter Number.Area Number.Subdivision of the Area

Thus, Rule 8.5B3 is derived from Chapter 8 ("Graphic Materials") and addresses the physical description (Area 5). The mnemonic transference of this number to other chapters means that the same rule for sound recordings would be Rule 6.5B2 (Chapter 6 being the chapter for sound recordings) and for three-dimensional realia and artefacts, 10.5B3. If a rule is not applicable to another chapter, that rule is eliminated, and the number remains unused.

0.24

The procedure that is to be followed in describing nonprint materials is to first apply the rules in the chapter dealing with the type of format to which the item belongs. This means the cataloger must determine the class of material to which the item in hand belongs according to the physical characteristics of the item and use that relevant chapter. Several parts of the rules may be used in recording the bibliographic information. Individual chapters for the description of nonprint materials will refer the cataloger to the general rules in Part I, Chapter 1. To provide a complete description, rules from other chapters in Part I may also have to be used. Although the form of the item in hand is the basis for the description, for some materials, that is, microforms, the original form of the item can be given in a note.

0.27

The use of notes for which rules are given in the individual chapters for the description of nonprint materials is optional unless the note is specifically required by a non-note rule. The greatly expanded coverage in *AACR 2* of the types of notes appropriate for nonprint materials is a great help to the cataloger in determining types of information to be given as notes and in determining the order in which to present this information. The liberal use of notes will increase the probability that needed information will appear in the catalog record.

0.29
This is the first mention in *AACR 2* of another important provision of this code—the three levels of description. This rule allows libraries to use the same level of detail for all types of materials or to use different levels of description for different types of materials. Additional discussion of the levels of description appear in *AACR 2* and in this text under Rule 1.0D.

AACR 2 CHAPTER 1: GENERAL RULES FOR DESCRIPTION

1.0 GENERAL RULES
The general rules given in the first chapter are applicable to all types of materials. When the item in hand necessitates more specific directions, as is usually the case with nonprint materials, the rules in subsequent chapters in Part I, appropriate to the type of format being cataloged, supersede and/or supplement the general rules presented here. It should be remembered that according to Rule 0.24, the description should be based on the rules in the chapter dealing with the class of material to which the item belongs.

1.0A SOURCES OF INFORMATION
This first general rule illustrates the above point. It instructs the cataloger to consult a specific chapter in Part I to determine the source of information for the description. It announces that each chapter will define the chief source of information for the type of item, rank them in order of preference when appropriate, and prescribe sources of information for each area of the description. Information taken from sources other than the prescribed sources should be enclosed in square brackets.

Items which lack suggested sources of information can have the information supplied by the cataloger with an indication in a note of the source of the information or an explanation of the source if it is not clear from the description. A note often found on LC copy reads: "Title from data sheet." This note is supplied by the LC cataloger because the cataloger did not have the item in hand and the title was taken from a source other than the prescribed source for a title, that is, the chief source of information—the item itself.

After a cataloger has identified the type of materials in hand, the next step is to select accurate and appropriate bibliographic information from the item. As anyone who has worked with nonprint materials knows, extracting this information can be a problem. Nonprint materials do not have title pages which give complete and succinct bibliographic information as do books. Information must be assembled from many sources, including parts of the item itself, labels, containers, study guides, etc. Numerous problems arise from the labeling of the item and the ways in which bibliographic information is given by the producers and publishers. Inaccurate, incomplete, and conflicting information can often be found in single part items. These problems are compounded when the nonprint material is in multiple parts.

The rules given in each chapter of *AACR 2* for determining the sources of information for various areas of the description are intended to provide a consistent and unique description for each item cataloged. Following *AACR 2*'s mnemonic numbering system, rules preceded by the chapter's number and followed by .0B1 define and limit the locations which are considered to be the chief sources of information. Rules preceded by the chapter number and followed by .0B2 indicate those sources which can be used to provide descriptive information for each of the areas of description. Because of differences in the materials themselves, the chief source(s) and other sources of information differ greatly from one chapter to another. A careful reading of these instructions is an essential step in constructing a catalog record.

General guidelines are given in Chapter 1, Rule 1.0H and in the 1983 Revisions to *AACR 2* for items with several chief sources of information. For single part items with several chief sources of information, use the first occurring chief source or the one designated as first except:

a.   with different works and no chief source of information pertaining to the whole item, use the multiple chief sources as if only a single source.

b.   with conflicting chief sources bearing different dates of publication, distribution, etc., use the source bearing the most recent date.

c.   when cataloging part of a multipart item singly, choose the chief source according to that information which relates to the single item being cataloged.

Two other parts of the rule deal with variations in language or script. For multipart items, use information found in the chief source for the first part. If there is no first part, choose a source which gives the most information, or, as a last resort, use a unifying element. The various sources used as prescribed sources of information for different elements of the description can be indicated in notes when this information is considered important. If other chapters in Part I are inconsistent with these general directions, the instructions in the chapter related to the item in hand, once again, take precedence.

Problems still exist with the rules for determining the chief source of information. These rules are not always clear, and in some cases, the prescribed chief source of information does not really provide the most accurate information. In the chapter on motion pictures and videorecordings, for example, directions are given to use the film itself and the container if the container is an integral part of the item. A film enclosed in a cartridge with one title or form of the title appearing on the cassette, another form of the title on the beginning title frames, and another appearing on the final frames of the film requires the cataloger to choose one title over another. In this case, the *AACR 2* guidelines do not provide a preferred order for the source of a title when the varying titles all come from the chief source of information. The cataloger's familiarity with the format of the material, the intent of the publisher, and the intent of the rules can help in determining which information to provide in the catalog record. In this instance, the producer's catalog or accompanying material, which may indicate the title chosen by the producer or publisher of the film, could be used to determine which title was actually considered the title of the work by the person(s) responsible for its content.

The importance of viewing or listening to materials and examining all parts of a multipart item cannot be stressed too much. Although *AACR 2* gives guidance in suggesting places to look for information, it cannot reconcile conflicting information given in various sources or help in determining which information is the most appropriate for the description. This is where the cataloger's understanding of the nature of the material and the ways in which media producers and publishers put together and label nonprint materials comes into play. In order to construct a good descriptive catalog entry, a cataloger must possess an understanding of the type of format being described, as well as the ability to locate relevant rules and apply them appropriately.

Catalogers should also be alert to the fact that some sources of cataloging copy contain bibliographic records which are not based on information from the item in hand, but are derived instead from information supplied to the cataloging agency by the producer or other intermediary. This is true of catalog copy from the Library of Congress and from the National Information Center for Educational Media (NICEM). Although often considered by other libraries as an authoritative source of information for bibliographic records for nonprint materials, these agencies may, in fact, produce records which are less accurate and complete than records produced by a cataloger working with the item in hand. Catalogers making use of LC copy must continually remind themselves that most of the cataloging of audiovisual materials done at LC uses information derived from data sheets. These data sheets contain information supplied by the publisher and may be significantly different from the information which actually appears on the item in hand. The data sheets contain information supplied by persons unfamiliar with the rules for extracting bibliographic information. This puts LC catalogers, and eventually catalog users, at a great disadvantage. One can only hope that eventually this situation will change.

Another problem is the large number of nonprint formats as well as the diverse content contained in these formats. Another problem is the availability of reference sources for different formats which will aid in the construction of complete and accurate descriptions. Having the item and a copy of the rules in hand is not enough. When bibliographic information is presented in conflicting forms and when needed information is totally missing for an item, other sources must be consulted in order to complete an entry. The rules allow the use of "any source" for several of the areas. This instruction most often applies to the Physical Description, Notes, Standard Number, and Terms of Availability areas. For help, the cataloger might maintain a file of catalogs from producers, publishers, manufacturers, and distributors. Both retrospective and current catalogs will be helpful.

Other sources which will assist the cataloger are reference materials which contain information concerning groups, individuals, companies, and associations related to the production and publication of nonprint materials. These reference sources should also be retrospective and current.

1.0B ORGANIZATION OF THE DESCRIPTION

The areas into which the descriptive elements are organized are dictated by ISBD(G), and are summarized under Rule 0.22 of this text. The terms used in the

ISBD(G) framework are general and apply to bibliographic information in both print and nonprint formats. Terms such as author, imprint, and collation have been renamed in *AACR 2* to reflect the different types of bibliographic information relevant to all forms of material. The first area of a description, 1, is designated as the Title and Statement of Responsibility Area. The relationships of individuals and groups responsible for nonprint material are considerably different from the relationship of an author to a printed work. The change in terminology for this area reflects this difference. Similarly, imprint has become the Publication, Distribution, etc., area and collation the Physical Description Area. Other areas which have retained their former terminology use terms that are appropriate for print and nonprint materials alike. These include 2, Edition Area; 6, Series Area; and 7, Note Area.

One of the most helpful features of *AACR 2* for catalogers of nonprint materials is the expansion of the treatment given to notes for the different media formats. As we shall see, notes are discussed in each chapter devoted to nonprint materials. For each media format, rules for choosing the information to be included in notes, the order of notes, and suggestions for the formulation of notes (Rule 1.7A3. Form of Notes) provide guidelines for giving important information not included in other parts of the description.

Four other areas of description demonstrate the accommodation of *AACR 2* to the special requirements of nonprint materials. One of these areas is Area 3, Material (or Type of Publication) Special Details, which is used with cartographic materials. Area 5, Physical Description, is one of the most important areas for nonprint materials. It is in this area that many of the characteristics of the physical entity are described in a standardized manner. This area now includes many specific details which can assist the user in determining the type of equipment required to use the item. The coordination of the information given in this area with notes about physical characteristics is a noteworthy improvement of *AACR 2*. The last area of description, the Standard Number and Terms of Availability (Area 8), provides a designated location in the description in which international standard identification numbers (i.e., ISBNs and ISSNs) are recorded. For nonprint and other types of materials, numbers which are not ISBNs or ISSNs are recorded in a note rather than in Area 8. This note rule appears in each chapter under the mnemonic subrule .7B19. Both types of numbers can be important elements of information and should be included in most cases.

1.0C PUNCTUATION

Rules for punctuation are also given in each chapter for description using the mnemonic rule numbering structure of

Chapter number.Area Number.A1

Thus, Rule 8.6A1 would provide punctuation instructions for the formulation of a series statement for graphic materials.

The general punctuation rules require the use of a period, space, dash, space between areas of the description except for the first area and for each note or standard number when they each begin a new paragraph. All marks of prescribed punctuation are preceded by a space and are followed by a space except for the comma and the period. The hyphen, parentheses, and square brackets are not preceded or followed by a space. Additional instructions are given in Rule 1.0C on the use of the mark of omission and the use of double punctuation.

This rule also indicates that a single set of square brackets can be used to enclose adjacent elements in an area providing all the data enclosed within the brackets require their use. The only exception to this is the general material designation (GMD) in Area 1, which must always be enclosed within its own set of square brackets. When adjacent elements in adjacent areas of description require the use of brackets, each area must use a separate set of brackets.

1.0D   LEVELS OF DETAIL IN THE DESCRIPTION

The elements to be included in each of the three levels of description are outlined in Rule 1.0D. It should be noted here that the elements set forth for each level are the minimum requirements. All of the required elements for a specific level must be recorded when they are applicable to the item in hand. In addition, other elements can be added to the chosen level at the discretion of the cataloger.

1.0D1   First Level of Description

Level one includes the title, first statement of responsibility (only if the form or number of the name is different from that of the main entry or if the item is entered under a title main entry), edition statement, material (or type of publication) specific details, first publisher, date of publication, extent of item (the number of physical units and the specific medium designation), notes, and standard number. A model of the elements in a level one description and the accompanying punctuation is given below.

> Title proper / 1st statement of responsibility. − Edition
> statement. − Material or type of publication specific details. − 1st
> publisher, distributor, etc., date of publication, etc.
>> Extent of item.
>
>> Note.
>> Note.
>> Standard number

The cataloger would add to this model an access point for the main entry of the work as well as additional access points for added entries. The following example is a complete minimum level one bibliographic record.

> The Confederacy / produced by Multi-Media Productions. −
> Multi-Media, c1972.
>> 4 filmstrips (ca. 37 fr. each)

Level one omits the general material designation which would provide an early indication of the item's format to the user. This level omits some statements of responsibility which can aid a teacher in determining the authority of the material. It also omits the place of publication, includes only the first named agency responsible for publication, and may omit other publication information which is significant for the unique identification of an item associated with more than one publisher. The physical description does not prescribe inclusion of all of the information needed for a user to be able to determine the type of equipment needed to use the item. It should be stressed again that any or all of these elements can be added selectively to level one or can be explained in notes. If the information is placed in the Note Area, however, it is given in a location on the bibliographic record which many users of the catalog never read. Also, when this information appears in notes it is often given in a much less formal and predictable manner which may be more confusing for the user than its inclusion in a prescribed order and form in other parts of the description.

Each library should set policies concerning levels of description based on the considerations discussed in chapter 1 of this text: the type of collection, the needs of the users, and the probability that cataloging records for materials in the collection will be shared with a bibliographic utility or other type of cooperative venture. Although librarians, especially those dealing with small collections and general users in small public libraries and school libraries, may be attracted by the simplicity of the first level of description, this level very often does not do justice to the nature of most nonprint material. Although level one is less confusing for a reader with low reading ability, it usually omits information which can be helpful for teachers, parents, and librarians working with children and young adults. This level of record also frequently omits information of use to the professional staff of the media center. Upgrading from a minimal level one description requires decisions to be made on an item-by-item basis. Thus, use of level one may result in more work and less uniform catalog records than if the next higher level of description had been used. Another factor to be considered in selecting a level one description is that level two is usually the recommended level of description for the entry of catalog records into the databases of the bibliographic utilities.

One final consideration in deciding whether to use a level one description is the effect it has upon access points provided for an item. Rule 21.29F essentially requires that access points must be related to some element already given in some form in the description. Specifically, it requires that the reason for an added entry should be apparent in the body of the description, that is, Areas 1 through 4. When this is not apparent, a note must be made to justify the access point. In the case of a level one description, the abridged nature of the statement of responsibility area and publication, distribution, etc., area often would result in no added entry being made for names or titles that might serve as useful access points to the material. The only way to alleviate that problem in level one situations would be to either upgrade the level one description or provide a note to justify the access point.

1.0D2 Second Level of Description

The second level of description prescribes most of the elements necessary for the unique identification of nonprint items. This is the level of description used by the Library of Congress for most of its cataloging of nonprint materials. Missing from level one, but included in level two is the general material designation (GMD). The list of these GMDs is found in Rule 1.1C1 and is discussed in more detail in this text under that rule. As previously mentioned, the chief obstacles to uniformity in nonprint material cataloging have been the different categorizations of media materials in cataloging codes and manuals and the different terminology applied to generic and specific categories of nonprint media. *AACR 2* provides a national and international standard for these bibliographic descriptions and should be applied to all collections. Continued variation from these standard terms can only cause continued confusion for the library user.

A model of a level two description and its accompanying punctuation is given below.

Title proper [general material designation] = parallel title : other title information / 1st statement of responsibility ; each subsequent statement of responsibility. — Edition statement / 1st statement of responsibility. — Material or type of publication specific details. — 1st place of publication, distribution, etc. : 1st publisher, distributor, etc., date of publication, etc.

Extent of item : other physical details ; dimensions. — (Title proper of series / statement of responsibility relating to series, ISSN of series ; numbering within the series. Title of subseries, ISSN of subseries ; numbering within subseries)

Notes.
Notes.
Standard Number

When this model is applied to a nonprint item, the minimum level two description is as follows:

The Confederacy [filmstrip] : the lost cause revisited / produced by Multi-Media Productions. — Stanford, CA : Multi-Media, c1972.

4 filmstrips (ca. 37 fr. each) : col. ; 35 mm. — (The Basis of our beliefs)

Several other elements important for the identification of nonprint materials and omitted from level one, are required in level two. The GMD and statements of responsibility, for individuals and groups responsible for the intellectual and artistic content of nonprint material, should be included in the body of the entry, rather than relegated to the notes. The place of publication and other publication information, omitted from level one, is also useful for these materials.

One important difference between level one and level two for nonprint material is the expanded physical description prescribed in level two. Physical details about the item are necessary to inform the user about the nature of the item and help determine the type of equipment needed for its use. Information about dimensions of some nonprint formats is useful in helping to determine the way in which materials can be used. Series information is also frequently necessary for proper identification. This is particularly the case when parts of a set are divided and cataloged separately with the set designated as a series. Both the series title and number are required in the catalog record. Level two is the level of description which most libraries should use to catalog the nonprint materials. This level is also the one that the Library of Congress has chosen for cataloging of most of its nonprint materials.

Perhaps the most important element not included in a level two description is the accompanying materials statement. This element is important because it frequently describes the audio accompaniment to filmstrips, slides, etc. The importance of this element has led the Library of Congress to include it in its augmented level two descriptions. Throughout this text, examples of the cataloging of nonprint materials will also include accompanying materials statements with level two descriptions.

1.0D3   Third Level of Description

Level three states that all elements of information that are required by a rule, including optional elements, must be included in the description. The cataloging record at level three for the *Confederacy Revisited* filmstrip would be as follows:

> The Confederacy [filmstrip] : the lost cause revisited / produced by Multi-Media Productions. — Stanford, CA : Multi-Media, c1972.
> 4 filmstrips (ca. 37 fr. each) : col. ; 35 mm. + 2 sound cassettes (37 min. 40 sec.) + 1 teacher's manual (6 p. ; 22 cm.). — (The Basis of our beliefs)
>
> Sound accompaniment compatible for manual and automatic operation.

It should be noted that the descriptive cataloging for many items at level two will be identical to that formulated under level three. This occurs in those situations where all the elements to be described are already mandatory for minimum level two. Thus, for some materials, one cannot always ascertain the level of description used by an examination of the bibliographic record.

Although some libraries may want to use level three for all their nonprint materials, others may want to use it for only selected types of formats, if at all. Most libraries will probably want to adopt level two and selectively add additional elements which supplement the information prescribed for that level, as in the case of accompanying materials mentioned previously.

1.0H   ITEMS WITH SEVERAL CHIEF SOURCES
OF INFORMATION

This rule, an important one for some nonprint formats, is discussed in detail in this text under 1.0A, Sources of Information. It can be used in choosing one chief source over another as the basis for description for either single part or multipart items when there are no more specific or conflicting guidelines concerning the choice of chief sources in Chapters 3-12 of *AACR 2*. This rule, revised in the *AACR 2 Revisions 1983*, addressed the issue of what to do when an item, consisting of different works, lacks a chief source of information which applied to the entire item. The revision indicated that the multiple chief sources of the individual parts were to be treated as if they were a single chief source of information. As with all other rules in Chapter 1 of *AACR 2*, if a more specific rule is provided in a chapter covering one of the formats being cataloged, the rule in the chapters covering that format takes precedence over a general rule in Chapter 1.

1.1 TITLE AND STATEMENT OF RESPONSIBILITY AREA

The general rules indicate the punctuation to be used in this area and instruct the cataloger to record the information from the chief source of information for the type of material being cataloged. Information derived from other sources must be enclosed in square brackets. Catalog records for nonprint materials frequently use information not derived from the chief source(s); therefore, brackets are often found in this and other areas of the description. Additional rules for choice of source of information are found in the specific descriptive chapters under mnemonic rule numbers .0B1 and .0B2. It should be remembered that the rules in these specific chapters take precedence over the general rules. The rules given in the general chapter can be used in the absence of a more specific rule for a nonprint format.

The title proper is the first element in this area. Included as a part of the title proper would be any alternative title (Rule 1.1B1). If an item lacks title information in the prescribed chief source(s) of information, a title can be supplied from another part of the item or from any source in which a title can be found. If a title from a source other than the chief source(s) or its substitute must be used, the information should appear in square brackets (Rule 1.1B7). If the item lacks a title and no title can be found in the reference sources, the cataloger must supply a title. This title should be a descriptive word or short phrase using terms which indicate, in the most specific way possible, the nature of the material. These supplied titles are most often supplied for locally produced items, naturally occurring objects, and multipart items of three-dimensional material. When the chief source of information is not the source from which the title was derived, the cataloger is instructed to include a note indicating the source of the title (mnemonic rule .7B3).

Many nonprint items are labeled with several different titles. According to Rule 1.1G1, when these items lack a collective title but have one part which predominates, the title of the predominant part serves as the title proper. The titles of the other parts are named in a contents note. More often, however, these items have no one part which predominates. When this occurs, Rule 1.1G2 (as revised in 1983) states that the item should be described either as a unit or each separately with the elements linked by the use of "with" notes. The rule further states that

> if describing the item as a unit, record the titles of the individually titled parts in the order in which they appear in the item if there is no single chief source of information. Separate the titles of the parts by semicolons if the parts are all the same person(s) or emanate from the same body (bodies), even if the titles are linked by a connecting word or phrase. If the individual parts are by different persons or emanate from different bodies, or in case of doubt, follow the title of each part by its parallel titles, other title information, and statements of responsibility, and a full stop followed by two spaces.

Items which lack a collective title but which have more than one item which predominates have the predominant parts and their associated statements of responsibility recorded in the body of the entry. The nonpredominant parts are given in a contents note.

1.1C OPTIONAL ADDITION. GENERAL MATERIAL DESIGNATION

The general material designation (GMD) appears in square brackets following the title proper and alternative title, but before parallel titles and other title information including subtitles. The placement of the GMD for nonprint materials insures an early indication to the catalog user of the document's format. The terms used as GMDs must be chosen from one of the two lists appearing in this rule and must always be given in the singular form.

The GMDs are an expansion of a similar statement used in earlier cataloging rules for nonprint materials. This statement, previously called the medium designator, always was written with the first letter uppercase and enclosed in either brackets or parentheses depending upon the cataloging rules used. Some of the terms used as medium designators differ slightly from those used as GMDs in *AACR 2*; that is, GMD "slide" prior to 1975 was represented by the term "slide set." Medium designators were placed following the last element of the title statement, including subtitles, rather than between the title proper and the other title information as are GMDs. The major difference, however, between medium designators and GMDs is in terms of their coverage and use. Medium designators were used only for nonprint materials and not for print materials. GMDs, on the other hand, exist for all forms of materials including textual materials in normal print form and braille. Additionally, when describing materials for which medium designators existed, the cataloger was mandated to use the designator. GMDs are an "optional addition" and thus can be used at the cataloger's discretion.

AACR 2 lists two sets of GMDs reflecting the development and use of different terms to describe media types on both sides of the Atlantic. The listing which uses more general terms is the British list (List 1), while the more specific listing of media formats is the North American list (List 2). This dual list approach is the result of many compromises during the course of the formulation of the rules. Upon first consideration by North American catalogers, these compromises may not seem to represent the best of all possible worlds.

For nonprint materials the North American GMDs include:

Chapter 1   **General Rules for Description—**
             Items Made Up of Several Types of Material
             kit

Chapter 3   **Cartographic Materials**
             map
             globe

Chapter 6   **Sound Recordings**
             sound recording

Chapter 7   Motion Pictures and Videorecordings
>   motion picture
>   videorecording

Chapter 8   Graphic Materials
>   art original
>   chart
>   filmstrip
>   flash card
>   picture
>   slide
>   technical drawing
>   transparency

Chapter 9   Computer Files
>   computer file
>   *[This chapter title and GMD reflects the 1987 revision of this chapter. Previously, the chapter title was "Machine-Readable Data Files" and the GMD "machine-readable data file".]*

Chapter 10   Three-Dimensional Artefacts and Realia
>   diorama
>   game
>   microscope slide
>   model
>   realia

Chapter 11   Microforms
>   microform

The GMD is chosen to describe the format in hand. For materials originally published in another format or available in another format the original format is not considered in choosing the designation. For example, materials in a microformat which are reproductions of works previously published as textual material are cataloged, according to *AACR 2*, as microforms. It should be noted, however, that there have been some changes to the application of this rule for microforms, which are discussed in detail in chapter 9 of this text. A graphic item appearing on a slide is generally categorized in the GMD as [slide] rather than [art original], [chart], etc. A kinescope recording is categorized as a videorecording rather than as a film.

Rules concerning the use of the term "kit" are discussed in *AACR 2* in a footnote to Rule 1.1C1 and in the next few pages of this text. The definition of the term kit used here is the same as that found in the definition of terms in the glossary to *AACR 2*. All of the terms used as GMDs are defined briefly in this glossary. Reference to each definition can also be found in the index to *AACR 2*, which provides useful access if there is confusion about the term or the category of materials appropriate for the item in hand. It should be noted that some of the definitions in *AACR 2* differ slightly from those in previous codes, which can affect the application of the rules.

The GMD following the title proper and the specific material designation (SMD) which appears as the first element of the physical description should work in concert to characterize the format and the extent of the format. For some materials (e.g., filmstrips), the GMD and the specific material designation are the same, while for other materials the terms differ; that is, videocassettes have the SMD videocassette and the GMD videorecording.

The first step in describing a nonprint item is to determine its GMD category so that a specific descriptive chapter in *AACR 2* can be identified to describe the item. These decisions are based on the glossary definition of GMD terms. The choice of GMDs will become standard if the definitions offered are carefully applied by all libraries.

As mentioned in the *AACR 2* introduction, it may be necessary to consult several chapters in formulating a description. The basic chapter to be consulted is the one which contains rules for the type of material designated in the GMD; for example, for a motion picture the basic chapter would be Chapter 7. This basic chapter for the format will refer the cataloger to rules in Chapter 1. In addition, other chapters may have to be consulted to make the description complete and accurate. These additional chapters may include Chapter 12, if the item is part of a serial publication, and Chapter 2, if the item is accompanied by monographic material which warrants a detailed description. If accompanied by another nonprint format, the basic chapter for that format may also need to be consulted.

The terminology for the GMDs is standardized and must be given in the singular form exactly as listed in Rule 1.1C. Specific material designations to be used with each of the GMDs are listed in the individual chapters covering nonprint materials. Some chapters provide a list of mandatory terms, which limits the terms that may be used as specific material designations. Other chapters provide only a suggested list of specific terms and allow the cataloger to supply a more specific term if none of the terms listed applies to the item in hand. Each cataloging agency will have to make some decisions about the terms which are chosen for specific material designations. One library may choose to apply consistently one of the suggested terms rather than choose others, while another library may want to use a combination of suggested terms and a few additional terms, the application of which is set forth in that library's policy. Another agency may, by choice or by default, leave the choice to the cataloger without internal guidelines. A logical starting point in the formulation of policies to guide the procedures in this and other matters would be the policy decisions made by the Library of Congress and recorded in the Library of Congress *Cataloging Service Bulletin*. See the bibliography of cataloging aids (appendix A) at the end of this text for a reference to this and other cataloging tools.

The following section is an alphabetical list of definitions of terms which are used as GMDs and a discussion of the various specific material designations which can be used in conjunction with each one. The definitions are taken from the *AACR 2* glossary. The specific material designations and the guidelines for the use of these terms as SMDs are not given in this text but appear in *AACR 2* under each chapter number followed by .5B1. In each chapter this is the part (Extent of the Item) of the Physical Description Area in which the specific material designation is addressed.

DEFINITIONS OF TERMS USED AS GMDs

[art original]

The original two- and three-dimensional work of art (other than an art print (q.v.) or a photograph) created by the artist, e.g., a painting, a drawing, or sculpture, as contrasted with a reproduction of it.

The term is applied only to items created by the artist. An art print which is defined as "printed from the plate prepared by the artist" is given the GMD [picture].

In describing a two-dimensional art original, the cataloger is instructed to choose one of the terms listed in Rule 8.5B1. The term, in most cases, will be the same as the GMD, but may be given in the plural. The optional rule which allows for the use of a more specific term can also be applied. The use of a more specific term may be particularly desirable for special libraries or libraries which collect a large number of different types of two-dimensional art works. This would include terms such as "woodcut," "painting," etc. The medium and the base given as other physical details can be used with either the given term or another term applied by the cataloger. Libraries with large collections of art originals and other graphics may also want to consider using the rules compiled by Elisabeth Betz of the Library of Congress's Prints and Photographs Division, published as *Graphic Materials: Rules for Describing Original Items and Historical Collections.* A discussion of these rules is given in chapter 6 of this text.

Some confusion arises in the application of this GMD term to three-dimensional objects such as sculpture, which, because of its three-dimensional physical characteristic, should be described according to the rules in Chapter 10 ("Three-Dimensional Artefacts and Realia") of *AACR 2.* Using Chapter 10, the GMD would still be [art original] and the specific designation would be covered by the provisions of Rule 10.5B1 which allows for the use of several listed terms or a more specific term for the object. An original sculpture could thus be given the specific material designation "sculpture" and then be further described by giving other physical details such as the material of which the object is made (e.g., 1 sculpture : bronze).

[chart]

1. An opaque sheet that exhibits data in graphic or tabular form, e.g., a wall chart. 2. In cartography, a special-purpose map generally designed for the use of navigators (e.g., an aeronautical chart, a nautical chart), although the word is also used to designate other types of special purpose maps, e.g., a celestial chart (i.e., a "star" map).

When used as a GMD, this term in the North American list applies to graphic material. The term "map" is to be used for cartographic materials rather than "chart."

The specific terms suggested in Rule 8.5B1 include "flip chart(s)" or "wall chart(s)," the two most common types. Other types can be described simply as "chart(s)."

[computer file]

Files that are encoded for manipulation by computer.

In 1987, this GMD replaced the original GMD "machine-readable data file." Although no definition was provided in the draft revision of Chapter 9 for the new GMD, the definition given here is derived from a statement in that revision. It should be noted that the earlier definition did not limit the use of this information to just computers, but rather to manipulation of the data by machine. The narrowing of the scope in the revision generally limits the format on which the information can be encoded to either tape or disk. There are four specific material designations which can be used, although new ones can be added. These four SMDs are: computer cartridge, computer cassette, computer disk, and computer reel. Under the earlier rules the scope of the chapter included aperture cards, punched cards, etc. These information carriers could still be covered under the new rules if they are sorted by computer rather than by sorting machines. The limitation of the SMDs in the revision to the ones given above indicates indirectly the change of the focus of this chapter to one of greater orientation towards computer manipulation of data.

[diorama]

A three-dimensional representation of a scene created by placing objects, figures, etc., in front of a two-dimensional painted background.

Although a diorama is used as an exhibit in most cases, it is a very specific term and can be used as both a GMD and as a SMD. The use of this term as a GMD reflects the fact that some GMDs apply to a broad category of materials while others are fairly specific.

[filmstrip]

A length of film containing a succession of images intended for projection one at a time, with or without recorded sound.

Single filmstrips and sets of filmstrips, whether accompanied by sound recorded on disc, tape, or other sound format, fall into this category. Because the visual component of a sound filmstrip combination is generally thought to carry the burden of the intellectual content while the sound is intended to be used to support the visual component, filmstrips accompanied by sound are categorized as graphic materials. See "kit" below for clarification of the use of that term in *AACR 2*.

"Filmslip(s)" and "filmstrip(s)" are two suggested terms which are applicable as specific material designations for these materials. Rule 8.5C4 instructs the cataloger to indicate, as "other physical details," the presence of sound if it is integral, that is, found on the physical item (e.g., a filmstrip with a soundtrack). Most sound filmstrip presentations do not have integral sound, so the sound accompanying the filmstrip(s) is described as accompanying material later in the Physical Description Area.

[flash card]

> A card or other opaque material printed with words, numerals, or pictures and designed for rapid display.

This definition demonstrates that the intended use for media materials often dictates their medium designation. A set of flash cards all containing pictures would be assigned the GMD "flash card" and not the term "picture." The specific term given in Rule 8.5B1 is the same as the GMD in this case, "flash card(s)," but, as with all specific material designations, it can be used in the singular or plural.

[game]

> A set of materials designed for play according to prescribed rules.

A definition as broad as this one allows the cataloger to assign this GMD to many types of nonprint media, some of which might consist of only printed material. The description of print material would be taken from the rules in Chapter 2, "Books, Pamphlets, and Printed Sheets." Games consisting of nonprint material would be described according to the rules in Chapter 10. It should be noted that the definition of a game was changed slightly from that given in *AACR 1* Revised Chapter 12. That definition required that a game must have been designed "for competitive play." This requirement is not present in the current definition.

[globe]

> A model of a celestial body, usually the earth or the celestial sphere, depicted on the surface of a sphere.

The two types of globes are differentiated in the specific designation as either "globe" or "celestial globe" according to Rule 3.5B1.

[kit]

> An item containing two or more categories of material, no one of which is identifiable as the predominant constituent of the item; also designated multimedia kit (q.v.).

Additional information about the use of this GMD is given in *AACR 2* in a note accompanying the list of GMDs in Rule 1.1C1. It explains that two types of formats are assigned this GMD, those in which the "relative predominance" of a part is not clear and those which are laboratory kits. If an item has a predominant component, such as a slide-tape presentation or a sound-filmstrip set, it is assigned the GMD appropriate for the part which carries the weight of the message. These examples would be cataloged as slides and filmstrips respectively in most instances, because the message is contained in the visual component. The sound serves as accompanying material to be used simultaneously with the visual medium. If the two items were to be used separately, they would fall within the definition of "kit" and would be assigned this term as the GMD. Not all multipart items, however, should automatically be assigned this designation. This will be a change for many libraries which have been following non-AACR guidelines which made extensive use of the term "kit" to describe all multipart items, especially sound filmstrips.

It should be noted that the rules for the initial description of kits appear in Chapter 1, "General Rules for Description," under Rule 1.10 Items Made Up of Several Types of Materials. They appear here because kits can contain formats of different types which are addressed in several different chapters. Three options are given for their physical description, and each option results in a different type of specific material designation. The first option, Rule 1.10C2 – method a. (revised), involves giving the extent of each group of items, such as ten activity cards, five rules, five thermometers, etc. The 1985 Revision to this rule makes a statement about the container an option to the rule rather than having this statement as a regular part of the rule. This option provides for the naming of the container followed by its dimensions as prescribed by Rule 1.5D2. This method for the description of a multipart item is adequate only if no further description of the physical characteristics of the components is deemed necessary. Because insufficient information is given to inform the user about the characteristics which make the use of different types of equipment necessary, this method omits information often vital to the successful use of the material. Some of this information could, however, be given as notes.

Method b. instructs the cataloger to give a physical description on separate lines for each item or group of items in the kit. In order to do this, the cataloger must consult each of the chapters containing rules for the types of material being described. Using this method, the specific material designation for each part of each type of format is presented. For example, if a kit contains filmstrips and a film, the specific material designations for the filmstrips would be chosen from the Physical Description Area for filmstrips (Rule 8.5) and from the list of specific material designations in Rule 8.5B1. The film would be described on a separate line with its own specific material designation chosen from the rules for film, Rule 7.5 Physical Description Area and from the list of specific material designations in Rule 7.5B1. Of the three methods, method b. provides the most detailed information about the individual components of the multipart item.

One final method given in this same rule, method c., is generally used for packages with a large number of different types of material. The rule instructs that the general term "various pieces," with or without the total number of pieces, should be used. This method, however, limits the use of the physical description and puts a great burden on the notes if any further physical information about the items in the package is to be a part of the catalog record.

[machine-readable data file]

[Cancelled by the 1987 revision to Chapter 9 and replaced by the GMD "computer file."]

[map]

> A representation, normally to scale and on a flat medium, of a selection of material or abstract features on, or in relation to, the surface of the earth or of another celestial body.

Many of the different types of maps are included in the list of suggested specific material designations. Rule 3.5B1 lists twenty-seven terms from which the choice of specific material designation can be made. This rule also allows for use of a more appropriate term if a specific material designation from one of the other chapters covering nonprint materials is the more logical choice for its description. It might be a better idea, however, to choose a term related to maps rather than one related to graphics for an item which, in the GMD, has been described as a map. If a map is a part of a more general graphic, the GMD [transparency] or [slide] or another GMD related to graphics might be applied to a map.

The rules allow the cataloger to decide which aspect is to be emphasized, the type of graphic in terms of its physical characteristics and use, or the type of a map which may be presented in several types of graphic formats, such as a transparency or slide. The choice of the GMD and specific material designation will determine the rest of the description. The choice should be made on the basis of the type of use to be made of the material and the type of collection for which it is being cataloged. Libraries which have a separate map collection will probably want to use Chapter 3 for these materials while other libraries with omnimedia collections which integrate maps with other types of material may want to describe maps which are specific types of graphics according to the provisions of Chapter 8.

[microform]

> A generic term for any medium, transparent or opaque, bearing microimages.

According to *AACR 2*, all materials in a microformat, either an original publication or a publication originally published in another form and filmed, should be assigned the GMD [microform] and cataloged according to the rules in Chapter 11. See chapter 9 of this text for the Library of Congress "rule interpretation" which changes this approach for microreproductions of previously published works. Specific material designations in Rule 11.5B1 include:

aperture card(s)
microfiche(s) plus cassette if appropriate
microfilm(s) plus cartridge, cassette, or reel, if appropriate
micropaque(s)

Optionally, the prefix "micro" can be dropped from the specific material designation if it is used in the GMD. The Library of Congress will not follow the practice of dropping the prefix, which is also probably the preferable practice for most libraries.

[microscope slide]

> A slide designed for holding a minute object to be viewed through a microscope or by a microprojector.

The reason why this type of slide is included in Chapter 10, rather than Chapter 8, which deals with photographic slides as graphic items, is implied in the definition. The microscope slide contains an object which is in reality three-dimensional. The same term used for the GMD is used for the specific material designation but may be in either the singular or plural form.

[model]

> A three-dimensional representation of a real thing, either of the exact size of the original or to scale.

Only two specific material material designation terms are suggested, "mock-up" or "model." Another term may be chosen, however, if it is more appropriate. Again, additional information about a model can be given in the notes. In the case of models, this information might be included in a summary note.

[motion picture]

> A length of film with or without recorded sound, bearing a sequence of images that create the illusion of movement when projected in rapid succession.

Several terms which cover the various containers for film are given as possible specific material designations in 7.5B1. They are:

film cartridge(s)   film loop(s)
film cassette(s)   film reel(s)

Optionally, the term "film" can be dropped from the specific material designation when it is used in the GMD. However, its retention as the prefix can aid the user in quickly identifying the format of the film and thus probably should be retained. The Library of Congress has indicated that it will not follow the option and will continue to retain the term "film."

[picture]

> A two-dimensional visual representation accessible to the naked eye and generally on an opaque backing.

This term is the most general of the GMDs applied to graphics and will be used for all visuals to which a more specific term does not accurately apply. According to 8.5B1, the specific material designations which can be used with the GMD [picture] include:

art reproduction(s)	poster(s)
photo(s)	radiograph(s)
picture(s)	stereograph(s)
postcard(s)	study print(s)

Two additional terms, "cartridge" and "reel," can be added to the specific material designations "filmstrip" and "stereograph" when appropriate. The cataloger is also allowed to add the trade name or technical specification to the term "stereograph." In all cases, the cataloger should use the most specific term applicable to all of the items in a package. In some instances, a package may contain several types of two-dimensional representations, and the term "picture" may be used as both the GMD and SMD.

[realia]

Actual objects (artefacts, specimens) as opposed to replicas.

Actual objects collected by a library can represent a broad range of different types of materials. Realia is the generic GMD to cover all of these materials. The specific material designations should be chosen by the cataloger and should consist of a one- or two-word designation, descriptive of a single item or individual parts which comprise a group of real items cataloged together according to Rule 10.5B1. An instructional package consisting only of realia and accompanied by printed material can be described as a kit or as realia with accompanying material. Most kits, however, contain other formats in addition to realia. If all of the objects in a multipart package are real objects, the more general term should be used as the specific material designation. A contents note or other type of note can be used to give detail about the parts. The nature of real materials makes it impractical to attempt to record and use controlled terms consistently in the specific material designation.

[slide]

Transparent material on which there is a two-dimensional image, usually held in a mount, and designed for use in a projector or viewer.

Individual slides, sets of slides, and slides accompanied by sound or with integral sound are all assigned the GMD [slide] and are also given the same specific material designation "slide(s)" according to Rule 8.5B1. Microscope slides are not included in this category.

[sound recording]

A recording on which sound vibrations have been registered by mechanical or electrical means so that the sound may be recorded.

Both musical and spoken word sound recordings are assigned this GMD. These recordings are produced in several different formats and both are found in current and archival collections. If the GMD is used, the cataloger may drop the term "sound" from the specific designation. Again, it is probably a better practice not to drop the term. The Library of Congress has indicated in a "rule interpretation" that it intends to use the GMD and the term "sound" in the SMD. The specific designations in Rule 6.5B1 include:

sound cartridge(s)   sound tape reel(s)
sound cassette(s)   sound track film reel(s)
sound disc(s)

The specific material designation "sound disc" can be used for both analog and digital discs. Although the rule does not specifically state that other terms can be used as specific designations, other terms could be used for types of material not covered in the list. An example of this would be wire recordings stored on spools, and piano and organ rolls which could make use of the term "rolls."

[technical drawing]

> A cross section, detail, diagram, elevation, perspective, plan, working plan, etc., made for use in an engineering or other technical context.

This GMD covers architectural renderings and other types of two-dimensional representations. Both the GMD and the SMD use the same term. Architectural models are cataloged as three-dimensional objects using Chapter 10.

[transparency]

> A sheet of transparent material bearing an image and designed for use with an overhead projector or a light box. It may be mounted in a frame.

Materials produced for use with an overhead projector are categorized in this group. Transparencies are assigned the same GMD and SMD. Although other photographic materials may be referred to as transparencies, they are not included here. Transparency masters on opaque material are not included and would use the term "pictures" as the GMD with the optional term "transparency master(s)" used for the specific material designation.

[videorecording]

> A recording on which visual images, usually in motion and accompanied by sound, have been registered; designed for play-back by means of a television set.

Specific types of videorecordings included in the specific designation, according to Rule 7.5B1, include:

videocartridge(s)   videodisc(s)
videocassette(s)   videoreel(s)

Optionally, the cataloger may drop the prefix "video" if it appears in the GMD. As with the term "film" and other similar specific material designations referred to previously, the dropping of the prefix "video" is probably not a good idea. The use of the term in both the GMD and the SMD will help to eliminate confusion on the part of the user of the catalog record.

Rule 7.5B1 suggests a variety of methods for cataloging a work recorded in several different videorecording formats which are owned by a library. One method is to use the term "videorecording" in the specific material designation and subsequently list in a note the various formats in which the item can be found. This is the method used by the Library of Congress. A second method uses the multilevel description found in Chapter 13, while the last method uses a separate description for each item. This latter method, a separate record for each item in the collection, is probably preferable from the user's point of view. With separate records, each item is assigned the appropriate specific material designation in the Physical Description Area. The catalog user will not have to interpret notes about availability in different formats. It is also quite possible that a library may acquire the same work in both film and video formats. Consistency and simplicity are enhanced by separate catalog records rather than multilevel descriptions or the use of notes to explain holdings.

Although this rule states that a more generic specific material designation can be used when an item is available for purchase in several different video formats, this practice is not encouraged. The primary objective of cataloging is to clearly and consistently describe the library's holdings. To accomplish this, each catalog record should be created to uniquely identify an item in the collection and should thus use the most specific material designation possible for the item. Because of incompatibility among videorecording systems, and in some cases film projection systems, information additional to that given in the specific material designation will often have to be given in the notes. Types of systems, but not a specific manufacturer's name unless it is the only one to produce needed equipment, should be given when terms such as "videocassette" or "film cartridge" are used as the specific material designation. In general, the use of the most specific term for the type of format for each item in the specific material designation is recommended. The type of system appropriate for the play of the item should be explained in a note under Rule 7.7B10(f).

1.1D-1.1G ELEMENTS FOLLOWING THE GMD

Rule 1.1D addresses the use of parallel titles—an element not frequently associated with nonprint materials. Rule 1.1E deals with "other title information." Unlike parallel titles, other title information in the form of subtitles is quite common for nonprint material. Rule 1.1E6 allows for the addition of an explanatory word or phrase as other title information. This rule can be very useful in indicating information about part of a work selected for inclusion in a media presentation when a uniform title is not used. This is particularly true for sound recordings.

Complete information about those responsible for nonprint items will increase the usefulness of the catalog records for many users. Previous cataloging rules have been criticized for not including enough information about individuals and bodies having some responsibility for the creation of media materials. The current rules allow for recording of this kind of information in two ways—in a formal statement of responsibility and in statement of responsibility notes.

According to Rule 1.1F1, statements of responsibility from the chief source(s) are recorded when they appear "prominently" in the item. The term "prominently" is defined in the General Introduction, Rule 0.8, as being a formal statement found in one of the prescribed sources of information for Area 1 or Area 2 for the type of material being described. There is a distinction being drawn in this definition which is not clearly stated. Although the prescribed sources of information for a statement of responsibility are the prescribed sources for Area 1, the information for a statement of responsibility can come from a prominent statement in a prescribed source of either Area 1 or Area 2. Thus, statements of responsibility prominently stated on an Area 1 prescribed source are recorded normally. Statements of responsibility prominently stated only in an Area 2 prescribed source can be recorded as statements of responsibility but must be enclosed in square brackets because they are not from the prescribed source of a statement of responsibility. Statements of responsibility which are not recorded prominently on the prescribed sources for either Area 1 or Area 2 can be recorded only in the notes. The cataloger thus must decide which individuals and groups are named prominently and record only those in the statement of responsibility. Other individuals and corporate bodies associated with the authorship, performance, publication, production, etc., of an item can be named in one of several categories of notes. Notes related to responsibility generally are placed in mnemonic rule .7B6. In some chapters, these note rules specify types of associated responsibility such as cast or credits.

The Library of Congress, in a rule interpretation to Rule 1.1F1, states that the objective of this rule is to record only those statements that are considered to have bibliographic significance in terms of the intellectual or artistic content of the item. LC further advises its catalogers that when there is doubt as to whether a statement has bibliographic significance, the presence of the statement on the chief source of information should lead to its inclusion in the statement of responsibility. Likewise, its absence from the chief source of information should lead to its exclusion from this area.

If a statement of responsibility is given, the phrasing found on the item will provide the most accurate indication of the relationship of those responsible for the item. Here again, there frequently is conflicting information in different parts of the nonprint item. If possible, the chief source(s) of information is preferred as the source of information for this area. If the cataloger determines that several groups and individuals should be named in the statement, their order is determined by their order in the chief source (Rule 1.1F6). When this order is not clear, the statements can be given in an order which makes the most sense. If the phrasing on the item does not make clear the relationship of the person or body to the work, the cataloger can add an explanatory word or phrase, in square brackets, to the statement (Rule 1.1F8).

Because of possible differences in interpretation of what constitutes prominent statements of responsibility and differences in the selection of sources of information, the catalog records for some nonprint materials may differ significantly from one cataloging agency to another. Large reference libraries may often want to include more information in the body of the catalog entry than will smaller libraries.

1.2 EDITION AREA

The general rules in this section, in most cases, cover the edition requirements of nonprint materials. Although nonprint materials, in general, are not
published in multiple editions with the regularity of print materials, information
about their edition and history of publication may be of value to users. Nonprint
items are often reissued in a slightly different format, reissued with a title change,
repackaged with or without a change in the title or contents, or otherwise altered
and presented as a new publication. In some instances, parts of a package are first
published as separate works, then subsequently collected into a single unit and
presented as a new work. Statements found on these items seldom reflect these or
other similar conditions. When this type of information is given in a prescribed
source of information, it should be given in the Edition Area. When this
information is derived from other sources, it should be recorded in the Note Area
instead. Specific rules relating to the use of edition statements are found in some
of the chapters dealing with specific nonprint formats. Some materials which are
easily edited, such as motion pictures and videorecordings, may have significant
changes in their content, although no edition statement is given indicating that a
change has occurred. When such a condition is recognized, the cataloger can, as
an option, provide within square brackets a brief statement in the language and
script of the title proper which indicates the new edition status (Rule 7.2B3). The
Library of Congress, however, has indicated that it will not exercise this option.
If the edition statement cannot be stated succinctly, it can be explained in a note
as illustrated by the examples to Rule 7.7B7. This information, when given in a
note, can be derived from any source.

1.3 MATERIAL (OR TYPE OF PUBLICATION) SPECIFIC DETAILS AREA

No general rules for this area are given in Chapter 1. For its use with cartographic materials see Chapter 3 in *AACR 2*. For its use with nonprint materials
which are published as serials, see Chapter 12 in *AACR 2*. For the rule revision
which allows its use for machine-readable data files (Chapter 9 in *AACR 2*) see
chapter 7 in this text.

1.4 PUBLICATION, DISTRIBUTION, ETC., AREA

According to Rule 1.4B1, "all information about the place, name, and date
of all types of publishing, distribution, releasing and issuing activities" is to be
recorded in this area. The nature of the contributions to the artistic and
intellectual content of nonprint material by individuals and groups associated
with their production and the prominent way this information is recorded on the
items may influence catalogers to incorrectly record this information as
statements of responsibility. Area 4 should be used instead to record the names
and designate the functions of those involved in the publication, distribution,
etc., of the item. In general, publishers of nonprint materials are more closely
related to the content of nonprint materials than are publishers of print materials.
The importance of this relationship for nonprint materials is reflected in the ways
in which users seek access to the bibliographic records and, as a result, is also
reflected in the access points created by the cataloger for the bibliographic record.
The names of individuals and groups associated with production of these
materials should be included in the statement of responsibility only when their
function goes beyond that normally associated with a nonprint publisher. In

recording this information the cataloger should provide as much explanation about the relationship of the name to the item as allowed by the rules. Rule 1.4D3 provides for the inclusion of a word or phrase found on the item which explains the relationship. Rule 1.4E allows the "optional addition" of a statement of function for a publisher, distributor, producer, and production company unless the phrase naming the body includes an indication of the function performed or the function is evident from the context in which the name is used. The clarification provided by the application of this option is considered desirable and is recommended for use when appropriate. Publishers, distributors, etc., already named in the title or statement of responsibility must be repeated here. Their names, however, are given a shortened form (Rule 1.4D4).

Information about the manufacture of an item can also be included in Area 4 according to Rule 1.4B2. This rule states that a manufacturer can be named, although Rule 1.4G1 limits its mandatory inclusion to those situations where the name of the publisher is unknown (Rule 1.4G1). The cataloger is given an *option* in Rule 1.4G4 to record this information even when there is a publisher, distributor, etc., if that information is considered important and if the manufacturer is not also the publisher or distributor. When doubt exists as to whether an agency is the publisher or manufacturer, Rule 1.4D7 instructs that the agency should be treated as the publisher. Also, Rule 1.4E1 does not include an "optional addition" of the term "manufacturer" to the statement naming a publisher, distributor, etc. The use of the place, name, and date of manufacture is probably best reserved for catalog records of items containing no publication information, or for items which prominently provide information about manufacture which differs in place, name, and date from the place, name, or date of the publication of the item. The latter situation is covered in the optional Rule 1.4G4.

1.4F DATE OF PUBLICATION, DISTRIBUTION, ETC.

In determining the date of publication of a nonprint item, the cataloger often must choose among dates given on several chief sources of information. For a single part item, refer to the chief source bearing a later date of publication and that part of the item which corresponds to the aspect in which the item is being treated. For example, for a study print with a copyright date for pictorial material and a later copyright date for instructional content, the cataloger would give the later date. That date represents the copyright of the item as a study print rather than just the previously copyrighted graphic. The date associated with the package, as it is designed to be used, is the date of copyright of the package.

Often multipart items bear several dates. The date chosen should be taken from a chief source of information, if possible, or from a unifying element for the package which indicates the copyright date of the publication of all parts as a package (see 1.0H). *AACR 2* chapters dealing with the description of different types of nonprint formats include rules for determining and transcribing dates associated with those specific types of media.

1.5 PHYSICAL DESCRIPTION AREA

For nonprint materials, this area of the description requires the use of many detailed rules which appear later in the individual chapters for description of nonprint materials. Several general rules should be noted, however. Rule 1.5A3 and a related note, Rule 1.7B16, provide an optional opportunity for recording information about additional formats other than the format in hand in which the item is available. The Library of Congress applies the optional use of the note. Most libraries will, however, probably determine that this note is unnecessary for their needs and may actually mislead patrons. Unless the note makes it clear whether it is the library which has the various formats available or only the publisher, the information is of limited usefulness to the user. Information related only to the existence of the other formats from the publisher often can be confusing to the user of the bibliographic record because it does not directly relate to the item actually available in the library.

The rule covering the various ways in which accompanying material can be described, Rule 1.5E, is important for nonprint materials. Four alternative methods are given. Any library may choose to use any one approach or all four in various situations. The four approaches are:

a. to make a separate entry in the catalog for each piece of material.

b. to use multilevel description found in Chapter 13.

c. to record details in a note.

d. to record the name of one or more types of accompanying materials at the end of the physical description for the one type of material being described as the dominant form.

An "optional addition" to method d. allows for the inclusion of further physical description for each type of material. These physical descriptions are based on the rules for physical description found in the appropriate chapter for that type of format.

Method a. is probably not a good idea for many libraries. It provides separate entries for parts of an item intended to be used together, and fails to provide complete information on one record for a multipart item. It also adds many records to the catalog, which is more of a problem for card catalogs than automated ones with large storage capacity. Method b. may be used for some types of nonprint materials but is time-consuming, difficult to consistently apply, and confusing to the user. Method c. places a heavy burden on the notes and omits basic information about the parts of a nonprint item from the physical description. If all of the information necessary for the use of the parts can be worked into the notes, this method can be a good choice.

Method d. allows for the inclusion of some information about all of the parts of a nonprint package and provides for the optional expansion of basic information about the physical description. If the option is applied to any or all parts of a multipart item which consists of basically one type of format accompanied by a number of dependent parts, the description can become quite long and complicated. It should be remembered that this rule does not apply to the description of kits, where individual parts are not dependent. The nature of accompanying material requires that it is to be used with the predominant type of material contained in the package. There are some specific rules in later chapters which more adequately cover certain types of multipart packages, such as games and realia.

1.6 SERIES AREA

A series, as it applies to nonprint materials, is defined by the *AACR 2* glossary as:

1. A group of separate items related to one another by the fact that each item bears, in addition to its own title proper, a collective title applying to the group as a whole. The individual items may or may not be numbered.

(or)

3. A separately numbered sequence of volumes within a series or serial.

Single and multipart nonprint items containing parts in either the same or different formats are frequently published in series. Information about the series should be included in the description according to the rules for Area 6.

Sets of nonprint materials are also frequently published as parts of series. A set of materials is a group of items in the same format, usually with a collective title, published and packaged together. An example of a set would be four filmstrips with accompanying sound which are published and packaged together. These sets may also be part of a series of sets which have a collective series title. When cataloging such a set as a package rather than as individual items, the collective set title and the numbering of that particular set within the series of sets is recorded as series information. When individual nonprint items in a set are cataloged separately, the set title and number and the series title and number are recorded as series and subseries respectively. In most instances, however, a set is cataloged as one multipart item.

An examination of publishers' catalogs will reveal that some publishers list the same item as part of various "pseudo-series," mainly for marketing purposes. These "pseudo-series" often lack collective titles and/or numbering and are referred to as "related materials." This type of publisher's series is often too loosely related to be considered a series and is not described in the Series Area. If it is to be mentioned at all, it can be placed in a note.

1.7 NOTE AREA

Information presented in the Note Area can be taken from any source. This freedom of source of information allows a great deal of useful information about nonprint material to be presented here which could not be given elsewhere in the entry, with or without brackets, because of the restrictions on the sources of information for these areas. Notes relating to the statement of responsibility can present relevant information not found in a "prominent" source of information. Also, information related to the physical characteristics of an item can be expanded and explained in the notes. Specific instructions about the types and order of notes appear in Chapters 2-12 of *AACR 2*. Some general guidelines on the use of notes are given in Rule 1.7A3 and Rule 1.7A4.

Information in a note is given in the same order in which that information is recorded in the other areas of description. Whenever possible, the appropriate ISBD style of punctuation is used between elements, except that a full stop (a period) is used to separate information from different areas of the description rather than a full stop, space, dash, space. When multiple notes are used the order of notes follows the order of the note rules. Several notes can be combined into a single note whenever appropriate.

Quotations from an item can be used to clarify information of interest to the user. These quoted notes must provide the source of the quotation unless the quotation is taken from the chief source of information for that type of material (Rule 1.7A3).

Formal notes, that is, those notes which are preceded by a consistently applied word or phrase, aid the user in understanding the categories of information presented in the notes. Their use should be considered by those who set policy for cataloging practice within a library. Some note rules specify an introductory phrase which should be used to precede certain information, that is, cast and credits notes, contents notes, and "with" notes. The Library of Congress Rule Interpretations indicate numerous situations where LC has prepared formal note wording not called for in *AACR 2*. One type of note where a consistently used phrase can be helpful is the audience note. A library may choose to consistently use the phrase "audience" to precede all types of information given in this note.

1.8 STANDARD NUMBER AND TERMS OF AVAILABILITY AREA

Unlike books, which frequently carry an International Standard Book Number (ISBN), most nonprint materials have not yet been assigned standard numbers. Thus, the use of this area is seldom appropriate for nonprint materials. Some nonprint materials have a number assigned to them by the publisher which is useful in uniquely identifying the item. This number is recorded in the Note Area (Rule 1.7B19 and its equivalents in specific chapters for description) rather than in Area 8. Rule 1,8B3, however, does refer the cataloger to the use of this note. Rule 1.8D provides for the "optional addition" of terms of availability. This can include information about the price of the item, its availability through cooperating agencies or rental, and its price. This area can be used to give information about nonprint items which are not necessarily part of the local collection but which can be obtained by the library for patron use.

1.10 ITEMS MADE UP OF SEVERAL TYPES OF MATERIAL

These rules, which apply to multimedia kits and to items made up of one predominant format accompanied by another, are of prime interest to catalogers of nonprint materials. These rules appear in Chapter 1 because kits can be composed of numerous types of materials which might be covered by several different chapters for description. Rule 1.10B reiterates the directions for treating an item with one predominant component—first describe the predominant part in the physical description, then give the details of the nonpredominant material, either: (1) following the description of the predominant component in the physical description preceded by a space, plus sign, space, or (2) in a note. Information on these approaches is given in greater detail in Rule 1.5E (for placement in the physical description) and Rule 1.7B11 (for placement in the notes).

The rules for multimedia kits with two or more types of materials with no predominant component are in Rule 1.10C. In describing items lacking a collective title, the individual titles can be recorded in sequence with the appropriate GMD recorded after each title proper. Few items, however, will need to be handled in this way. The more common situation involves works which have a collective title. In these situations, the GMD [kit] is recorded following the collective title. In British libraries the GMD "multimedia" would be used rather than the GMD "kit." It should be remembered that when more specific rules are given in other chapters for description in *AACR 2*, as in the case of games and multipart packages of realia in Chapter 10, those rules take precedence over the general directions in Chapter 1.

Rule 1.10C2 identifies three methods which can be used in describing multipart items made up of two or more formats. The first method is the least detailed, allowing for the enumeration of each part. The terms to be used can be derived from the specific material designations in appropriate chapters covering different types of nonprint materials or can be any other terms which apply to the materials in the package. This method is used only if no further details about the physical description of each of the types of nonprint material are desired although notes can always be used to give additional information about the component parts. The 1985 Revision to this rule makes the identification of any associated container and its dimensions an "option." Previously this information was required. This information is recorded under the guidelines given in Rule 1.5D2.

The second method provides a physical description for each part or group of parts on a separate line. This method is used when it is necessary to give additional details about the physical characteristics for each part. This method is best used for nonprint component parts which would necessitate the use of different types of equipment for one or more of the parts. To describe each type of material, rules from the specific chapters for each type of material are used. For example, a kit containing a filmstrip, a videotape, and a sound recording would have three separate physical descriptions. The filmstrip would be recorded according to Chapter 8, the videotape according to Chapter 7, and the sound recording, Chapter 6. The Library of Congress has instructed its catalogers not to use this method.

The third method simply designates the number of items in the package or indicates that the package contains an undetermined number of pieces which are assumed to be heterogeneous. This method is best used when a package contains a large number of pieces or a variety of different types of materials and when the parts do not necessitate use of different types of equipment.

Notes related to the multipart items are given together in one paragraph following the physical description (Rule 1.10C3). Individual notes are separated by a full stop (a period), space, dash, space. This structure is different from that normally used for notes where each note generally appears as a separate paragraph.

If it is desired to catalog the parts of a multipart item separately, the rules in Chapter 13 should be followed. In most cases, however, packages of multimedia material should be cataloged as a unit, and one of the three methods in Rule 1.10C2 should be applied.

3
Description of
Cartographic Materials

3.0 GENERAL RULES

3.0A SCOPE

The description of the types of cartographic materials covered by this rule is fairly complete. The rule includes examples of some of the many types of items which fall within the scope of this chapter. Both two- and three-dimensional representations of the earth, or any other celestial body, can be described under the rules in this chapter. Maps published in formats covered by other chapters in *AACR 2*, such as Chapter 8 (slides and transparencies), Chapter 11 (microforms), etc., can be described using this chapter; however, rules from several chapters can be combined to provide a more complete description of the item. These catalog records would provide a physical description which emphasizes the microform, slide, or transparency nature of the item.

The purpose of this chapter of this text is to provide an approach to the handling of cartographic materials in a general multimedia collection. It is not intended to serve the highly sophisticated cataloging needs of a specialized cartographic collection. Additional works which will assist both the general multimedia cataloger and the cartographic cataloging specialist are listed in appendix A. *Cartographic Materials: A Manual of Interpretation for AACR 2* is the most significant of the works. Produced by an international committee formed in 1979, it illustrates, clarifies, and expands upon the rules given in Chapter 3 of *AACR 2*, indicates the position of the Library of Congress regarding the application of optional rules, and provides guidance in the selection of access points. This work is an essential tool for anyone cataloging a sizable collection of cartographic materials, and it also provides valuable assistance to the cataloger of smaller cartographic collections.

Examples provided at the end of this chapter illustrate the application of the rules as presently stated in *AACR 2*, with modifications to reflect rule revisions and LC Rule Interpretations. These items used as examples represent the types of cartographic materials found in a general multimedia collection rather than those found in an extensive cartographic collection. Generally, a level one description provides the degree of detail required by users of these general collections. Therefore, the examples appearing at the end of this chapter were developed as level one descriptions augmented with selective additional information.

3.0B   SOURCES OF INFORMATION

3.0B1   [Atlases]
The fact that atlases are books results in the use of the same sources of information for atlases as are used for books (Rule 2.0B).

3.0B2   Chief Source of Information
Two different sources can serve as the chief source of information for nonatlas cartographic items — (1) the item(s) themselves or (2) the container. For globes, the cradle and stand also serve as the chief source of information. Preference is given, however, to the item itself as the chief source of information. Although not specifically stated in the rules, the container, case, cradle or stand, used as the chief source of information, should have been issued by the publisher or manufacturer of the cartographic item. For cartographic works in several parts, all the parts should be treated collectively as a single item.

3.0B3   Prescribed Sources of Information
For each area of the description there are different prescribed source(s) from which information can be taken without having to enclose it in square brackets. For the Title and Statement of Responsibility Area, the chief source of information is the prescribed source of information. For some other areas of description (e.g., Edition, Mathematical Data, and Series), the chief source of information is one of several acceptable prescribed sources, although it is the preferred source. In cases where different prescribed sources provide conflicting information, the sources should be given preference based upon the order in which they are given in the rules. Other areas of description (e.g., Physical Description, Notes, Standard Number), allow their information to be derived from any source.

3.0D   LEVELS OF DETAIL IN THE DESCRIPTION
Many multimedia libraries have small collections of maps which, because of the nature of their use and the limited needs of patrons, require less than complete bibliographic description. These libraries may wish to adopt level one for maps and selectively augment this level with additional information according to their needs. Thus, the level of description chosen for maps may differ from that used for other types of nonprint and print publications.

It should be noted that one area not used for most other nonprint materials, Area 3 (Mathematical Data Area), is required for all levels of description when cataloging cartographic materials. While all three levels require the recording of the scale of the item, only levels two and three require the provision of additional information in this area. See Rule 3.3 for more detailed information about the requirements for the Mathematical Data Area.

3.0J   DESCRIPTION OF WHOLE OR PART
When a group of maps has a collective title, three options are available for their description. These options can be used regardless of the level of description employed. The first option involves the description of the collection as a whole. If this option is chosen, the generous use of notes is recommended to describe the parts. The items within the collection can be specifically identified using a contents note. The second option involves the creation of separate catalog

records for each map. If this option is chosen, the collective title of the set is treated as a series title. When a cataloger cannot decide whether to treat a collection of maps collectively or separately, *AACR 2* instructs that the collective option be chosen.

The third option is the use of multilevel description. Although this type of description has not been recommended for other types of nonprint materials, it may be the most useful description for cartographic materials by providing somewhat detailed information about the collection in general and each item within it without having to create separate records for each. In a multilevel description, the cataloging record is structured so that information relating to the collection is given first, followed by that related to the individual parts. Catalogers using a multilevel description for cartographic materials will need to use both Chapters 3 and 13 (Analysis) in *AACR 2*.

There is no requirement that a library exclusively use one method of description for collections. Thus, a cataloger may wish to evaluate all three approaches before selecting the one most appropriate for the item being cataloged.

3.1 TITLE AND STATEMENT OF RESPONSIBILITY AREA

3.1B TITLE PROPER
Title information is recorded as instructed in Rule 1.1B.

3.1B2
If the title proper includes a statement of scale, this information should be recorded as part of the title.

3.1B4
Cartographic materials which lack a title should have a title supplied as instructed by Rule 1.1B7. Unlike other materials, however, the cartographic cataloger is further instructed to include in the supplied title the name of the geographic area covered by the item.

3.1C *OPTIONAL ADDITION.* GENERAL MATERIAL DESIGNATION
Unlike some other types of nonprint materials, no equivalent of a GMD existed under earlier cataloging codes for cartographic materials. The two terms most often used as GMDs are "map" and "globe," although maps published in formats covered by other chapters for description can be assigned a GMD other than "map" or "globe." For cartographic charts, the GMD "map" should be used rather than "chart." Likewise, atlases use the GMD "map" rather than "text." Although the Library of Congress has chosen not to use a GMD for cartographic materials, libraries integrating catalog records for these materials into a catalog with records for other print and nonprint items should seriously consider applying the "optional addition" and use a GMD.

3.1E OTHER TITLE INFORMATION
Other title information is recorded as instructed by Rule 1.1E. Other title information is preceded by a space, colon, space. Note that the position of "other title information" follows the GMD.

3.1F   STATEMENTS OF RESPONSIBILITY

Cartographers and other individuals named on an item who are associated with some facet of responsibility, such as editor, are recorded here. Corporate bodies are generally only recorded here if the intellectual or artistic responsibility is attributed to them and they appear prominently in the chief source of information. If these conditions are not met, or if the nature of the responsibility is considered secondary or is unclear, they should be recorded in the Publication, Distribution, Etc., Area or a note (Rule 3.7B6), if at all.

3.1G   ITEMS WITHOUT A COLLECTIVE TITLE

A collection of cartographic items which lacks a collective title can have a description created for the collection (Rules 3.1G2 and 3.1G3) or for each separately titled part (Rule 3.1G4). Although not specifically mentioned in this section of the rules, items for which a collective title is supplied can be described using a multilevel description.

3.1G2

When describing as a unit a collection which lacks a collective title, the titles of the individual items within the collection are recorded according to the provisions of Rule 1.1G. The resulting description can produce a Title and Statement of Responsibility Area which is potentially very confusing to the user. This confusion occurs because much of the information regarding the relationship of one title statement to another is borne by the punctuation used, that is, a space, color, space indicates that the following title is "other title information" while a space, semicolon, space indicates that the subsequent title statement is the title of another part. This type of description can become additionally confusing when separate statements of responsibility are supplied for the individual parts (Rule 3.1G3).

3.1G4

For most libraries, the creation of a separate description for each individual part of an untitled collection is the preferred alternative to cataloging the collection as a unit. This is particularly true if the individual parts are not related in content. Care should be exercised in constructing the physical description for each part to ensure that the information being provided pertains to that part rather than to the collection as a whole. The separate descriptions should be linked with a "with" note according to the provisions of Rule 3.7B21.

3.2   EDITION AREA

Edition statements are recorded as instructed by Rule 1.2. The "optional addition" to provide an edition statement not found on the item will not be employed by the Library of Congress but will be given instead in a note. This practice by LC is one which should also be seriously considered for adoption by other libraries.

3.3   MATHEMATICAL DATA AREA

Information in this area is recorded in English regardless of the language of the item. Abbreviations are used whenever permissible (appendix B). As was indicated previously, the first element in this area, the scale of the item, must be given even when using only a level one description. The other elements in this area are required for level two and level three descriptions.

3.3B STATEMENT OF SCALE

This element is always present in the description of cartographic material regardless of the level of description used. If the scale has already been given in recording the title, it should be recorded again here. The scale should be expressed as a representative fraction using a 1:x ratio preceded by the word "scale." If the ratio is not derived from the chief source of information, or is calculated from a verbal scale, it should be placed within square brackets. If the scale is calculated from other than a verbal scale, the abbreviation "ca." precedes the scale. For assistance in calculating scales, the aid listed at the end of this chapter can prove most useful. If no scale can be determined, the statement "Scale indeterminable" is given.

The Library of Congress has indicated that it will follow a practice different from that called for by *AACR 2* for those situations where no scale can be determined. LC will not normally determine the scale of an item by the comparison of it to another for which the scale is known. LC will attempt to calculate a scale from bar scales, grids, etc., on the item. When this cannot be done, the statement "Scale not given" will be used. LC will only use the "Scale indeterminable" statement in those few cases in which all the methods to determine scale given in the rule prove unsuccessful.

3.3B2 *Optional Addition*

Additional scale information given by the item can be recorded as an option. Whenever possible, numerals and approved abbreviations should be used in place of words. Scale information can be quoted directly from the item, if this provides greater clarity, or if the information is unusual and cannot be verified by the cataloger. If multiple additional scale statements are recorded, each additional statement should be preceded by a full stop.

The Library of Congress has indicated that it will apply this option. This additional scale information is often more easily understood by the noncartographic specialist than the ratio information which must be recorded, and thus has potential usefulness for many library users regardless of the level of description used.

3.3B4

If a multipart item has two scales, both should be given. The largest of the two scales is recorded first.

3.3B5

If there are three or more scales associated with a multipart item, the statement "Scales vary" should be used rather than the specific scale information.

3.3B7

For items not drawn to scale, the statement "Not drawn to scale" is required.

3.3C STATEMENT OF PROJECTION

The statement of projection is required for descriptions developed using level two or level three. It can, however, be provided optionally in a level one description. This statement, derived from the item, its container or accompanying material, should be recorded using approved abbreviations and numerals whenever possible. The statement is preceded by a space, semicolon, space.

3.3C2 *Optional Addition*

Additional statements related to the projection which appear on the item, its container, or accompanying material can be added at the cataloger's option. These statements frequently deal with meridians and parallels. The Library of Congress applies this option.

3.3D *Optional Addition. Statement of Coordinates and Equinox*

3.3D1 [Coordinates]

This option allows the cataloger to record the coordinates of the item. These coordinates, enclosed within parentheses, are to be expressed in degrees, minutes, and seconds with each coordinate preceded by the appropriate designation, "W," "E," "N," or "S," in that order. Each longitude and latitude should be separated from its counterpart by a dash, while a diagonal slash is used to separate longitude from latitude. The Library of Congress will apply this optional addition whenever the information is readily available.

This rule also provides the cataloger with the option of recording other meridians found on the item in the Note Area (Rule 3.7B8). LC applies this option.

3.4 PUBLICATION, DISTRIBUTION, ETC., AREA

The provisions of Rule 1.4 are followed in recording publication, distribution, etc., information for cartographic materials. Additionally, the Library of Congress exercises the option to Rule 3.4D1 of supplying the name of the distributor in addition to the name of the publisher. LC also applies the option to Rule 3.4E1 of adding to the name of a publisher, distributor, etc., the statement of function, if that information is needed for clarification and is readily available. Rule 3.4G2 allows the optional recording of information about the printer (place, name, date) when that information differs from that of the publisher and is found on the item, its container, or accompanying material. The Library of Congress applies this option.

3.5 PHYSICAL DESCRIPTION AREA

The definitions to terms which may be used as specific material designations (Rule 3.5B1) can be found in most general dictionaries although better explanations are usually found in reference tools for cartographic materials. If these terms do not adequately identify the nature of an item, other terms can be used (e.g., flip chart, wall chart, slide, transparency, microfiche, etc.). *AACR 2* advises the cataloger to prefer a term used as a SMD in another chapter for description (subrule .5B in each chapter). In many cases, these terms will be SMDs from Chapter 8 ("Graphic Materials"). This particular situation will most likely occur when maps, published in another format, are cataloged according to Chapter 3 and assigned the GMD "map."

3.5C   OTHER PHYSICAL DETAILS

The "other physical details" to be recorded for cartographic materials are:

number of maps in an atlas

color

material

mounting

These elements must be given in this order with each element separated by a comma. No indication of the material of which an item has been made should be given unless that information is considered significant (e.g., no mention would be made of the material if a map is printed on paper). Mountings are indicated regardless of whether the mounting was part of the publication process or done subsequently.

3.5D   DIMENSIONS

The rules for recording the dimensions of a cartographic item are quite detailed. For two-dimensional items, both the height and width are given in centimeters, while for globes the diameter is recorded in centimeters (Rule 3.5D4). When measuring a map, the face of the map is the area to be measured. The face of the map is the area enclosed within the "neat lines," that is, the grid or graticule lines which enclose the map. In some situations, the size of the sheet on which the map is printed will also need to be measured, particularly if the dimensions of the map are significantly different from those of the sheet. If a map is intended to be folded, the folded size is given following the size of the item. For relief models (Rule 3.5D3), the cataloger is given the option of recording the depth in addition to the height and width. The Library of Congress applies this option. LC also applies the option of recording the dimensions of a container (Rule 3.5D5).

3.5E   ACCOMPANYING MATERIAL

The name of accompanying material should be recorded and, optionally, its physical description. This option should generally be applied, particularly if equipment is required for the use of the accompanying material. The provisions of Rule 1.5 should be used to record the information about the accompanying material.

3.6   SERIES AREA

Series information for cartographic materials is recorded as instructed in Rule 1.6.

3.7   NOTE AREA

A great deal of information about cartographic items can be given in the Note Area. Notes are particularly useful to a library with a limited cartographic collection where level one descriptions are used.

3.7B1   Nature and Scope of the Item

This type of note can address various aspects of the material, particularly unexpected aspects; however, it should not be used to record information related to the item's physical characteristics. This information would be given in Rule 3.7B10. This note should also not be used if another part of the description provides the information. Nature and scope information is frequently covered by other parts of the description, particularly the title proper, other title information, and the contents note.

Although not specifically stated in the rule, this note is also used to identify the date of situation and the method of relief portrayal. A date of situation note should always be given if that date is different from the publication date of the item. Catalogers not familiar with the terminology used to describe methods of relief portrayal should consult *Cartographic Materials.* It contains excellent definitions of these methods as well as illustrations (following p. 150) of many of them.

Shows flood control dams, reservoirs, and benefitted areas.

Shows land use.

Does not show military positions, movements, or fortifications.

Based on the latest Geological Survey quadrangles.

"Compiled January, 1985."

"Date of photography, May, 1983."

Information as of March, 1963.

Depths shown by contours and soundings.

Relief shown by gradient tints.

Relief shown by land form drawings and spot heights.

3.7B2   Language

The language or languages of the textual parts of an item(s) should be identified unless the other parts of the description make them apparent. This note is particularly important for maps which provide place names in a language different from that of the title. The Library of Congress gives the predominant language first, followed by the other languages in alphabetical order. If there is no predominant language, the languages are given in alphabetical order.

French and German.

Legend in Arabic and French.

Panel title and legend in English, German and Russian.

Place names on maps in English and German.

Publication statement in English and Welsh.

3.7B3   Source of Title Proper
If the title is derived from other than the chief source of information, this source must be given in this note.

Cover title.

Panel title.

Title from portfolio cover.

Title from producer's catalog.

Title from slip case.

**3.7B4   Variations in Title; 3.7B5 Parallel Titles and
Other Title Information**
Title notes are often needed because titles may appear in different forms in various places on cartographic items. These two notes aid in the unique identification of items and facilitate access to them if an access point is to be provided for the titles in the catalog.

Alternate title: Downtown in Atlanta.

Caption title: World atlas & gazetteer.

Cover title: Gregory's street directory, Greater Brisbane.

Panel title: La Porte : 1979 street map.

Title in upper left corner: Ocean Drive, Atlantic City-Cape May.

Title on container: Bett's patent portable globe.

3.7B6   Statements of Responsibility
Although many individuals and groups may be named on cartographic material, relatively few are recorded in the statement of responsibility. Those not chosen to be named in Area 1 can be named in this note, either as individual notes or grouped into one note. The contribution of the individuals or group to the item should be made clear in the note. This note can also be used to record variant names of persons or bodies already named in the statement of responsibility as well as persons or bodies related to previous editions. As was the case with title notes, this note may be used to justify the creation of an access point for them.

At head of title: Kisatchi-Delta Regional Planning and Development District, Inc.

At head of title: UNESCO.

"Base map prepared and copyrighted by the Delaware Department of Transportation."

On each map: Prepared by Michael Baker, III, P.E.

On some maps: "Prepared by the Wyoming Highway Department, Planning and Research Division in cooperation with the U.S. Department of Transportation, Federal Highway Administration, Bureau of Public Roads."

"Sponsored by His Majesty's Government, National Council for Science and Technology Mapping Subcommittee." — P.v.

3.7B7 Edition and History

This note is important because the information it provides is significant to the content of the item. Relatively liberal use should be made of this type of note.

"Base compiled from 1:500,000 U.S.G.S. state base map ..."

Base map title: State of Wisconsin.

Previously published as: General highway maps of New Jersey (by counties), 1947.

Revision of: The 1978 atlas of Greene County, Iowa.

Source: USGS base map and official highway map of South Dakota; watershed information from field technicians.

Supplement to National geographic, Feb. 1983, p. 144A, Vol. 163, no. 2.

3.7B8 Mathematical and Other Cartographic Data

These notes provide data which are supplementary to, or elaborate upon, the information reported in Area 3. For celestial charts, this note is used to record magnitude. When a level one description is used and only the scale has been given in the body of the description, the other information omitted from Area 3 (i.e., projection, coordinates, equinox) can be given in this note if it is deemed important or useful. It should be noted, however, that this information could have been placed in Area 3 when using level one.

National grid.

U.T.M. grid.

Oriented with north to right.

3.7B9 Publication, Distribution, Etc.

Important information not recorded in the Publication, Distribution, Etc., Area can be given here.

"Published by Arnold D. Baldwin."

"Published by the National Museum of Wales in conjunction with Wales Gas."

Stamped on: Vassar Chamber of Commerce.

"April, 1980."

Maps dated from 1921 to 1923.

Date from Map 21N.

Date stamped on.

Maps engraved and printed by the U.S. Geological Survey.

3.7B11   Accompanying Material
Noncartographic accompanying material is given in this note. It can be used to identify materials not mentioned in the Accompanying Materials Statement as well as to expand upon materials already mentioned there. When separate entries or multilevel descriptions are not used to describe collections, this note and the contents note carry the burden of description for the items in the collection.

Accompanied by text (72 p. : maps (some col.) ; 21 cm.)

Course and bearing finder in pocket.

Text in case.

3.7B18   Contents
The contents of an item may be given either completely or partially. The indication of contents should include a statement of scale when this scale is "consistent."
When collections are described as a unit, this note provides information about all its parts. This note should indicate the state of the collection at the time of cataloging as well as the nature of the entire collection. When the collection is complete, the note should be revised to reflect the completed status. Generally, items with a collective title with some unity of contents can adequately be covered by a contents note. However, collections of diverse materials pose complex description problems and are generally better cataloged separately or with multi-level description.

Contents: Town of Bar Harbor — Downtown Bar Harbor.

Contents: The Oxford map of Egypt — The Nile Valley.

Maps on verso: Street map of Watchung and parts of Warren Township — The Summit area and vicinity — Roads from New York to Summit and adjoining areas.

Distance chart and road map of southern Nigeria, 1:1,000,000, on verso.

Advertisements on verso.

Includes distance chart and key to abbreviations.

Includes location map, statistical table, "List of rightholders," and table of "Summary of activity during 1984."

Indexed for points of interest.

3.7B19 Numbers
This note is used to record important numbers on an item which are not ISBNs or ISSNs. The presence of numbers on cartographic items is rather common, but care should be exercised to ensure that the numbers being recorded are not, in fact, numbers associated with a series.

"Best. — Nr. 10 0412." "DA TM 5-241, plate 1."

Publisher's number: 50 2020.

Sheets numbered "Map no. 1-17" thru "Map no. 13."

3.7B21 "With" Notes
When individually titled parts of a collection are given separate descriptions, this note is used to link the parts. The items should be listed in the order of their occurrence on the item. Although not specifically required by the rule, this note traditionally begins with the word "with."

EXAMPLES: Descriptive Cataloging for Cartographic Materials

All of the following examples, except the last, have been developed using augmented level one descriptions. Additional data elements added, when appropriate, to the minimal level one description include "other title information," place of publication, "other physical details," dimensions, and series. The last example is a level two description.

Hammond large type world atlas [map]. — Scales vary. —
Maplewood, N.J. : Hammond, 1979.
1 atlas (144 p.) : 51 col. maps ; 32 cm.

Audience: Visually handicapped.
ISBN 0-8437-1246-5

I. Hammond Incorporated.

Comment	— Atlases are described like book material with the following exceptions:
Area 3	— The scale is indicated.
Area 5	— Some variation appears in the extent of item to indicate the map content of the item.
Added Entry	— This entry is at the discretion of the cataloger.

Tennessee. Division of Geology.
Generalized geologic map of Tennessee [map] / State
of Tennessee, Department of Conservation, Division of
Geology. — Scale ca. 1:2,851,200. — [Nashville,
Tenn.] : The Division, 1970.
1 map : col. ; 22x28 cm.

Scale 1 in. to ca. 45 miles.
Robert E. Hershey, director and state geologist.

I. Hershey, Robert E. II. Title.

Main Entry	— Entry under the corporate body responsible for more than the mere publication of the item. (Rule 21.1B2f).
Area 3	— Scale given for level one. Scale is approximate.
Area 4	— Place of publication is not given on the item.
	— Publisher's name given in shortened form because it was already recorded more fully in the statement of responsibility.
Area 7	— Additional scale. This scale could have been recorded in Area 3.
	— Statement of responsibility note.
Added Entries	— Entry made at the discretion of the cataloger. The value of the entry is heavily dependent upon the nature of the cartographic collection and its users.

Forest, J.
France [map] : agriculture, industrie, et commerce /
par J. Forest. — Scale 1:1,200,000. — Paris : Girard
et Barrere, [196-] (Paris : Imprimeries Michard,
1966)
1 map : col. ; 93x120 cm.

Text in French.
Dépôt légal no. 590.

I. Title.

Main Entry	—Entry under the cartographer named on the item.
Areas 1 & 4	—Language of the description is that of the item.
Area 4	—"Optional addition" of information about the printing.
Area 7	—Notes written by the cataloger are given in the language of the catalog users.
	—Number given on the item.

United States. Forest Service. Eastern Region.
Chequamegon National Forest, Hayward, Washburn,
Glidden Ranger Districts [map] : Wisconsin fourth
principal meridian / U.S. Department of Agriculture,
Forest Service. — Scale 1:126,720 ; Polyconic proj.
1927 North American Datum. — [Washington] : The
Service : U.S.G.P.O. [distributor], 1977.
1 map : col. ; 111x75 cm.

Compiled at the Regional Office, Milwaukee, Wis-
consin, 1966 from U.S. Geological Survey quadrangles.
Updated revisions made from 1976 U.S. Forest
Service township maps and the latest U.S. Geological
Survey quadrangles.
GPO no.: 1978-753 463.

I. Title.

Main Entry	—Entry under the corporate body responsible for more than the mere publication of the item (Rule 21.1B2f).
Area 1	—Other title information explains the title proper.
	—Statement of responsibility as given on the item.
Area 3	—Both scale and projection were taken from item.
Area 4	—Publisher's name given in shortened form because it was already recorded more fully in the statement of responsibility.
	—U.S.G.P.O. is not the publisher, only the distributor. This is indicated in the optional statement of function.

Area 7   — Indication of the base maps for this item.
                    — Number appearing on the item.

Tsopelas, D.
     Road map of Greece [map] / D. Tsopelas, cartog-
rapher. — No. 32. — Scale 1:1,230,000. — Athens :
National Tourist Organization of Greece, 1972.
     1 map : col. ; 62x74 cm. folded to 22x12 cm.

     Relief shown by shading and spot heights.
     Place names in Greek, legend in English.
     Title on outside of folded map: Map of Greece.
     Inset on front: Map of communications in Greece.
     Includes list of N.T.O.G. offices and distance chart.
     On verso: Maps of 6 regions (Scale 1:500,000), "Key
to maps" and location map.

     I. Hellenikos Organismos Tourismou. II. Title.
III. Title: Map of Greece.

Main Entry   — Entry under cartographer prominently named on
                   item.
Area 2   — Although this number might appear to be a series-
                   related number, it actually identifies the edition of
                   the item.
Area 3   — Scale given on the item.
Area 7   — Language notes.
                   — Inset map noted.
                   — Regional maps with different scale included in note
                   only because of their importance to general map.
Added Entries — Entry for the publisher is to provide an access point
                   for an element which could be confused as having
                   some responsibility for the item. *AACR 2* (Rule
                   24.3A) requires that the name be recorded in the
                   language predominantly used on items issued by the
                   body. Multimedia libraries may wish to deviate from
                   this rule and list the corporate body in English as:
                   National Tourist Organization of Greece.
                   — Entry for the variant title.

Arkansas. State Highway and Transportation Department. Division of Planning and Research.
    1979 highway map of Arkansas [map] / prepared
and issued by the Arkansas State Highway and
Transportation Department, Division of Planning
and Research. — Scale 1:316,800. — Little Rock,
Ark. : The Dept., [197-]
    1 map : col. ; 53x58 cm. on sheet 56x81 cm. folded
to 19x14 cm.

    On verso: Enlargements of 16 major cities and
Interstate Highways 30, 40, and 55.
    Indicates public recreation areas and state mileage
chart.

    I. Title.   II. Title: Highway map of Arkansas.

Area 1   —Title, including the date, is recorded as appears on
              the item.
Area 4   —Decade certain, year uncertain.
Area 5   —Size of main map given because it differs significant-
              ly from the sheet size.

United States. Army Topographic Command.
    The world [map] / by the U.S. Army Topographic
Command and the U.S. Naval Oceanographic
Office. — 1st ed. — Scale 1:11,000,000. — [Wash-
ington, D.C.] : Dept. of Defense, [1972]
    9 maps : col. ; 104x134 cm. or smaller.

    Shows average limits of ice.
    "International boundaries information ... as of
May 1972."
    Relief shown by contours, gradient tints, shading,
and spot heights.
    Depth shown by gradient tints.
    Scale: 1 in. = 174 statute miles at the equator ;
Mercator projection.
    Includes sheet index.
    Series 1142.

    I. United States. Naval Oceanographic Office.
    II. Title.

Comment   —A collection of maps with a collective title on the
              item.
Main Entry   —Entry under the first named corporate body respon-
              sible for the item (Rule 21.1B2f).
Area 2   —Edition statement on the item.

Area 3 —Scale given in body of entry with additional scale information placed in the Note Area. The additional scale information could have been recorded in Area 3.

Area 5 —Map sizes vary. Because there were more than two maps, the height of the tallest and the width of the widest were given along with the statement "or smaller."

Area 7 —Projection is recorded as a note because the entry is a level one description. This information could have been recorded in Area 3. If placed there, it would have been recorded as: Scale 1:11,000,000. 1 in. to 174 statute miles at the equator ; Mercator proj.

Added Entries—Tracing made for the second named corporate body responsible for the item.

United States. Bureau of the Census.
 Population distribution, urban and rural in the United States, 1960 [map] / prepared by Geography Division, Bureau of the Census, U.S. Department of Commerce. — Scale 1:5,000,000. — Washington, D.C. : The Bureau ; For sale by the Supt. of Docs., U.S.G.P.O., [1963]
 1 map : col. ; 66x99 cm. — (United States maps / Bureau of the Census ; GE-50, no. 1)

"Albers equal-area projection."
"Subject data from the 1960 Census of Population."
Includes legend.
GPO. no.: 1963 0-706-712.

I. Title. II. Series: United States. Bureau of the Census. United States maps ; GE-50, no. 1.

Area 1 —Statement of responsibility elements recorded in the order in which they appear on the item. No elements were removed from the hierarchical order here as is done for the heading of the corporate body.

Area 4 —Distributor statement recorded using the wording of the item. This is slightly different from the way it was recorded on one of the previous examples.
 —Data derived from the G.P.O. stock number. It appears in brackets because it can be considered only a "probable" date of publication.

Area 6 —Map series. The series required the use of a series statement of responsibility because the relatively common title was not considered sufficient to identify the series.

(Explanation continues on page 60.)

Added Entries — Series entered under the corporate body because of
Rule 21.1B2. Series had to be traced explicitly
because it varied in structure from the series
statement.

Bolton, Herbert Eugene, 1870-1953.
  Struggle for independence [map] = Lucha por la
independencia / Herbert Eugene Bolton, James F.
King ; L. P. Denoyer, geographer ; drawn by
R. B. Blair. — Scale 1:15,800,000. — Chicago :
Denoyer-Geppert, c1942.
  3 maps on 1 sheet ; col. ; 73x103 cm. — (Hispanic
America series = Serie Hispanoamericano ; HA 9)

  Includes legends.
  Contents: Mexico and Central America = México y
Centro América — Hispanic America, 1830 = Hispano
América, 1830 — Hispanic America and Wars of
Independence = Hispanoamérica y las Guerras
de Independencia.

  I. King, James F. II. Denoyer-Geppert Company. III. Title. IV. Title: Lucha por la independencia. V. Series.

Main Entry	— Entry under the person shown to be principally responsible by typography.
Area 1	— Parallel title.
	— GMD precedes parallel title.
Area 4	— No publication date available, copyright date recorded.
Area 5	— Multiple maps on one sheet.
Area 6	— Parallel series title.
Area 7	— Parallel titles for the parts of the item.
Added Entries	— Entries made for the other person stated prominently on the item.
	— Entry could have been made for the geographer and drawer at the discretion of the cataloger.
	— Entry for the publisher. This entry is discretionary.
	— Entry for the parallel title. LC advises this practice.
	— Series entry traced as it appears in the series statement.

Pennsylvania. Topographic and Geologic Survey.
    Geological map of Pennsylvania / Commonwealth
of Pennsylvania, Department of Environmental
Resources, Topographic and Geologic Survey. —
Scale 1:250,000. 1 in. to ca. 4 miles.
(E 73°30' — E 80°30'/N 42°15' — N 40°15') —
[Harrisburg, Pa.] : The Survey, 1960.
    1 map in 2 sections : col. ; 145x201 cm., sections
each 149x105 cm. folded to 28x21 cm. — (Pennsylvania
geological survey ; 4th series)

    Relief shown by gradient tints and shading.
    Compiled and edited by Carlyle Gray, V.C.
Shepps ... [et al.] ; A.E. Van Olden, draftsman.
    "Third printing, 1979."
    "Base compiled from Army Map Service 1:250,000
scale map sheets."
    Issued in envelope.
    Includes 4 cross sections, source of data index map
and legend.

    I. Title. II. Series: Pennsylvania Topographical and
Geologic Survey. Pennsylvania geological survey ; 4th
series)

Comment	— This is a level two description.
Main Entry	— Main entry under corporate body considered responsible for the content of the item (Rule 21.1B2). Corporate body given precedence over the persons associated with the item.
Area 3	— Alternative scale recorded. This could have been given in a note.
	— Coordinates recorded as an "optional addition."
Area 4	— Place of publication not given on the item.
Area 5	— Item consists of two sections which, when placed together, form one map.
	— Size of the complete map, the sections, and the folded sections is recorded.
Area 6	— Map series.
Area 7	— Statement of responsibility note records names which were not treated as prominently on the item as those recorded in the statement of responsibility.
	— "Et al." used because a total of fifteen names was listed, with two more prominently stated than the others.
	— Printing date recorded because it is significantly different from the date of original publication. Printing date could also have been recorded in Area 4.

(Explanation continues on page 62.)

> —Container indicated.
>
> Added Entries—Series traced differently from the way it is recorded in Area 6.
>
> —Added entries could have been made for the two individuals given in the statement of responsibility note.

4

Description of Sound Recordings

6.0 GENERAL RULES

6.0A SCOPE
This chapter covers sound discs, tapes, rolls, and film on which only sound is recorded. It can also be used for various types of archival recordings, including wire recordings, and nonprocessed sound recordings, although some alteration of the elements of the Publication, Distribution, etc., and the Physical Description areas are required. Music videos are covered by Chapter 7 of *AACR 2*. In this chapter of this text, the *AACR 2* requirements for the description of published sound recordings will be emphasized because they are the major type of sound recordings held by most multimedia libraries.

Because of the nature of the material found on sound recordings, several other parts of *AACR 2* must be used when developing a bibliographic record for them. Nonmusical recordings, musical recordings, and recordings which are a combination of the two often can be assigned a uniform title. The revised definition in *AACR 2* for a "uniform title" is:

> The particular title by which a work is to be identified for cataloging purposes.
>
> The particular title used to distinguish the heading for a work from the heading for a different work.
>
> A conventional collective title used to collocate publications of an author, composer, or corporate body containing several works or extracts, etc., from several works, e.g., complete works, several works in a particular literary or musical form.

The basic purpose of a uniform title is to bring together in the catalog all of the varying forms of a work with the elements of the description providing for unique identification of the item. The uniform title aids in access, particularly in cases where the title proper does not give sufficient information for identification, or where the title by which an item is known differs from the title proper. Uniform titles can be used for both musical and nonmusical sound recordings although their use is far more frequent for musical works. *AACR 2* Chapter 25 provides rules for the application and formation of uniform titles.

The decision to apply a uniform title should be based on considerations outlined in Rule 25.1. These considerations are:

- "how well the work is known"

- "how many manifestations [i.e., editions, translations] of the work are involved"

- "whether the main entry is under title"

- "whether the work was originally in another language"

- "the extent to which the catalogue is used for research purposes."

In deciding to use uniform titles, the weight to be given to these considerations must be determined by each library based on the needs of its clientele. Even in a small collection, the use of uniform titles can be an important element in the identification of a work. As the sharing of resources between libraries of different types increases, a consistent policy of application of uniform titles can certainly aid in providing access to recorded sound materials for library patrons with different information needs.

According to Rule 25.2A, the uniform title should be enclosed within square brackets and be placed before the title proper. As an option, if the uniform title is the main entry heading, it can be recorded without brackets. This approach is followed by the Library of Congress. Whenever a uniform title is used as an entry element, an added entry is provided for the title proper only when the uniform title is not a "conventionalized" uniform title. *Sonatas, Symphonies, Concertos, Orchestra works* and *Piano music* are all examples of "conventionalized uniform titles" whereas *Musique de table, Romeo et Juliette* and *Rosenkavalier* are examples of uniform titles which are not "conventionalized."

The great majority of sound recordings to which uniform titles are applied are musical in nature. The formation of uniform titles for these works is covered by the basic uniform title rules for individual and collective titles, Rules 25.1 to 25.12, as well as Rules 25.25 to 25.36, which deal specifically with music.

As previously indicated, the rules in Part I of *AACR 2* do not deal with choice of access points or with the form of headings. Rules for these aspects, including uniform titles and references, headings for both print and nonprint materials, appear in Part II of *AACR 2*. Because of their unique nature, sound recordings are addressed separately from other materials in terms of the choice of their main entry (Rule 21.23). For a more thorough discussion of access points as they pertain to sound recordings, see Chapter 10, "Access Points for Nonprint Material."

Like other chapters for the description of nonprint materials, some of the rules in *AACR 2* Chapter 6 have had Library of Congress rule interpretations issued for them. Unlike other *AACR 2* chapters, however, the rules in Chapter 6 are also affected by other rule decisions made by LC. These "cataloging decisions" are published in the *Music Cataloging Bulletin (MCB)* published by the Music Cataloging Association. Generally, these "cataloging decisions" are not as comprehensive in their scope as are the more widely distributed LC Rule Interpretations, and thus mainly affect those individuals who specialize in the cataloging of music and sound recordings. In this chapter, LC policy expressed as "cataloging decisions" will be indicated as such.

6.0B SOURCES OF INFORMATION

6.0B1 Chief Source of Information
The chief source of information differs among the various types of sound recording formats. In all cases though, information in textual form is preferred over that conveyed in audio form. For all types of sound recordings the label affixed to the item is the chief source of information. Additionally, the following sources are also considered the chief source of information for these sound recording formats:

Sound Recording Type	Chief Source of Information
Open reel-to-reel tape	the reel
Tape cassette	the cassette
Tape cartridge	the cartridge
Sound recording on film	the container

If there are two or more chief sources of information, for example, information on both the label and cassette of a tape cassette, they should be treated as a single chief source of information.

When information is not available from the chief source of information, it can be taken from:

- accompanying material

- a container which is not an integral part of the item

- other sources.

These sources are listed in their order of preference for use.

In the case of multipart items, the labels on the parts should be treated as the chief source of information if they provide a collective title. If these labels do not provide a collective title, any accompanying textual material or a unifying container should be treated as the chief source of information if they provide such a title. In this situation, a note (rule 6.7B3) should be made indicating the source of the title.

In a "cataloging decision" to this rule, LC has stated a policy for sound recordings consisting of two works of one type by the same composer which lack a collective title. For these works, a title on the accompanying material made up of the name of the type of music combined with the serial number and/or the opus number, thematic number or key (e.g., *Symphonies no. 3 in F major, op. 90 and no. 4, op. 98 in E minor*) should be used in place of a collective title for the sound recording.

6.0B2 Prescribed Sources of Information

For each area of the description, there are different prescribed source(s) from which information can be taken without having to enclose it in square brackets. For the Title and Statement of Responsibility Area, the chief source of information serves as the prescribed source of information. For some of the areas (Edition, Publication, Distribution, etc., and Series) the chief source of information and any accompanying material or container are prescribed sources, although the chief source of information remains the preferred source. Other areas of the description (Physical Description, Notes, and Standard Number) allow the information to be derived from any source.

In all but a few cases, information required by the chosen level of description can be taken from any source provided that the information is placed within square brackets. Additionally, catalogers are always free to record information in a note without the need of brackets.

6.1 TITLE AND STATEMENT OF RESPONSIBILITY AREA

6.1B TITLE PROPER

Determining the extent of the title proper for sound recordings can be difficult because of the many elements which can be used to create a title. The identification of the title proper is important, however, because of the placement of the GMD immediately after it, preceding other title information and parallel titles. It is also important because in many online catalogs only the title proper is indexed. If one incorrectly places elements of the title proper in another location or an element that is not a part of the title proper in the title proper location, it can seriously affect the retrievability of the catalog record.

The titles proper of nonmusical sound recordings are transcribed under the provisions of Rule 1.1B. An alternative title and the name of a person whose name is an integral part of the title are considered part of the title proper. Lengthy titles proper can be abridged (Rule 1.1B4).

Information to be recorded as part of the title proper for a musical sound recording is governed by Rule 5.1B1 as revised in 1982. Musical titles can be distinctive titles unrelated to the type of composition or production, or they can be titles descriptive of the type of composition. These latter titles, consisting of a generic term (e.g., "symphony," "quartets," "choral"), are combined with other distinguishing descriptive elements such as medium of performance, key, and numbers associated with the composition. If the title consists of the name of one or more types of compositions in combination with other descriptive elements, all of this information is considered part of the title proper. This is because all of these elements are important to uniquely identify a work.

When the condition mentioned in the paragraph above, that is, the presence of the name of a type of composition, does not exist, the distinguishing elements should be recorded as other title information. If there is doubt about whether the required condition has been met, the distinguishing elements should be treated as part of the title proper.

Some musical works are known by both a formal title and also by a popular title (e.g., Schubert's Symphony no. 8 in B, D. 759 is also known as the "Unfinished" Symphony). Although no rule indicates how to deal with these popular titles, catalog records from the Library of Congress indicate that it treats the popular title as "other title information" if it is given as a second title on the chief source of information.

The Library of Congress has provided further instruction to its catalogers when dealing with serial numbers which appear in conjunction with a title. These numbers, if they are not preceded by "no." or its equivalent (e.g., Dance service II), are considered by LC to be part of the title proper.

Often, some or all of the information in the title proper will be used in the uniform title. The difference between these two titles is usually in the order of the elements, a difference which affects filing location or indexing. While the uniform title uniquely identifies a composition from other compositions, the title proper helps to uniquely identify the specific item being cataloged. Many libraries consider the use of both types of titles to be necessary in order to adequately describe a work and retrieve its catalog record.

According to Rule 1.1B1, the title proper should be recorded from the prescribed source of information exactly as it appears in terms of its wording, order, and spelling. Punctuation and capitalization of the title on the item can be changed by the cataloger but do not have to be. These changes are often necessary and desirable, however, because context and meaning can be portrayed in the layout of the item in other than a linear fashion, making the use of punctuation often unnecessary. On the catalog record, however, the linear order restriction makes the use of additional punctuation often mandatory in order to convey the proper meaning. In terms of changing capitalization, the type used to record the title on the item (e.g., all letters on all words capitalized) may not be appropriate to the "sentence-like" style used on a catalog record.

Whenever a cataloger must devise a title for a musical sound recording (Rule 6.1B2), all of the elements prescribed for the uniform title of the work should be used to create the supplied title. These title elements should be recorded in the order in which they are used for the uniform title. This devised title must be recorded within square brackets. The cataloger must also indicate the source of the title in a note (Rule 6.7B3).

Don Juan ballettmusik

Sonate pour violon et piano en la majeur

L'elistir d'amore-highlights

Sinfonias op. 6, 8, 9

Also sprach Karl Farkas

Music for solo flute

Quartet in G minor for piano and strings, K. 478

The six viola quintets

Concerto for violin and orchestra in B minor, op. 61

[Germelshausen]
  [Title from narration.]

6.1C OPTIONAL ADDITION. GENERAL MATERIAL DESIGNATION

The general material designation follows the title proper. For all types of sound recordings the GMD "sound recording" is used. Parallel titles, "other title information," and their associated punctuation follow the GMD.

Particular care needs to be exercised in the placement of GMDs for sound recordings. Their location is determined by whether the sound recording consists of a single work, multiple works by the same composer, or multiple works by different composers. Rule 1.1C2 provides specific instructions for these situations. The constructs which result from the application of this rule are as follows:

> Title proper [GMD] / statement of responsibility.
> *[One work.]*

> First title proper ; Second title proper [GMD] / statement of responsibility.
> *[Separate works by the same individual.]*

> First title proper / statement of responsibility for the first work.
> Second title proper / statement of responsibility for the second work [GMD].
> *[Separate works each by different individuals.]*

Rule 25.5E provides catalogers with the option of using a GMD in the uniform title. When this is done, the GMD begins with an uppercase letter and is enclosed in the same set of brackets used for the uniform title. The Library of Congress, however, does not follow this option. For most multimedia libraries, it would probably be best to follow LC's decision for reasons of consistency. Libraries with extensive holdings of printed music and sound recording may, however, wish to deviate from LC's practice in order to provide a differentiation in the uniform title between a score and a recording of a work.

6.1D PARALLEL TITLES

Musical sound recordings are frequently published with titles in several languages, usually with the title proper given in both the language of the market in which the publisher expects the largest sales and the language of the original composition. While a uniform title is formulated using the language of the composer's original title, or optionally, a better known title in another language (Rule 25.27A), the title proper is usually the first title or most prominent title given on the chief source of information. The remaining titles in other languages, i.e., parallel titles, are recorded as instructed in Rule 1.1D. For a level two description, only the first parallel title is recorded as well as a subsequent parallel title in English. Rule 1.1D should be consulted for specific instructions when the title proper appears in a nonroman script.

> La fille du regiment [sound recording] = The daughter of the regiment

> Les amants turcs [sound recording] = I traci amanti

> Highlights from Le nozze di Figaro [sound recording] = The marriage of Figaro

6.1E OTHER TITLE INFORMATION

Both musical and nonmusical sound recordings often have other title information which augments the title proper, usually with a descriptive phrase. This other title information should be recorded according to the provisions of Rule 1.1E. Lengthy other title information can be abridged (Rule 1.1E3) or given in a note (Rule 6.7B11). In addition, a word or words explaining the title proper can be added in square brackets as other title information according to Rule 1.1E6. These words should be in the language of the title proper. Information of this nature is best recorded, however, in a summary or contents note:

The starlight express [sound recording] : incidental music, op. 78

Social orchestra [sound recording] : a collection of popular melodies published in 1854

Developments in civil procedure, 1979 [sound recording] : a one-hour discussion

Zarzuela [sound recording] : Jose Carreras sings Spanish arias

Die Walküre : ride of the Valkyries ; Tristan und Isolde : prelude to Act I ; Götterdämmerung : Siegfried's funeral music ; Siegfried : forest murmers [sound recording]

6.1F STATEMENTS OF RESPONSIBILITY

The names of persons or corporate bodies responsible for the intellectual or musical content are recorded here. Excluded from the statement of responsibility are persons or corporate bodies responsible only for the performance or production of the work. Performers are only mentioned here when their contribution extends beyond mere "performance, execution, or interpretation." This can include unique performances of contemporary music where the performance constitutes the event being recorded. In its instructions to its catalogers, LC instructs that only the "most obvious cases" of contributions extending beyond performance should be included in the statement of responsibility. Performers, because they are important in the identification of a work and its retrieval, should be given in a note (Rule 6.7B6). According to Rule 6.1F3, a word or phrase explaining the nature of the responsibility of persons or groups named in the statement of responsibility can be added in square brackets. In a MCB announced "cataloging decision," LC indicated that it has instructed its catalogers to add such a phrase to the names of performers which can appear in the statement of responsibility when other parts of the description (e.g., a statement of responsibility notes or the contents note, etc.) do not show that their contribution is one of performance.

Contours for orchestra [sound recording] / Hale Smith. —

Annie [sound recording] : a new Broadway musical / lyrics by Martin Charnin ; music by Charles Strouse ; book by Thomas Meehan. —

Diverse ayres on sundrie notions, (S. 99 44/100) [sound recording] : for bargain counter tenor and keyboard / P.D.Q. Bach ; cunningly transcribed by Peter Schickele. —

Creativity [sound recording] : reflections and reminations / [lecture by] Winston Weathers. —

Address to the U.S. Congress, 1941 [sound recording] / Winston Churchill. —

Goodbye, Columbus [sound recording] : music from the sound track of the motion picture / featuring songs composed and performed by The Association. —

Close encounters of the third kind [sound recording] : original sound-track / composed by Johnny Williams. —

6.1G ITEMS WITHOUT A COLLECTIVE TITLE

Sound recordings, particularly those with musical content, commonly contain diverse works for which a collective title is either inappropriate or not given. Care must be exercised to ensure that adequate description and access are provided for all of the works on the recording. *AACR 2* provides two approaches to the description of items of this type: they can be described either as a unit or as separate pieces. Adequate access is possible under either method, provided the cataloging agency does not limit the number of access points that may be assigned to a single bibliographic record. Cataloging records for items described as a unit are more complicated to use and may not be as clear to the user. They do, however, usually require fewer cards in a card catalog and fewer records in an automated catalog, although the number of access points should be the same. Items described separately present fewer problems for the cataloger and may make access easier for the user. They do increase the total number of cards in the catalog, however. Rules 6.1G2 and 6.1G4 provide specific instructions on the use of both cataloging approaches.

Although some nonprint materials, particularly those which are educationally oriented, are best handled in the unit form in which they were published, users of sound recordings are usually interested in an individual work rather than in the collective unit. This factor may help a cataloging agency decide the way in which multipart works which lack collective titles will be handled. This decision may be made for all items of this type encountered or by instituting a policy of deciding on a case-by-case basis. In either case, the library should consider the options provided by the rules and try to consistently apply their policy. The Library of Congress policy on this issue is to catalog these works as a unit. This policy, implemented with the adoption of *AACR 2*, is a departure from the previous policy of cataloging each work separately, linking the records with the use of "with" notes. This LC policy is another factor libraries will wish to consider in making or reevaluating their policy on this issue.

6.1G2

This rule indicates that titles for collections lacking a collective title that are to be cataloged as a unit should be recorded according to the provisions of

Rule 1.1G. The recording of all the titles in Area 1 often can produce a lengthy and complicated title statement. Although subsets of that rule indicate that a predominant part (Rule 1.1G1) or parts (Rule 1.1G4) of an item lacking a collective title can be used as the title proper, with the other parts named in a contents note, this approach is inadequate for sound recordings. Although one part may seem predominant by virtue of its duration in relation to other parts, information about other seemingly minor parts may be important for the user and may not be described in sufficient detail in a contents note.

Items without a collective title described as a unit

Rhapsody in blue ; An American in Paris [sound recording] / George Gershwin. —

Die Walküre : ride of the Valkyries ; Tristan und Isolde : prelude to Act I ; Götterdämmerung : Siegfried's funeral music ; Siegfried : forest murmers [sound recording] / Richard Wagner. —

Quartet in G minor for piano and strings, K. 478 ; Quintet in E-flat for piano and winds, K. 452 [sound recording] / Mozart. —

Concerto in D major for cello & orchestra, op. 101 / Haydn. Concerto no. 1 in a minor for cello & orchestra, op. 33 / Saint-Saens [sound recording]. —

6.1G4
Instead of recording all of the titles in a collection lacking a collective title as a unit, a library may choose to provide a catalog record for each titled part. This method of cataloging has the advantage of producing less complicated title and responsibility statements. If this approach is followed, care must be taken to provide a physical description which relates only to the separate part being cataloged (Rule 6.5B3). The descriptions for each of the separate parts should be linked with a "with" note (Rule 6.7B21). As indicated earlier, this separate catalog record approach has been abandoned by LC with its adoption of *AACR 2*.

Items without a collective title described as separate parts
[Each of the examples below represents a separate catalog record.]

Rhapsody in blue [sound recording] / George Gershwin. —

An American in Paris [sound recording] / George Gershwin. —

Die Walküre [sound recording] : ride of the Valkyries / Richard Wagner. —

Tristan und Isolde [sound recording] : prelude to Act I / Richard Wagner. —

Quartet in G minor for piano and strings, K. 478 [sound recording] / Mozart. —

Quintet in E-flat for piano and winds, K. 452 [sound recording] / Mozart. –

Concerto in D major for cello & orchestra, op. 101 [sound recording] / Haydn. –

Concerto no. 1 in a minor for cello & orchestra, op. 33 [sound recording] / Saint-Saens. –

6.2   EDITION AREA

Information concerning the edition of a sound recording should be recorded as instructed in Rule 1.2B. These edition statements may indicate that differences exist between it and other editions or that it is a "named" reissue. The use of edition statements for sound recordings is relatively rare compared to its use for books. Catalogers should be aware that some statements which appear on a sound recording may indicate the quality line of a recording and are not considered edition statements.

6.2B4   *Optional Addition*

The Library of Congress does not apply the option of providing an edition statement for an item which does not have an edition statement even though it might contain changes from a previous edition. It is strongly suggested that multimedia libraries follow LC's policy. This information, if considered important, can be given in a note (Rule 6.7B7).

6.2B5   [Items Without a Collective Title]

Items without a collective title which are described as a unit may have different edition statements for each part. When this occurs, these edition statements should follow the title and statement of responsibility with which they are associated. This structure does have the disadvantage of becoming exceedingly lengthy and complicated. Its use demonstrates to many libraries the advisability of continuing to describe this type of material with separate catalog records despite LC's policy.

6.4   PUBLICATION, DISTRIBUTION, ETC., AREA

In this area of the description, the information provided should be for the item in hand as originally published. Care should be exercised that information sources used to obtain information about publication, distribution, etc., identify the work as originally published. If it is determined from these sources that the place, publisher, distributor, etc., of the item have changed, that information can be given in a note.

6.4C   PLACE OF PUBLICATION, DISTRIBUTION, ETC.

The place of publication, distribution, etc., of a published sound recording should be recorded as instructed in Rule 1.4C. This information should be taken from the item, its accompanying material, or container, in that order of preference. If the information is not available from these sources, reference sources should be consulted. The reference sources listed in the bibliography of cataloging aids (appendix A) at the end of this text should provide some of this information. Conjectural information about the place of publication, distribution, etc., should be followed by a question mark with the entire statement enclosed within square brackets (Rule 1.4C6).

For nonprocessed sound recordings, the 1985 Revision to *AACR 2* (Rule 6.4C2) indicates that no place of publication, distribution, etc., should be recorded.

6.4D NAME OF PUBLISHER, DISTRIBUTOR, ETC.

The names of both the publisher and distributor should be recorded according to Rule 1.4D. Although only optional, recording the name of the distributor can be important for sound recordings and the Library of Congress exercises this option. It is recommended that other multimedia libraries follow LC's practice.

6.4D2

When recording the name of a publisher, the name of a subdivision of a company associated with the publication, when stated on the item, should be recorded rather than the name of its parent organization. Frequently this subdivision name will be either the trade name or the brand name used by the company. Care should be taken to ensure that the subdivision is a functional organization rather than a series under which a number of recordings have been issued by the company. This latter type of statement should be given as a series statement. Most of these series statements will be unnumbered, but they do constitute a sound recording series. This is a somewhat different concept of series from that used for other types of nonprint materials. It is sometimes difficult to differentiate between a series and a trade name or brand name of a publisher. The publisher's catalog or a reference source, particularly the *Schwann Catalog*, can help to clarify the facts of publication.

6.4D4

For nonprocessed sound recordings, the 1985 Revision to *AACR 2* indicates that no publisher, distributor, etc., should be recorded.

6.4E *OPTIONAL ADDITION.* STATEMENT OF FUNCTION OF PUBLISHER, DISTRIBUTOR, ETC.

It may be necessary to record the names of several corporate bodies in this location. The use of this optional addition to record a statement of function can help to clarify the information for the user. It is recommended that it always be used in cases where function is not clear. The Library of Congress exercises this option, but not necessarily uniformly. For major companies, the indication of function may not be necessary, while for less well known organizations, it may be essential.

6.4F DATE OF PUBLICATION, DISTRIBUTION, ETC.

Several dates associated with the performance, recording, pressing, and copyright of the sound recording may appear in one or several of the prescribed sources of information. The date of publication, distribution, etc., should be recorded according to the provisions of Rule 1.4F. A revision to Rule 6.4F2 instructs that the date of recording, as opposed to a date of publication, of a published sound recording be given in a note (Rule 6.7B7) rather than in Area 4.

Generally, the most common date to be found on a sound recording is a date of copyright. The previous cataloging code, *AACR 1* Revised Chapter 14, had required that the copyright date of a sound recording be preceded by a lowercase "p". Because *AACR 2* does not specifically address the issue of how to record sound recording copyright dates, the implication was that they were to be recorded like copyright dates for other materials — preceded by a lowercase "c". This implication was strengthened by an early LC Rule Interpretation that called for sound recording copyright dates to be preceded by the "c". Eventually, the confusion was resolved when a revision was issued to Rule 6.4F1 which added an additional example that used a "p" for a copyright date. Although this method of stating a rule would seem to violate the principle that the examples in *AACR 2* are "illustrative and not prescriptive," the point was made that the practice of the previous cataloging code for recording copyright dates was being continued.

For nonprocessed sound recordings, the 1985 Revision to *AACR 2* (Rule 6.4F3) indicates that the date of recording should be recorded as instructed in Rule 4.4B1. That rule, written for manuscripts, calls for giving the date or dates of a collection unless already given in the title. This date should be recorded as either a single year or a range of years. For single works, an option to the rule allows the inclusion of the month and day. When this option is exercised, the order of elements is: Year Month Day.

6.4G PLACE OF MANUFACTURE, NAME OF MANUFACTURER, DATE OF MANUFACTURE

If the name of the publisher is unknown, and information about the manufacturer of the item is available, this information should be recorded, in parentheses, following the date.

6.4G2 *Optional Addition*

As an option, information about the manufacture of an item (place, name, and date) can be given if it is different from that of the publisher. LC will apply the option on a selective basis. For most users of multimedia libraries this information has little if any value, and thus the option should probably not be exercised.

New Rochelle, N.Y. : Spoken Arts, 1956.

New York : Caedmon Records, 1973.

Berkeley, Calif. : Pacifica Archive, 1968.

[London] : Angel, 1968.

[New York?] : RCA Victor, 1962.

[New York] : RCA Red Seal, 1978.

Norwalk, Conn. : Cook Laboratories, p1976.

Tulsa, Okla. : J. Nickols, p1978.

Brooklyn, N.Y. : Produced and distributed by 3R Sound, 1972.

Santa Barbara, Calif. : Center for the Study of Democratic Institutions, [1976]

North Hollywood, Calif. : Bowman, [196-?]

New York : Sesame Street Records : Manufactured and distributed by Distinguished Productions, 1978.

Santa Monica, Calif. : BFA Educational Media ; [New York : Holt Information Systems, distributor, 1972]

Hollywood, Calif. : Discreet, 1974 ([New York] : Warner Bros. Records)

6.5 PHYSICAL DESCRIPTION AREA

The physical characteristics of sound recordings must be considered when constructing a complete and accurate physical description. While all types of materials covered in this chapter have recorded sound, their physical characteristics can vary markedly. In presenting the information requirements for Area 5, rules which are pertinent to all sound record formats will be discussed first, followed by those rules which only apply to specific types of sound recordings.

6.5B EXTENT OF ITEM (INCLUDING SPECIFIC MATERIAL DESIGNATION)

The total number of physical units of the sound recording being described, followed by a specific material designation, are the first two elements in this area. The specific material designations for sound recordings are generally limited to the following phrases:

sound cartridge	sound tape reel
sound cassette	sound track film
sound disc	

Additionally, the terms such as "piano roll," "organ roll," etc., can be used as SMDs for roll recordings.

In a "cataloging decision," the Library of Congress instructed that, if the number of discographic units differs from the number of physical units, the number of physical units should be given here and the number of discographic units recorded in a note (Rule 6.7B10).

As an option, a cataloger may drop the designation "sound" from the specific material designation if the GMD "sound recording" has been used. The Library of Congress is not following this option and, for the benefit of users, most multimedia libraries will probably find it best to follow LC's policy.

6.5B2 [Playing Time]

The 1985 Revision to *AACR 2* deleted the original *AACR 2* rule for recording playing time and replaced it with a new rule. This new rule instructs catalogers to follow the provisions of Rule 1.5B4. That rule, also revised in 1985, provides several ways to record the playing time. In a Rule Interpretation to the original *AACR 2* rule, LC further stated that the duration should be given here only if the sound recording is one work as defined by Rule 25.26B (i.e., a single unit intended for performance as a whole, a set of works with a group title, or a group of works with a single opus number).

If the time is stated on the item, it should be recorded as given. The old *AACR 2* rule had required that the playing time for a sound recording under five minutes in duration had to be recorded in terms of minutes and seconds. The revised rule allows recording playing time in minutes and seconds, without any maximum duration limit, provided that the playing time is given that way on the item.

There are two options to this rule for approximating the playing time of an item and for recording the time of multipart items. These options are not followed by the Library of Congress since it has issued several Rule Interpretations. LC instructs that, when the total playing time is not given but the playing times of the parts are, they may be added together at the discretion of the cataloger to obtain the total playing time. When that sum exceeds five minutes, the total should be rounded to the next minute.

Catalogers at the Library of Congress do not precede a statement of playing time by "ca." unless the playing time stated on the item is an approximation. The "ca." is also not used when playing time has been rounded to the nearest minute or when the total playing time has been computed from the durations of the parts.

The Library of Congress does not provide a duration statement if no playing time has been given with the work or if the playing times of some, but not all, of the parts of a work are given and there is no overall playing time available. LC cautions its catalogers against approximating the playing time from the physical characteristics of the item, such as the length of tape on a cassette, the number of bands on a disc, etc.

6.5B3

Sound recordings which (1) consist of separately titled parts, (2) lack a collective title, and (3) are cataloged as separate units, should have their extent of item expressed in terms of the fraction of the work represented by each cataloged unit. This statement should be written using one of two constructs. If the physical parts of the item are numbered or lettered, the following construct would be used.

> on side [number or letter] of [number] sound [format],
>   e.g., on side 1 of 1 sound disc

If physical parts have no numbering or lettering the statement would be written as:

> on [number] side of [number] sound [format]
>   e.g., on 1 side of 1 sound disc

This information is followed by the playing time, within parentheses, if it is known.

6.5C OTHER PHYSICAL DETAILS

A variety of elements constitute "other physical details" for the various types of sound recordings. Excluding those elements appropriate only to sound track films, these elements are:

- Type of recording
- Playing speed
- Groove characteristics (discs only)
- Number of tracks (tape only)
- Number of sound channels
- Recording and reproduction characteristics (tapes only)

6.5C2 Type of Recording

This rule originally addressed only sound track films. A 1985 decision of the Joint Steering Committee for Revision of AACR (JSCAACR) deleted the original rule and replaced it with one which expanded coverage to include disc and tape sound recordings. This was done to accommodate the newest form of sound recording, the compact disc. Under this revised rule, the way in which the sound is registered on either a disc or tape (i.e., analog or digital) must be recorded. This information is separated from the next element, playing speed, by a comma. Because these two terms may not be familiar to all catalogers, the revision also included an addition to the *AACR 2* glossary to define them. These definitions are:

Analog sound recording

A sound recording on which vibrations have been registered in a form analogous to the manner in which sound is perceived by the human ear; that is, a mechanical, electrical, or magnetic fluctuation that follows the air pressure variations by which the human ear experiences sound.

Digital sound recording

A sound recording in which vibrations have been registered by encoding, mechanically or magnetically, a series of numbers (digits) that describe the sound completely.

1 sound disc (32 min.) : analog

1 sound disc (47 min.) : digital

1 sound tape (23 min.) : analog

on side 1 of 2 sound discs (21 min.) : analog

6.5C3   Playing Speed

According to the 1985 Revision to *AACR 2* approved by JSCAACR, the playing speed of a sound recording should be given if the speed is other than the standard for that type of recording. See the sections "Sound Recording Discs" and "Sound Recording Tapes" that follow for specific instructions on recording the playing speed for each type of recording.

6.5C7   Number of Sound Channels

This rule, as revised in 1985, calls for recording of the number of sound channels (i.e., mono., stereo., quad.) when that information is "readily available." This revised rule is different from the original version in that the original did not include the qualification to record this information only when it was "readily available." In a "cataloging decision" to the original rule, LC had stated that the number of sound channels should only be given if they were stated "explicitly."

Sound recording discs

The physical characteristics of disc sound recordings are fairly standardized and do not present many problems for description. In addition to the physical characteristics common to all sound recordings given previously, characteristics specific to sound discs are addressed by the following rules.

6.5C3   Playing Speed

Generally, the playing speed of a sound recording in disc form should be recorded if there is no standard speed for that format. The way this information is recorded has changed from the way it was originally stated in *AACR 2* to allow for differences introduced by digital discs. For analog discs the speed should be expressed in terms of revolutions per minute (rpm). Because there is no standard speed for analog discs, the playing speed is always given. For digital discs the expression of speed is changed to meters per second (m. per sec.). If the playing speed is 1.4 meters per second, no playing speed should be recorded.

6.5C4   Groove Characteristics

The groove characteristic of a sound disc should only be given if it is other than the standard characteristic for that type of disc. The standard groove size on stereo recordings is .0007. The information that a disc's groove size is other than standard is important for several reasons. Although stereo recordings can be played on a disc player equipped with a stylus or needle appropriate for microgroove recordings, the difference in the size of the needle can cause wear on the recording and will not produce maximum sound fidelity.

Sound recording tape

Sound tape is first described in terms of the type of integral container—cartridge, cassette, or open reel. A cartridge contains a continuous loop of tape and requires no rewinding, while a cassette contains two reels with the tape transported across the playing head in both directions, thus requiring rewinding. All magnetic tape is recorded on only one side. Although often marked on the label as side one or side two, the actual recording is located on different parts of the same side of the tape. To play side two, the container is turned over if in cassette form.

6.5C3   Playing Speed

The playing speed of a tape is always recorded in terms of inches per second (ips). Open reel tape is commonly recorded at 1⅞, 3¾, or 7½ inches per second. Generally speaking, the faster the speed and the wider the area for recording, the better the fidelity of the recording. The playing speed of a sound tape in open reel format is always recorded because there is no standard.

The playing speed of cassettes or cartridges is only expressed if the speed is other than the standard speed for that format. Sound cassettes are generally recorded at 1⅞ inches per second, and cartridges at 3¾ inches per second.

6.5C6   Number of Tracks

Several types of materials are used as the base for blank tape intended for magnetic recording. The type of material used for tape is irrelevant to the cataloger describing the tape sound recording. Although all tape is similar, it can be recorded in a number of different track configurations. The method used to record the sound signals on a tape determines both its tracking and speed. This information is important to the user, and thus also the cataloger, because the equipment used for playback must be compatible with the characteristics with which the sound was recorded.

There are a number of tracking characteristics which are common to certain types of integral containers of the tape. These tracking characteristics are determined by the recording equipment. Open reel tape can be recorded in a full track mode: one sound track recorded across the full width of the tape; two sound tracks, each recorded on one-half of the width of the tape; or four sound tracks, each recorded on one-fourth of the width of the tape. These tracking configurations are described as one track (sometimes also called single or full track), two track, or four track.

A monophonic recording indicates that the sound is recorded from one source. These recordings can be one track or two track where one-half of the tape is used for a sound track recorded in one direction while the other half is used for another sound track recorded in the other direction. In the latter situation, the cassette is turned over to play the second track. A similar procedure is used to play both halves of a two track monophonic open reel tape. A stereophonic tape recording indicates that sound is recorded from two main sources while quadra-phonic indicates four sources. Stereo and quadraphonic recordings cannot be one track because, by their very number of sound sources, the number of tracks must exceed one. Stereo tape recordings may be two track, four track, or, in the case of cartridge recordings, eight track. Quadraphonic recordings must be at least four track.

In recording tracking information, *AACR 2* instructs that the number of tracks should be recorded only if the number of tracks is not standard for that type of item. In a footnote, *AACR 2* indicates that four tracks is the standard for cassettes and eight tracks the standard for cartridges. It is generally rare to see an indication of the number of tracks on a LC catalog record for a sound cassette. No standard number is suggested by the rules for open reel tape.

6.5C8 *Optional Addition.* Recording and Reproduction Characteristics

For tapes, specific information on the recording and reproduction characteristics of the work should be given following the statement of the number of sound channels. In many cases, this information will be the trade name of a process. This information should be separated from the previous statement by a comma. In a "cataloging decision," the Library of Congress instructed its catalogers that this information should be supplied whenever it is needed to select appropriate equipment to obtain the "full audio" effect. This information would be provided even if the tape could be played on another type of equipment without the "full audio" effect.

6.5D DIMENSIONS

Although the thickness of sound recording tape varies, because this does not affect the selection of playback equipment, this information is not provided. The thickness of the tape does determine the amount of tape that can be put on a reel or in a container. The length of the tape plus its speed determine the playing time.

The dimensions of sound cartridges are given in terms of both the size of the cartridge and the width of the tape. This information is only recorded, however, if the dimensions are other than the standard. The standard size of a cartridge is 5¾x3⅞ inches and the standard width of its tape is ¼ inch.

A practice similar to that used for sound cartridges is followed for sound cassettes. The standard size of a sound cassette is 3⅞x2½ inches and the standard width of its tape is ⅛ inch.

The dimensions of open reel tape are given in terms of the diameter of the reel expressed in inches. If the size of the tape is other than the standard, ¼ inch, that information should be recorded.

A sound disc's dimensions should be given in terms of its diameter in inches.

6.5E ACCOMPANYING MATERIAL

The name of material accompanying a sound recording should be recorded and, optionally, the material's physical description. This option should generally be applied if the size of the material is considered significant. The provisions of Rule 1.5E should be used to record the information about the accompanying material. If it is considered necessary to indicate the location of the accompanying material, a note (Rule 6.7B11) should be used. Usually, a statement about the existence of program notes is also recorded in a note rather than in the Physical Description Area. In a "cataloging decision" in MCB, LC has stated that if there is a need to state more about accompanying material than can be done using option "d" of Rule 1.5E1, the cataloger should give this information in an accompanying material note and record nothing about it in this area.

Sound recordings on disc

1 sound disc (42 min.) : analog, 33⅓ rpm, stereo. ; 12 in. + 1 teacher's guide.

on side 1 of 1 sound disc (22 min.) : analog, 33⅓ rpm ; 12 in.

1 sound disc (48 min.) : analog, 33⅓ rpm, mono. ; 10 in.

1 sound disc (ca. 15 min.) : analog, 45 rpm ; 7 in.

10 sound discs (449 min.) : analog, 33⅓ rpm, stereo. ; 12 in.

1 sound disc : digital, stereo. ; 4¾ in.

Sound recordings on tape

1 sound cassette (18 min.) : analog.

1 sound cassette (34 min.) : analog, 3¾ ips

1 sound cassette (48 min.) : analog + 1 teacher's guide.

1 sound cassette (60 min.) : analog + 1 syllabus (v, 26 p. ; 23 cm.)

3 sound cassettes (62 min.) : analog, stereo.

1 sound cartridge (ca. 50 min.) : analog, stereo.

1 sound tape reel (28 min.) : 3¾ ips, analog, 2 track, mono. ; 5 in.

1 sound tape reel (25 min.) : 7½ ips, analog, 4 track, stereo. ; 7 in.

6.6 SERIES AREA

6.6B SERIES STATEMENTS
Some sound recordings are published in series and should be treated normally. Other series, usually not numbered, often consist of works which are not related in content to other works in the series. These series are generally nothing more than marketing devices for a publisher for a group of unrelated recordings. Information about this type of series should also be recorded as a series statement. However, when a trade name is associated with a group of recordings and it is a functioning subdivision of a publisher, it should be recorded in Area 4 as the publisher rather than as a series. If the subdivision function of a publisher is not present, then that information should be recorded as a series statement.

(Modern American poetry criticism)

(Retrospect series)

(Recorded anthology of American music)

(Music from Ravinia ; v. 3)

(Richard Strauss Edition Bühnenwerke = Opera liriche ; 4)

When individual items in a set are cataloged separately, the title of the set can also be given as the series statement. If the set is part of another series, the name of that series can be given as the series title with the set title given as a subseries (but not as the subtitle to the series).

6.7 NOTE AREA

6.7B19 Notes on Publishers' Numbers

This rule calls for recording alphabetic and/or numeric designations given to a sound recording by its publisher. These instructions call for the numbers to be preceded by the label name of the publisher, followed by a colon (no space). In cases where there are two or more numbers, only the principal number should be recorded.

If no principal number can be determined, *AACR 2* requires that all the numbers should be given. If one of these numbers applies to the entire set, it should be given first. LC practice in this situation differs in that it records only the set number unless it is not given on the individual items. In this latter situation, the LC gives the set number first followed by the individual numbers within parentheses. *AACR 2* also indicates that when an item consists of separately numbered units which are numbered consecutively, they should be recorded as a continuous sequence, giving only the first and last numbers separated by a dash.

Because of the importance of the publisher's number in identification of the item, LC has indicated that this number should be the first note given on a catalog record. For the same reason, it is strongly recommended that multimedia libraries follow LC's practice in the location of this note. LC has further instructed its catalogers to transcribe spaces and hyphens on the catalog record the way they are given on the recording.

In some cases, sound recordings will contain a number that identifies the master from which the recording was made. These numbers are known as matrix numbers. The Library of Congress records matrix numbers only when they are the only number given on the work. When matrix numbers are given, LC follows each number with the word "matrix" enclosed within parentheses.

World Records: SH116.

Seraphim: S 60343

Deutsche Grammophon: 2531199.

Folkways: 8772E.

London: 99451

Historic Masters: HMB 8.

Musical Heritage Society: MHS 834308 (MHS 4308 — MHS 4310).

Additional numbers on container: TC-LFP 80165 — TC-LPF 80166.

Melodiia: C10 06767 (matrix) — C10 06768 (matrix)

6.7B1 Nature or Artistic Form and Medium of Performance

This note is used to record information about the form of a literary work, the type of musical work, or other statements which help to clarify the nature of a work. Some of this information may already have been given in the Title and Statement of Responsibility Area and should not be repeated here. Sometimes, this information may be mentioned on a work but not included in Area 1 because it did not appear on the chief source of information for that sound recording format. In these cases, this note should be used to record that information.

Interview.

Lecture with question and answer segments.

Radio drama recorded from broadcast made Dec. 20, 1937.

"A structured learning approach to teaching prosocial skills"— Container.

Excerpts from the ballet.

The first work: excerpts from a film score, the 2nd: opera excerpts.

For 2 trumpets, tympani, 2 violins, chorus and continuo.

Orchestral arrangements of arias from operas.

Suites from the ballet.

The complete ballet.

The second work is a suite.

Vocal ensembles, songs, and harpsichord music.

6.7B2   Language
The language of the content, whether spoken or sung, of a sound recording should be indicated in this note if it differs from the language of the rest of the description. If only the language of the accompanying material is different from that of the work and the rest of the description, that should be indicated in an accompanying material note (rule 6.7B11).

Sung in Latin.

Sung in English, French and Latin.

Songs sung in German and (principally) Swedish.

Each selection sung in original language.

Read in French with English translation following each poem.

6.7B3   Source of Title Proper
Anytime a title has been taken from a source other than the chief source of information or its substitute, that source should be indicated in this note. The most common occurrence of the use of this note is to indicate that the title has been taken from the container.

Title from accompanying material.

Title from container.

Title from distributor's catalog.

6.7B4 Variations in Title;
6.7B5 Parallel Titles and Other Title Information
Frequently, titles appear in variant forms on different prescribed sources of information and, sometimes, in variant forms within the same prescribed source. This is particularly a problem for sound recording formats where the chief source of information for the title is a rather small label. The limited space available there often dictates that a title be given in far less detail than the form in which it is given on the container. It is particularly important to note the form of a title on a container if it differs significantly from the form on the chief source of information because it is the container title which will be most visible to the user. In these cases, it is also essential to make an access point for the variant title in addition to identifying it in this note.

Although not specifically instructed to do so in a Library of Congress Rule Interpretation, catalogers may wish to "borrow" the Interpretation used for Rule 7.7B4, which formalized the LC decision process as to when variant title notes should be made. Under that interpretation, LC indicates that the first step in the process is to determine whether an additional access point is desired for the title variation. This determination is based upon the conditions given in Rule 21.2 (Changes in Title Proper). These conditions are:

- a change occurs in the first five words of the title (exclusive of initial articles in the nominative case), or

- the addition, deletion or change of important words in the title, or

- a change occurs in word order.

If, based on these conditions, a decision is made that an additional access point is necessary, then a variation in title note should be made to justify the use of the added entry. If the decision to make an additional access point is negative, then the variation in title note should not be made.

Title on container: McNamera on torts.

Title on container: Edward Woodward reads The African Queen.

Title on container: Magnus Magnusson reads Tales from Viking times.

Title on container: The Murray Hill Radio Theatre presents The Green Hornet.

Title on container: Swedish dances = Danses suédoises.

Added title on container: The unicorn, or, The triumph of chastity.

Parallel title on container: The barber of Seville.

6.7B6 Statements of Responsibility
The limitations placed upon recording the names of performers in the body of the description necessitate the use of this note to provide complete information about them and their medium of performance. This note can also be used to record information about other important persons or corporate bodies related to the work which were not recorded in Area 1. This includes information about the work upon which a sound recording is based. Unfortunately, *AACR 2* does not provide specific instructions for recording or categorizing this information. Generally, it is best to group together those names associated with similar functions into a single paragraph. For the members of a cast on a nonmusical sound recording, a LC Rule Interpretation instructs its catalogers to begin the note with the word "Cast." When appropriate, LC's catalogers also add the role or the part played, within parentheses, after the name of the performer.
When some, or all, of the performers are not related to all of the works on a sound recording and these works are listed in a contents note (Rule 6.7B18), the performers' names should be recorded in the contents note in association with the appropriate title(s).

Joan Sutherland, soprano ; New Philharmonia Orchestra ; Richard Bonynge, conductor.

Lee Morgan, trumpet ; David "Fathead" Newman, tenor saxophone ; Cedar Walton, piano ; Ron Carter, bass ; Billy Higgins, drums.

Jessye Norman, Mirella Freni, Yvonne Minton, sopranos ; Ingvar Wixell, baritone ; Wladimiro Ganzarollik, bass ; BBC Symphony Orchestra and Chorus ; Colin Davis, conductor.

Lucy Shelton, soprano (1st work) ; St. Louis Symphony Orchestra ; Leonard Slatkin, conductor.

Philadelphia String Quartet.

Aeolian String Quartet ; with Thea King, clarinet in first work.

Ed Ames with orchestra.

Arranged by Bruno Reibold.

Libretto by the composer, based on the play by Artturi Järviluoma.

Background music performed by Gviomar Novaes.

Lecture by the author.

Read by James Mason.

Stuart Finley, narrator.

Host: David Prowitt ; guests, Paul Kurtz ... [et al.].

Text of 4th movement by J.C.F. von Schiller.

Cast: First work: Mary Ann Strossner, Yolanda Marquez, Mary Thomas Barry. Second work: Gregg A. Roebuck, Barry Cooper, Bernard Erhardt, Roger Harkenrider.
First work: Director, Christy Simmens. Second work, Director, Michael Amundsen.
[Two separate statement of responsibility notes for the same work.]

6.7B7 Edition and History

This note is used to record information about the history of the recording or the edition being described. It should not be used to give information about the material in another format on which the sound recording was based. That information should be recorded in the previous note (Rule 6.7B6).

For nonprocessed sound recordings, the 1985 Revision to *AACR 2* indicates that the details of the event being recorded should be given in this note.

The 2nd work originally for horn, violoncello, or violin and piano.

Works realized at the Columbia-Princeton Electronic Music Center.

Recorded on the E.G. & G. Hook Organ, Church of Immaculate Conception, Boston.

Edited from the Pacem in Terris IV Convocation, Washington, D.C., Dec., 1975.

Recorded between 1947 and 1958.

Recording of radio broadcast May 23, 1979.

Recorded May 3, 1981.

"Direct disc recording, limited edition, recorded July 18 & 20, 1977 at M.G.M. Studio, Culver City, Calif."

Ed. recorded: Helicon Music (1st work) ; Merion Music (2nd work).

Previously released as DG 2531 and DG 2531 354.

6.7B9 Publication, Distribution, etc.

Important publication, distribution, etc., information that was not given previously in Area 5 is recorded in this note. Catalogers should ensure that the information is related to the item in hand and not a previous recording of the work which is only related to the one in hand.

Issued by the British Institute of Recorded Sound in collaboration with EMI Records (The Gramophone Co.).

"Produced by Charndos Records, Ltd." — Container.

Discs manufactured by Vic, Toshiba Records, Polydor, King and CBSSony Special Projects with various label nos.

"Co-production with … VEB Deutsche Schallplatten Berlin/DDR" — Container.

Licensed from Erato: 70912.

Distributor from label on container.

6.7B10 Physical Description

This note is used to record information about the physical characteristics of the item not previously given in Area 5. The rule specifically excludes its use to record information that is standard to the item being described. LC has issued a "cataloging decision" which states that information about the presence of containers should only be given if the number of containers is not clear from the rest of the description.

This note is also the place where catalogers should indicate that an analog or digital recording was made from a master registered in the other form (e.g., a digital recording made from an analog master). Although the indication of "sound disc" combined with the dimension "4¾ in." indirectly indicates that a work is a compact disc, this note is frequently used by the Library of Congress to more directly indicate that it is a compact disc.

Compact disc.

Digital recording.
[Used to indicate that an analog recording was made from a digital master.]

Analog recording.
[Used to indicate that a digital recording was made from an analog master.]

Digitally remastered recording.

In part mono.

"Electronically reprocessed to simulate stereo."

Manual sequence.

Segments recorded at 3¾ ips for special effects.

Sound recorded on track 1 only.

Disc made of flexible plastic.

In container (14 cm.).

Set in container (25 cm.).

In addition to the general instructions in this rule to record physical characteristics, specific instructions are also given for using this note to give the
duration of the parts of a multipart item, lacking a collective title, that has been
cataloged as a unit. LC has provided additional instructions for recording these
durations. It indicates that this note should be used only if the titles of the parts
are given in the Title and Statement of Responsibility Area. If the titles are given
instead in a contents note, their durations should be given as a part of that note
(Rule 6.7B18).

When recording durations, LC indicates that they should be recorded as they
are given on the item in terms of hours, minutes, and seconds. A LC "cataloging
decision" in MCB provides additional guidance on formatting the duration note.
It indicates that the digits representing hours, minutes, and seconds should be
preceded by a colon.

When the duration is represented only in seconds, it should also be preceded
by a colon. When the durations of individual parts of a work are given on the
recording, if desired, a cataloger may add the durations and record the total in
minutes, rounded to the next minute.

Whenever a duration statement gives only an approximate time it should be
preceded by "ca." This should not be done, however, when the duration has been
developed from adding the times of parts or when rounding the total to the next
minute. LC instructs its catalogers not to give a duration statement if the duration
is not stated on the item or if only the durations of some of the parts are stated.
LC will not approximate durations from the physical features of a work, such as
the number of sides, the length of tape, etc.

Durations: 33:00; 17:00.

Durations: 10:56; 12:24; 12:38; 20:33.

Durations: 15:00 each.

Duration: ca. 65:00.

Durations on labels.

6.7B11 Accompanying Material

The location and type of textual or other types of accompanying material
and their characteristics can be described in detail in this note.

Booklet (128 p. ; 14 cm.)

Booklet contains text in German and English.

Lyrics on inner sleeve.

Synopsis by E. Spielberg on container.

Program notes by Lionel Stater on container.

Program notes by Joan Chissell in English, German and French on container.

Program notes by Phillip Ramex on container and text of the 1st work with English translation ([1] p.) inserted in container.

Booklet containing words of the songs and historical notes (12 p.) inserted in the container.

Text of last work in German with English translations on container.

Notes inserted in container.

6.7B14 Audience

As with other chapters, the intended audience or the intellectual level of the audience can be given in this note provided that the information is taken from the item, its container, or accompanying textual material. Whenever possible, it is best to take the audience statement from the item itself using the terms it used. Before 1985, the Library of Congress generally prefaced this note with the phrase "intended audience." Since then, LC has prefaced this note with the word "Audience."

Audience: Continuing education for the legal profession.

Audience: Elementary grades.

Audience: Ages 16 through adult.

For broadcast use only.

Made for use of the American Armed Forces.

6.7B16 Other Formats Available

This note is intended to alert the user about other formats in which the item is available. The Library of Congress will use this note to indicate the availability of the item in other formats whenever this information is known. It prefaces the note with the term "Issued."

In most other libraries, the use of this note should be restricted to providing information about other formats of the same title which are available in the library, rather than about formats available for purchase but not held. This latter information is confusing to the user trying to identify the holdings of a library. If a library collection contains the same work in different formats, the best way to describe each one is with a separate catalog entry.

Issued also as sound tape reel.

Issued also as sound disc.

Issued also as cassette 3343 526.

Issued also as videorecording, edited for classroom use.

Issued also as transcript no. 1016 and 1027.

6.7B17   Summary

When other parts of the description, especially the title statement and titles recorded in a contents note, do not sufficiently explain the type of material, the scope, the point of view of the material, or significant artistic characteristics, this information can be given in a summary. This note is sometimes also the most appropriate place to explain the relationship of a person(s) named in the statement of responsibility, or in a related note, to the work. It also can be used to indicate the responsibility of an individual who was not mentioned previously in the description.

The summary note should be both brief and objective. Information in the summary note can be taken from other sources without attribution. Although this rule limits the use of a summary note to works that are either entirely or predominantly nonmusical, it can be applied, if necessary, to both types of sound recordings.

Summary: Tom Bradley, Mayor of Los Angeles, calls for an urban recovery program. Points out federal government's neglect and offers remedies.

Summary: T.M. Aluko discusses themes in his novels focusing on the interaction between African culture and "imported" European culture.

Summary: Greek language instruction for the English speaking with phrases and sentences in each language.
[Includes an indication of the intended audience.]

6.7B18   Contents

A contents note is essential for sound recordings issued under a collective title which are cataloged as a unit. The information provided should include statements of responsibility not previously given in Area 1 as well as the duration of individual works, when known. Titles transcribed in the contents note should be the titles proper taken from the chief source of information for the item.

In a "cataloging decision," the Library of Congress has instructed its catalogers that the duration of individual parts can be recorded in parentheses, after the title of the part. If the number of physical units for a part is more than one, the number of units can also be given within parentheses, for example, (4 discs).

In addition to the more formal contents note which begins with the term "Contents:", catalogers may also use formal partial contents notes and indicate additional contents with the use of a more informal contents note written by the cataloger. Partial contents notes, prefaced by the term "Partial Contents:", are very rarely used by the Library of Congress. The use of the informal contents note is less common for sound recordings than it is for other types of nonprint materials.

Contents: Jerusalem blues — Careless love — Dippemouth blues — Ain't gonna give nobody none of my jelly roll — Dallas blues — Tin roof blues.

Contents: Tannhauser overture / Wagner — Der Freischutz overture / Weber — Merry Wives of Windsor overture / Nicolai Ruy — Blas overture, op. 95 / Mendelssohn — Hansel and Gretel overture / Humperdinck.

Contents: 1. Management of problem behaviors : introduction to structured learning — 2. Management of problem behaviors : structured learning in use — 3. Management of problem behaviors in the structured learning group.

Contents: Op. 90 (D.899). No. 1 in C minor (10:38) ; No. 2 in E flat major (4:37) ; No. 3 in G flat major (6:28) ; No. 4 in A flat major (8:13) — Op posth. 142 (D.935). No. 1 in F minor (10:00) ; No. 2 in A flat major (7:27) ; No. 3 in B flat major (11:39) ; No. 4 in F minor (6:59).

Contents: The saucier's apprentice (15:00) — Cloudland revisited (16:34) — Acres and pains 1-2 (4:11 ; 4:52) — Swiss family Perelman, Rancors aweigh (20:53).

Partial Contents: Mastersingers of Nuremberg, Act 3, Prelude: Dance of the apprentices ; Entry of the masters.

6.7B19 Notes on Publishers' Numbers
As previously mentioned, these notes will be given as the first note by the Library of Congress. See the first note discussed under Rule 6.7 in this text. When the number being recorded is not a publisher's number, it should be recorded in this note in its normal location.

"1"—Container.

6.7B21 "With" notes
When multipart items lacking a collective title are cataloged separately, the use of this note is essential. Prior to their adoption of *AACR 2*, the use of "with" notes by the Library of Congress for this type of work was the norm. Since then, LC's decision to catalog these works as one unit has virtually eliminated the use of "with" notes for sound recordings cataloged by LC.

If a "with" note is used, it must begin with the term "With:", followed by the other titles listed in their order of occurrence on the item. Although the example in the *AACR 2* text gives only the title proper, the Library of Congress has issued a Rule Interpretation to Rule 1.7A4 which has a direct bearing upon the form of the title in a "with" note. This Interpretation, applying to nonserial items, instructs that when citing another work in a note, the uniform title of the work should be recorded provided one has been assigned to the work. Only when the work does not have a uniform title associated with it will the title proper of the other work be transcribed.

> With: Concertos, violoncello, orchestra, H. VIIb, 2, D major / Joseph Haydn.

> With: Concertos, guitar, orchestra, no. 1, op. 30, A major, arr. / Mauro G. Giuliani.

> With: Speech at the National Press Club luncheon, Washington, June 9, 1954 / C.S. Cameron.

> With: Peter Gynt. Suite no. 1 ; Peter Gynt. Suite no. 2 / Edward Grieg — Till Eulenspiegels lustige Streiche / Richard Strauss.
> *[This is the example used in AACR 2. It has been modified to show uniform titles in the "with" note.]*

6.10   ITEMS MADE UP OF SEVERAL TYPES OF MATERIAL

Even sound recordings accompanied by several different types of material (e.g., a book, a script, extensive commentary), should be described as sound recordings when the main burden of intellectual or artistic content is assigned to the recording. Only when the intellectual or artistic content cannot be assigned to one predominant item should this rule be implemented and the work cataloged as a kit.

6.11   NONPROCESSED SOUND RECORDINGS

The 1985 Revision to *AACR 2* removed this rule and incorporated its provisions into the following rules: 6.1B1, 6.4C2, 6.4D4, 6.4F3 and 6.7B7. See those rules (except 6.1B1) in this text for the treatment of unpublished sound recordings.

EXAMPLES: Descriptive Cataloging for Sound Recordings

Musical Sound Recordings

>   Beethoven, Ludwig van, 1770-1827.
>   [Concertos, piano, orchestra, no. 1, op. 15, C major]
>   Concerto no. 1 in C, op. 15 ; Leonore overture
>   no. 3, op. 72a [sound recording] / Beethoven. — New
>   York : RCA Victrola, p1970.
>   1 sound disc : analog, 33⅓ rpm, mono. ; 12 in. —
>   (Immortal performances)
>
>   Victrola: Vic-1521.
>   Arturo Toscanini, conductor ; NBC Symphony
>   Orchestra. Concerto no. 1, Ania Dorfman, piano.
>   Concerto no. 1 recorded Aug. 9, 1945 in Carnegie
>   Hall. Leonore overture no. 3 recorded from the NBC
>   broadcast of Nov. 4, 1939.
>   Durations: 32:00; 13:00.
>   Program notes on container.
>
>   I. Toscanini, Arturo, 1867-1957. II. Dorfman, Ania.
>   III. Beethoven, Ludwig van, 1770-1827. Leonore.
>   Ouverture no. 3. 1970. IV. NBC Symphony Orchestra.

Comment	—Musical sound recording, consisting of multiple works by a single composer.
Main Entry	—Entry under the composer.
	—GMD omitted after the uniform title to conform with LC practice.
	—Publisher's number positioned as the first note in accordance with LC practice.
Area 7	—Statement of responsibility note indicates the relationship of a performer to only one of the two works.
	—History of the recordings noted.
	—Duration recorded for each work using the "hour:minute:second" structure.
Added Entries	—Order of the added entries follows the LC policy of listing personal name added entries before Name. Title added entries. Corporate name added entries follow personal name added entries.
	—Name. Uniform Title added entry for the second work. To conform with LC practice, no GMD was used in the added entry. LC adds the date of publication to the uniform title to provide an element for subarranging multiple recordings of the same work.
	—Access points provided for the notable performers, including the orchestra.

(Explanation continues on page 94.)

—No access point provided for the titles proper in accordance with Rule 21.30J which prohibits the use of an added entry for a title proper if a conventionalized uniform title has been used in an entry for a musical sound recording.

Bach, Johann Sebastian, 1685-1750.
   [Concertos, harpsichord, string orchestra, BWV 1052, D minor]
   Concerto no. 1 in D minor for piano, S. 1052 / J.S. Bach. Concerto no. 20 in D minor for piano, K. 466 / Mozart [sound recording]. — [New York] : Vox, p1972.
   1 sound disc : analog, 33⅓ rpm, stereo. ; 12 in.

   Vox: STPL 513 410.
   Sviatoslav Richter, pianist ; Kurt Sanderling, conductor. Concerto no. 1 by the U.S.S.R. State Symphony Orchestra. Concerto no. 20 by the National Philharmonic Orchestra.
   Electronically reprocessed to simulate stereo.
   Durations: 27:00; 34:00.
   Program notes on container.

   I. Richter, Sviatoslav, 1915-   II. Sanderling, Kurt. III. Mozart, Wolfgang Amadeus, 1756-1791. Concertos, piano, orchestra, K. 466, D minor. 1972. IV. Gosudarstvennaẙ i simfonicheskĭ orkester SSSR. V. Moskovskaiâ gosudarstvennaiâ filarmoniiâ.

Comment	—Musical sound recording, lacking a collective title, described as a unit.
Main Entry	—Entry under the composer of the first work.
Uniform Title	—Uniform titles employing thematic numbers exclude serial and/or opus numbers (Rule 25.31A4).
Area 7	—Statement of responsibility note indicates that different orchestras performed the works.
Added Entries	—Name. Uniform Title added entry for the second work. Date added for subarrangement in accordance with LC practice.
	—Entries for the performing orchestras are recorded in Russian to comply with the *AACR 2* instruction to use the form of a corporate name the way it appears in works issued in its language (Rule 24.1). Names have been romanized in accordance with Rule 24.1A. Many multimedia libraries, if not all, would probably prefer to ignore this rule and use an English form of the name—one that library users would most

likely use, over that of the authorized name in Russian. If the Russian form of the name is used, a reference should be made from the English form of the name.

Tchaikovsky, Peter Ilich, 1840-1893.
   [Shchelkunchik. Suite]
     Nutcracker suite, op. 71a [sound recording] / Tchaikovsky. — [New York] : Columbia, [1961]
     On side 2 of 1 sound disc : analog, 33⅓ rpm, stereo. ; 12 in.

   Columbia: MS 6193.
   New York Philharmonic, Leonard Bernstein, conductor.
   Program notes on liner.
   Contents: Miniature overture (3:00) — Danses characteristics (11:00) — Waltz of the flowers (6:00)
   With: Petia i volk / Prokofiev.

   I. Bernstein, Leonard, 1918-   II. New York Philharmonic. III. Title.

Comment	—Musical sound recording, lacking a collective title, with the parts described separately. The uniform title, title proper, and physical description refer only to that part. Under *AACR 2*, the Library of Congress would have cataloged this work as a unit.
Main Entry	—Entry under the composer of the part.
Uniform Title	—A uniform title is generally the title originally given the work by the composer in the language in which it was formulated. Many multimedia libraries not specializing in musical study may wish to deviate from *AACR 2* and create a uniform title in English, e.g., [The nutcracker. Suite]
Area 5	—Playing time is not recorded in this area when the playing time of parts is recorded in a durations note (Rule 6.7B10) or in a contents note (Rule 6.7B18)
Area 7	—Contents note with durations as stated on item.
	—"With" note linking this work to the other on the sound disc. The title used is the uniform title.
Added Entries	—Entries for the performers.
	—Access point provided for the title proper because the uniform title is not a "conventionalized" uniform title.
	—No entry is provided for the work mentioned in the "with" note. This work will be identified instead by the catalog record created for that part.

Prokofiev, Sergey, 1891-1952.
  [Petĩa i volk]
    Peter and the wolf, op. 67 [sound recording] /
Prokofiev. — [New York] : Columbia, [1961]
    On side 1 of 1 sound disc : analog, 33⅓ rpm,
stereo. ; 12 in.

    Columbia: MS 6193.
    New York Philharmonic, Leonard Bernstein,
conductor.
    Program notes on liner.
    With: Shchelkunchik. Suite / Tchaikovsky.

    I. New York Philharmonic. II. Bernstein, Leonard,
  1918-   III. Title.

Comment   —Catalog record for the other work on the sound
          recording.

Vivaldi, Antonio, 1678-1741.
  [Cimento dell'armonia e dell'inventione. N. 1-4]
    The four seasons [sound recording] / Vivaldi. —
Cleveland, Ohio : Telarc, [1984?], p1982.
    1 sound disc : digital, stereo. ; 4¾ in.

    Telarc: CD-80070.
    String orchestra acc.
    Joseph Silverstein, violin ; Boston Symphony
Orchestra ; Seiji Ozawa, conductor.
    Recorded Oct. 10, 1981, Houghton Chapel, Welles-
ley College, Wellesley, Mass.
    Compact disc.
    Contents: La primavera = Spring : concerto no. 1
in E major, op. 8, no. 1/RV 269 (11:00) — L'estate =
Summer : concerto no. 2 in G minor, op. 8, no. 2/RV
315 (11:00) — L'autumno = Autumn : concerto no. 3
in F minor, op. 8, no. 3/RV 293 (11:00) — L'inverno =
Winter : concerto no. 4 in F minor, op. 8, no. 4/RV
297 (9:00).

    I. Silverstein, Joseph, 1932-   II. Ozawa, Seiji,
  1935-   III. Boston Symphony Orchestra. IV. Title.
  V. Title: 4 seasons.

Area 5   —Dimension of the digital disc recorded.
Area 7   —Note indicates that this is a compact disc, not just a
          conventional disc with the sound registered in digital
          form.

—Contents note gives a parallel title for each of the parts. The parallel titles include both the title proper and other title information.

Added Entries—Access points provided for the principal soloist, the orchestra, and the conductor.

—Access point provided for the title proper even though a uniform title was used, because the uniform title is not a "conventionalized" uniform title.

—Additional access point provided for the title with the first word expressed by a numeral rather than a word. This conforms with LC policy for a title which begins with a number.

Moody Blues (Musical group)
    In search of the lost chord [sound recording] /
Moody Blues. — [United States] : Deram, [1968?]
    1 sound cartridge : analog, stereo.

    Deram: DER M,77817.
    Contents: Departure — Ride my see-saw — Living-stone, I presume — House of four doors — Legend of the mind — Voices in the sky — The best way to travel — Visions of paradise — The actor — The word — Om.

    I. Title.

Main Entry —Entry under the principal performer—the performing group.
Area 1 —Statement of responsibility for the performing group because their involvement was more than mere performance, that is, the group composed many of the songs.
Area 4 —City of publication unknown. Country known.
—Date of publication uncertain.
Area 5 —No number of tracks was given because they are standard for a sound cartridge (eight tracks).
—No dimensions were given because this cartridge is the standard size.
—Listing of the songs on a collection is at the option of the library. Many libraries would not describe popular music to this level of detail.

Holly, Buddy, 1936-1959.
    20 golden greats [sound recording] / Buddy Holly,
the Crickets. — University City, Calif. : MCA
Records, p1978.
    1 sound disc : analog, 33⅓ rpm, stereo. ; 12 in.

    MCA Records: MCA 3040.
    Contents: That'll be the day (2:16) — Peggy Sue
(2:35) — Words of love (2:01) — Everyday
(2:12) — Not fade away (2:25) — Oh boy (2:11) —
Maybe baby (2:06) — Listen to me (3:26) —
Heartbeat (2:13) — Think it over (2:50) — It doesn't
matter any more (2:16) — It's so easy (2:14) — Well
... allright (2:18) — Rave on (1:53) — Raining in
my heart (2:52) — True love ways (2:51) — Peggy
Sue got married (2:10) — Bo Diddley (2:24) — Brown
eyed handsome man (2:07) — Wishing (2:08)

    I. Crickets (Musical group). II. Title. III. Title:
Twenty golden greats.

Main Entry   — Entry provided for the person named with the group.
              The LC Rule Interpretation to Rule 21.23C indicates
              that the name of a person which appears in con-
              junction with the name of the group is not con-
              sidered part of the group's name but rather the name
              of a person.
Added Entries— "(Musical group)" added to the corporate name of
              the performing group to clarify its corporate nature.
              — Additional title access point provided for the title
              with the number expressed as words rather than
              numerals. This is in accordance with LC policy.

Springsteen, Bruce.
>   The river [sound recording] / Bruce Springsteen. —
> New York : Columbia, p1980.
>   2 sound discs : analog, 33⅓ rpm, stereo. ; 12 in.

>   Columbia: PC2 36854.
>   Bruce Springsteen, vocals and guitar ; Clarence
> Clemons, saxophone ; Max Weinberg, drums ; Steve
> Van Zandt, guitar ; Roy Brittan, piano ; Danny
> Federici, organ ; Garry Tallent, bass.
>   Contents: The ties that bind (3:33) — Sherry
> darling (4:02) — Jackson Cage (3:04) — Independence
> day (4:45) — Hungry heart (3:19) — Out in the
> street (4:17) — Crush on you (3:40) — You can
> look (but you better not touch) (2:36) — I wanna
> marry you (3:26) — The river (4:59) — Point
> blank (6:05) — Cadillac ranch (3:02) — I'm a
> rocker (3:34) — Fade away (4:40) — Stolen car
> (3:53) — Ramrod (4:04) — The price you pay
> (5:27) — Drive all night (8:26) — Wreck on the
> highway (3:53).

>   I. Clemons, Clarence. II. Weinberg, Max. III. Van
> Zandt, Steve. IV. Brittan, Roy. V. Federici, Danny.
> VI. Tallent, Gary. VII. Title.

Main Entry   —Entry under the principal performer.
Added Entries—Access points provided for each of the performers. If
the performers were identified by the name of a
group, entry would have been made under the
corporate name of the group, with no entry under
persons other than for the principal performer.

Webber, Andrew Lloyd, 1948-
  [Joseph and the amazing Technicolor dreamcoat
  (Opera) Selections]
    Joseph and the amazing Technicolor dreamcoat
  [sound recording] / music by Andrew Lloyd Webber ;
  lyrics by Tim Rice. — Los Angeles, Calif. : Chrysalis,
  p1982.
    1 sound disc : 33⅓ rpm, stereo. ; 12 in.

    Chrysalis: CHR 1387.
    "Original Broadway cast": Bill Hutton, David
  Ardao, Laurie Beechman, Tom Carder, other artists,
  with orchestra.
    Recorded at the Power Station, New York, Feb.
  1982.
    Durations on labels.
    Lyrics on inner sleeve.

    I. Rice, Tim. II. Hutton, Bill, 1950-   III. Ardao,
  David. IV. Beechman, Laurie. V. Carder, Tom.
  VI. Title.

Main Entry   — Entry under the composer of the work.
Area 7   — "Cast" statement has been modified to show that this
                is the original cast. Normally, a cast note would be-
                gin with the word "Cast:" in accordance with LC
                policy.
              — Early LC *AACR 2* catalog copy placed a space semi-
                colon space between the names of all individuals
                named in a statement of responsibility note. LC has
                since modified this to apply ISBD spacing and punc-
                tuation in only those locations where it is required,
                that is, between the names of individuals performing
                different functions.
              — Location of accompanying material indicated.
Added Entries — Access point under the author of the libretto.
              — Access provided to the work through the names of
                the principal members of the cast. These added
                entries are made at the discretion of the cataloger.

The World of marches [sound recording]. — North
Hollywood, Calif. : Bowmar Records, [19--]
1 sound disc (ca. 50 min.) : analog, 33⅓ rpm, mono. ;
12 in.

Bowmar: 2051.
City of Los Angeles Concert Band, Gabriel Bartold,
conductor.
Contents: National emblem / Bagley — Aguero /
Franco — March from Aida / Verdi-Bartold —
British Eighth / Elliott — French national defile /
Turlet — Einzugs march / Strauss — Entry of the
gladiators / Fucik-Laurendeau — Parade of the
charioteers / Ronza — Colonel Bogey / Alford —
Third of February march / Roncal — Under the
double eagle / Wagner.

I. Bowmar Records.

Comment   — Musical recording with a collective title.
Area 7   — Names of the parts are recorded in the contents notes
                 along with the statement of responsibility for the
                 composers as they appeared on the item.
Added Entries— Added entries could be given for individual works if
                 they are considered important to the library's users.
               — The unique nature of Bowmar records might make it
                 useful for some libraries to provide an access point
                 for the publisher. This would be at the discretion of
                 the cataloger.

Nonmusical Sound Recordings

>Stallman, Lou.
>
>   Let's act as consumers [sound recording] / original words and music by Lou Stallman and Bob Susser. — Roslyn Heights, N.Y. : Stallman-Susser Educational Systems, 1972.
>
>   1 sound disc (ca. 45 min.) : analog, 33⅓ rpm ; 12 in.
>
>   Stallman-Susser Educational Systems: LPED 129A.
>   Songs sung by Lou Stallman.
>   Produced by Lou Stallman and Bob Susser.
>   Teacher's guide on container.
>   Audience: Children.
>   Summary: A one-act play that deals with purchasing to teach consumer awareness.
>   Contents: The book sale — I'm a consumer — More for my money — Here are some rules — I want what I want — Consumer test.
>
>   I. Susser, Bob. II. Title.

Comment	—Nonmusical sound recording not requiring a uniform title.
Area 1	—Statement of responsibility is taken from the item.
Area 7	—Statement of responsibility notes related to the performer and production.
	—Indication of the accompanying material and its location are given in a note rather than in the physical description.
	—Intended audience taken from the program notes.
	—Summary note was necessary to clarify the nature of the item (i.e., a drama). This could also have been indicated using a "nature or artistic form and medium of performance" note.
Added Entries	—Access point provided for the second named individual.

DeRegniers, Beatrice Schenk.
    May I bring a friend [sound recording] / [book by
Schenk de Regniers and Montresor ; composed and
sung by Albert Hague]. — Weston, Conn. : Weston
Woods, 1973.
    1 sound cassette (7 min.) : analog, 2 track, mono.

    Weston Woods: LTR 164C.
    Text from the book of the same title published by
Atheneum, 1964.
    Side 1 with inaudible signal, side 2 with audible
signal.
    Summary: The king and queen are surprised at the
strange friends a little boy brings to visit each day of
the week.

    I. Montresor, Beni. II. Hague, Albert. III. Title.

Main Entry	— Entry under the author prominently named on container.
Area 1	— Composer is named in statement of responsibility because of the importance of his contribution to the sound recording.
Area 5	— Speed of the tape was not given because it is the standard speed for a sound cassette.
	— Track configuration was given because it is not the standard for a sound cassette (four track).
	— Dimensions of the cassette were not given because they are the standard for a sound cassette.
Area 7	— Use is partly determined by use of automatic advance signals indicated in the physical description note.
	— Summaries frequently are useful for children's sound recordings.

Hale, Lucretia Peabody, 1820-1900.
    The Peterkin papers [sound recording] / by
Lucretia P. Hale. — New York : Caedmon Records,
1973.
    1 sound disc : analog, 33⅓ rpm, stereo. ; 12 in.

    Caedmon: TC 1377.
    Read by Cathleen Nesbitt.
    Descriptive notes by P. Kresh on container.
    Audience: Elementary grades.
    Contents: The lady who put salt in her coffee
(12:00) — About Elizabeth Eliza's piano (2:37) — The
Peterkins try to become wise (7:00) — The Peterkins
at home (3:49) — The Peterkins snowed-up (11:00) —
The Peterkins' picnic (15:00)

    I. Nesibtt, Cathleen, 1888-   II. Caedmon
Records. III. Title.

Main Entry	—Entry under prominently named author.
	—Form of the name is Library of Congress "*AACR 2* compatible".
Area 5	—Duration of the entire recording is not given here because the durations of the parts are given in the contents note.
Area 7	—Performer named.
	—Audience stated on the item.
	—Duration of the individual parts included in the contents note.
Added Entries	—Access provided to this work through the name of the narrator.
	—Access point provided for the name of the publisher because of the type of record it produces. This is provided at the option of the cataloger.

Wagner, Linda Welshimer.
William Carlos Williams [sound recording] / lecturer, Linda Wagner. — Deland, Fla. : E. Edwards, 1972.
1 sound cassette (28 min.) : analog, 2 track, mono. — (Modern American poetry criticism)

Everett Edwards: 808.

I. Title. II. Series.

Main Entry — Entry is under the lecturer.
— Form of the name is the *AACR 2* authorized form.
Area 5 — LC seldom gives the track configuration of a sound cassette.
Area 7 — No summary note was needed because the content is clear from the rest of the description.
Added Entries — Access point provided for the series because of the subject indication in its title.

Doyle, Arthur Conan, Sir, 1859-1930.
Favorite tales of Sherlock Holmes [sound recording] / by Sir Arthur Conan Doyle. — Old Greenwich, Conn. : Listening Library, p1959.
2 sound discs : analog, 16⅔ rpm, mono. ; 12 in. — (Talking books)

Listening Library: A 1608.
Title on container: Tales of Sherlock Holmes.
Read by John Brewster.
Text from the original issues of the Strand magazine for 1891, 1892 and 1893.
Program notes on container.
Contents: A scandal in Bohemia — The Red-headed league — The speckled band — The final problem.

I. Brewster, John. II. Title. III. Title: Tales of Sherlock Holmes.

Main Entry — Entry under the person responsible for the intellectual content of the work.
— Form of the name is LC "*AACR 2* compatible". *AACR 2* form would be: Doyle, Sir A. Conan (Arthur Conan), 1859-1930.
— "Sir" moved to the end of the name, rather than preceding the forename as called for in *AACR 2*, in accordance with LC policy.
Area 1 — "Sir" retained in the statement of responsibility in accordance with Rule 1.1F7.

(Explanation continues on page 106.)

Area 5   — Care must be taken in recording the playing speed.
                This work physically appears to be a 33⅓ rpm re-
                cording. Only an examination of the label reveals the
                actual playing speed of 16⅔ rpm.
Area 7   — Note provided for the variant title.
Added Entries — Access provided to the work through the variant
                title.

World War I [sound recording] : historic music and
  voices / written and produced by Robert Lewis
  Shayon. — New York : American Heritage, p1964.
  1 sound disc : analog, 33⅓ rpm, mono. ; 12 in.

    Charles Collingwood, narrator ; Charles Paul,
music director.
    Companion to: The American Heritage history of
World War I / S.L.A. Marshall.
    Program notes on container.
    Summary: Recounts the history of World War I
through recordings of actual events and the music of
the war period.

    I. Shayon, Robert Lewis. II. Collingwood, Charles.
III. Paul, Charles. IV. Marshall, S.L.A. (Samuel
Lyman Atwood), 1900-1977. The American heritage
history of World War I.

Main Entry   — Entry under title because the contributions to the
                work were considered to be too diffuse to attribute
                the work to a single individual.
Area 7   — No publisher's number is associated with this work.
                — Indication of a related work.
Added Entries — Access point provided to the entry (Name. Title) for
                the related work.

Labor relations and employment law for the corporate
counsel and the general practitioner [sound record-
ing] : ALI-ABA course of study. — Philadelphia,
Pa. : American Law Institute-American Bar Association Committee on Continuing Professional Education, p1979.
13 sound cassettes

American Law Institute-American Bar Association Committee on Continuing Professional Education: V 476.
Panel discussions, lectures and questions and
answers.
Recorded in Atlanta, Ga., Jan. 18-20, 1979.
In loose-leaf binder with study materials (29 cm.)
Audience: Lawyers.
Summary: Discusses equal employment obligations,
agency investigations, affirmative action programs,
labor relations law, defense of unfair labor practices, negotiating a labor agreements, etc.

I. American Law Institute-American Bar Association Committee on Continuing Professional Education.

Area 5 — No information available on playing time, track configuration, or sound characteristics.
Area 7 — Name of the publisher given even though it is exceedingly lengthy.
— Information about the container and other accompanying material given in one note.

5
Description of
Motion Pictures and Videorecordings

---

*AACR 2 CHAPTER 7: MOTION PICTURES AND
VIDEORECORDINGS*

7.0   GENERAL RULES

7.0A   SCOPE

The scope of this chapter includes many different types of images on film and videotape which simulate motion. Motion pictures of varying length, from short film clips, both edited and unedited, to full-length theatrical productions, are included. Single-concept film loops, standard 8mm, and super 8mm films in cartridges and on reels are also covered, as are videocassettes and videodiscs, including music videos. Sound track films (i.e., films on which no visual images appear) are not covered by this chapter but are addressed in Chapter 6 of *AACR 2*.

This chapter in *AACR 2* has rule provisions for special types of motion pictures and videorecordings (e.g., newsfilm, stock shots, commercials, trailers, unedited material, etc.), some of which are not likely to be a part of typical multimedia collections. This chapter will concentrate upon those types of motion pictures and videorecordings most likely to be held in these collections and will not address the more unique materials covered by *AACR 2*.

Many libraries have established procedures for providing for the motion picture and video needs of their patrons that are different from those used for other forms of print and nonprint materials. School and public libraries often omit motion pictures and videorecordings from their local collection. Instead, these items are often cataloged, stored, and circulated from a central agency, either a school district film center, a district media center, a central public library, or a state library film collection. Many universities also have centralized their film services outside the library. Many of these film agencies, providing either motion picture or videorecordings or both, do not provide complete descriptive cataloging for their materials, providing instead some form of film catalog. Typically, these catalogs enter the film under its title, give a brief synopsis, and classify the collection into a limited number of subject categories. Many film agencies, particularly those which rent motion pictures and videorecordings and publish catalogs of their rental holdings, may want to continue their current practices, rather than adopt the more detailed approach to them provided by *AACR 2*.

Providing bibliographic access through a unified media catalog, using standard descriptive cataloging techniques, however, can significantly increase the informativeness of the catalog and thus potentially increase the availability of these materials. Much of the description, particularly the notes, given for motion pictures and videorecordings provides valuable information for the user. This description enhances the user's ability to select materials by providing information often lacking in the typical film catalog in book form. Access points, based on this expanded description, increase the avenues by which users can gain direct access to these materials.

If the cataloging provided by film agencies was adequate for most types of users, the detailed *AACR 2* rules would not be necessary. In most cases, however, *AACR 2*-based cataloging provides more information than do most locally developed methods used for film catalogs. Film services that wish to continue publishing a catalog in book form could enhance its value by using access points derived from descriptive cataloging developed according to *AACR 2*. In developing these book catalog entries, catalogers can simply eliminate information deemed unnecessary from the *AACR 2* record. *AACR 2* provides for a synopsis or summary of a work's content. This type of summary can also be used in the film catalog. If *AACR 2*-generated catalog records are machine-readable, they can be used to create a film catalog in book form for distribution outside the library as well as a traditional catalog for library use.

In addition to the guidance given catalogers of motion pictures and video-recording by *AACR 2*, a manual published by the Library of Congress in 1984 is designed to assist catalogers in film and television archives in the description of their archival materials. This manual, *Archival Moving Image Materials: A Cataloging Manual*, compiled by Wendy White-Hensen, supplements rather than replaces information found in Chapter 7 of *AACR 2*. As in the case with other, similar manuals issued by LC, it follows the general structure of *AACR 2* but differs significantly in specific details. Catalogers of nonarchival works should become familiar with this manual, because it may provide useful approaches which can be applied to nonarchival works.

7.0B SOURCES OF INFORMATION

7.0B1 Chief Sources of Information

The chief source of information for both motion pictures and videorecordings is the item itself and its container, if that container is an integral part of the item, that is, physically inseparable for playback purposes. This includes cassettes or cartridges housing motion pictures or videorecordings. Also included as part of the chief source of information is any label permanently affixed to the container.

Although the preferred chief source of information on an item is the title frame, information important to the correct description of a work can appear at any point in the item. Catalogers should be aware that, to catalog this type of format adequately, it is necessary to scan the entire work to be sure that information appearing near the beginning or the end of the motion picture or videorecording has been evaluated for its usefulness in describing the work. Title frames, credits, and other valuable information normally appear at the beginning and at the end of these works.

When information is not available from the chief source of information, it can be taken from:

- accompanying textual material
- a container which is not an integral part of the item
- other sources

These sources should be consulted in this order of preference.

7.0B2 Prescribed Sources of Information

For each area of the description, there are different prescribed source(s) from which information can be taken without having to enclose it in square brackets. For the Title and Statement of Responsibility Area, the chief source of information serves as the prescribed source of information. For some of the areas (Edition, Publication, Distribution, etc., and Series) the chief source of information and any accompanying material are prescribed sources, although the chief source of information remains the preferred source. Other areas of the description (Physical Description, Notes, and Standard Number) allow the information to be derived from any source.

In all but a few cases, information required by the chosen level of description can be taken from any source provided that the information is placed within square brackets. Additionally, catalogers are always free to record information in a note without the need of brackets.

7.1 TITLE AND STATEMENT OF RESPONSIBILITY AREA

7.1B TITLE PROPER

The title proper should be recorded as instructed in Rule 1.1B. Information taken from sources other than the chief source of information, that is, the item itself and any integral container, must be enclosed within square brackets.

In an interpretation to Rule 7.1B1, the Library of Congress has instructed its catalogers not to consider a statement of credits, naming an individual or corporate body which precedes or follows the title, as part of the title proper. This instruction includes those situations where the language of the title "integrates" the credit statement into the title. The credit statement would, however, be treated as part of the title proper if the statement is: (1) "within" the title, (2) a "fanciful" statement mimicking a true credit, or (3) represented by the credit in the possessive case preceding the title proper.

Rule 7.1B2 instructs catalogers to supply a title, following the provisions of Rule 1.1B7, if the item lacks a title. This situation will occur far less frequently for materials covered by the chapter than it will for other forms of nonprint materials. This can, however, be a more frequent occurrence for materials covered by this chapter in *AACR 2* which are not commonly held by multimedia libraries, such as newsfilm, commercials, etc.

7.1C *OPTIONAL ADDITION.* **GENERAL MATERIAL DESIGNATION**

The General Material Designation follows the title proper. Either the GMD "motion picture" or "videorecording" can be used. Parallel titles, "other title information," and their associated punctuation follow the GMD.

7.1D PARALLEL TITLES

Parallel titles, that is, titles proper which appear in more than one language or script, are not all that uncommon for commercial, noneducational motion pictures and videorecordings. These titles are recorded following the title proper and the GMD according to the instructions given in Rule 1.1D. A parallel title is preceded by a space, equals sign, space. For level two descriptions, a cataloger must record the first parallel title. If a subsequent parallel title is in English, it must also be recorded.

Some complexities are introduced by motion pictures, originally recorded in one language, which are distributed in countries which use other languages. For films made originally in a language other than English, then subsequently dubbed in English, catalogers should record the English title as the title proper, if it is given in the chief source of information. The title in the language of the original, if given on the chief source of information, should be recorded as a parallel title following the GMD. If the title appears only in the non-English language, that title should be recorded as the title proper. No attempt should be made to translate it into English.

If a sound track is recorded in a non-English language and the title appears in that language on the chief source of information, which it usually does, that original title is the title proper. An English title, if it appears on the item, should be recorded as the parallel title. If a film in a non-English language has English subtitles, that fact can be given in a note (Rule 7.7B2).

Visit to the sepulcher [motion picture] = Visitatio sepulchri

Afterlife [videorecording] = Apres la vie

7.1E OTHER TITLE INFORMATION

Other title information, including subtitles, is recorded following the GMD. Rule 1.1E1 is the operative rule for recording this information. The position of this information is different from that used in *AACR 1* Revised Chapter 12, where it was placed before the GMD.

America in 1968 [motion picture] : people and culture

Asbestos [motion picture] : the way to dusty death

Glory was, glory is! [motion picture] : the Peloponnesus of Greece

Indian crafts [motion picture] : Hopi, Navajo, and Iroquois

Spirit catcher [videorecording] : the art of Betye Saar

7.1F STATEMENTS OF RESPONSIBILITY

In *AACR 2*, catalogers have to decide whether to record statements of responsibility in this area, in a statement of responsibility note, or ignore the statement entirely. This problem is more difficult for motion pictures and video-recordings than it is for books because, most often, numerous individuals are mentioned on the item as having some involvement in its production. In its interpretation to Rule 7.1F1, the Library of Congress indicated that statements of responsibility are generally made for persons who have had some degree of "overall" responsibility for the item. Generally, LC considers producers, directors, and writers to have had some degree of overall responsibility. Persons who do not meet this level of responsibility would be mentioned either in a statement of responsibility note or not mentioned at all. LC encourages its catalogers to be "liberal" in making exceptions to this general policy to allow for the inclusion of others who have made important, albeit partial, contributions to a work. The amount of information given in this area will depend upon the judgment of the cataloger and policy set by the library based upon the needs of the library's users.

Statements of responsibility are recorded as instructed in Rule 1.1F. In most cases, this excludes information found only in accompanying material and infor-mation found in sources outside the item. When recording a statement of responsibility, include the entire statement of responsibility, that is, phrases indicating the relationship between the title and the person or corporate body, rather than just the name, if the relationship is not clear.

The provision of statements of responsibility in *AACR 2* differs significant-ly from that prescribed by *AACR 1* Revised Chapter 12. That earlier code allowed for the transcription of a statement of responsibility only if the person or corporate body to be named was also the main entry, or if the statement was considered to be of "primary significance" in identifying the work. Under *AACR 2* these conditions are not a factor in determining whether to record a statement of responsibility or not.

AACR 1 Revised Chapter 12 included a rule which instructed catalogers to record in the statement of responsibility, the name of the person or corporate body responsible for the "physical process of production," if that person or body was different from the person or corporate body responsible for "originating" the work. In these situations, the person or body responsible for "originating" the work was recorded first, followed by the person or body responsible for the "physical process." The latter statement was to include any phrase indicating the function performed by the person or body. When no such function statement existed on the item, the cataloger was to add the phrase "[made by]" to that part of the statement of responsibility. Under these earlier rules, the use of this type of statement was rather commonplace. Cataloging developed under *AACR 2* does not provide specific instructions for this type of statement. In practice, however, the Library of Congress frequently records this type of information in the statement of responsibility using the phrase "[produced by]."

Notes related to the statement of responsibility are discussed under Rule 7.7B6. Individuals and groups related to a production who are omitted from the statement of responsibility can be named in notes. Those associated with the artistic and technical production can be included in statement of responsibility notes as can members of the cast. See examples under Rule 7.7B6 for this type of note.

7.1F2

If the relationship between the title and statement of responsibility is not clear, and no statement exists on the item, a short word or phrase, enclosed in square brackets, explaining the relationship should be added by the cataloger.

7.1F3

Give both the production agency and the organization for which an item is produced if both are named.

> Yours truly, Andrea G. Stern [motion picture] / by Susan Seidelman. — *[Main entry under Seidelman.]*

> Creative storytelling techniques [videorecording] : mixing the media / with Caroline Feller Bauer. —

> The Shores of the cosmic ocean [videorecording] / KCET-TV. —

> The National Bible quiz [motion picture] / Walter J. Klein, Co., Ltd. — *["Co." and "Ltd." were abbreviated on the item.]*

> Getting together [videorecording] : love / Educational Film Center and Ontario Educational Communications Authority. —

> The Body in question. Program 12, Heads and tails [videorecording] / BBC in association with KCET. —

> Hispanic America [videorecording] / CBS News ; with CBS News correspondents Walter Cronkite and Ed Rabel. —

> Doctor-patient relationships [videoreocrding] / Time-Life Video ; producer, director, and writer, David A. Taper. —

> Giving a complete bed bath [videorecording] / Miami-Dade Community College ; project director, Frances Britton ; project coordinator, Jeanne Stark. —

> Heredity [videorecording] / Encyclopaedia Britannica Educational Corporation ; [produced by] Acorn Films ; producer and writer, William Claiborne. —

> Her best interests [motion picture] / Chase Exchange and the Chase Manhattan Bank, N.A. ; [produced by] Film Counselors, Inc. —

> Via satellite [motion picture] / American Telephone and Telegraph Company ; [produced by] Aegis Productions. —

7.1G ITEMS WITHOUT A COLLECTIVE TITLE

If multiple works are recorded on a videotape or motion picture, they may be described either separately or as a unit. Generally, it is best to describe each item separately (Rule 7.1G4) and link the descriptions using a "with" note (Rule 7.7B21).

If, however, the works are conceptually related, or are related in terms of the person or group responsible for the intellectual content, a unit description (Rules 7.1G2 and 7.1G3) can prove satisfactory. The titles of the individual parts should be recorded according to the provisions of Rule 1.1G, with each title separated by a full stop. Statements of responsibility are recorded following the individual title with which they are associated. The GMD is recorded in brackets following the statement of responsibility of the last work.

7.2 EDITION AREA

7.2B EDITION STATEMENT

When recording information about the edition or a named reissue of a motion picture or videorecording, a cataloger must follow the provisions of Rule 1.2B. Generally, the nature of motion pictures and videorecordings is such that they seldom carry edition statements. Instead, when these materials have differences from other versions, the work is retitled without continuing the edition numbering of the previous edition.

7.2B3 *Optional Addition*

Catalogers have the option of adding an edition statement if the work is known to have "significant" changes from previous editions of the motion picture or videorecording. This statement, enclosed within square brackets, should be given in the language of the title. Catalogers should be aware, however, that the Library of Congress does not use this option. Instead, if a work is known to be a new edition but unnamed, this information is given in a note (Rule 7.7B7). It is probably a good idea for most multimedia libraries to follow LC's practice because these relationships between works, often difficult to describe succinctly, can be made more meaningful through the use of a note. See examples under Rule 7.7B7.

7.4 PUBLICATION, DISTRIBUTION, ETC., AREA

Information provided in this area for motion pictures and videorecordings differs somewhat from that recorded for other types of nonprint materials. The difference lies in the number of functions that can be recorded. For most nonprint materials, these functions are limited to the publisher and/or distributor of the item. For motion pictures and videorecordings, in addition to these two functions, are the functions of releasing agency, producer, production agency, etc.

The prescribed sources of information for this area are the chief source of information and any accompanying material. All of the places and names, usually of corporate bodies, associated with the publication, distribution, and release of an item should be given here. Agencies responsible for the production of an item which were not named in the statement of responsibility can also be named here. This approach is particularly appropriate if the production agency or producer is not mentioned prominently in the item.

Items originally made as motion pictures which are later issued in a video format should be described in terms of the agencies responsible for the videorecording. Information recorded in the statement of responsibility area most often will be related to the production of the original motion picture.

Details concerning manufacture and distribution should be related to the video-recording. Information about the manufacture and distribution of the motion picture, if considered important, can be recorded as a note (Rule 7.7B9). Many productions are now being offered in both video and motion picture formats. When cataloging these works, it should be remembered that it is the format in hand which should be described.

The punctuation of the information in this area can become complicated because these works will frequently contain several places, names, and dates. Rule 7.4A1 contains specific punctuation instructions for these situations. Examples for Area 4 in this chapter of *AACR 2* and Chapter 1 can be helpful in gaining an understanding of the punctuation used in different situations.

7.4C PLACE OF PUBLICATION, DISTRIBUTION, ETC.

The place of each of the agencies named in this area should be recorded following the instructions given in Rule 1.4C. In addition, Rule 1.4C7 provides an option to add the complete address of any of these agencies if this information is deemed useful and that the agency is not a "major trade" publisher. Generally, this information is of little value to a library's patrons, even for small publishers who are often difficult to locate in reference sources. Except in unusual cases, it is best not to apply this option. The Library of Congress does not apply this option for either motion pictures or videorecordings.

7.4D NAME OF PUBLISHER, DISTRIBUTOR, ETC.

The name of each of the agencies responsible for the work, except the manufacturer, not named in the statement of responsibility, should be recorded here. In recording this information, the provisions of Rule 1.4D must be followed.

7.4E *OPTIONAL ADDITION. STATEMENT OF FUNCTION OF PUBLISHER, DISTRIBUTOR, ETC.*

Because there are often several agencies associated with motion pictures and videorecordings performing these functions, an indication of the function of each agency is necessary unless each is fulfilling the same function. This indication can be done using a phrase from the item as instructed in Rule 1.4D3. In cases where a phrase indicating the function (1) is not available from the item, (2) is not recorded, or (3) in cases where the function is not clear from the context of the information given elsewhere in the body of the entry, the option to add a phrase indicating the function can be implemented. These phrases are provided according to the provisions of Rule 1.4E1.

This rule gives a cataloger four choices for a statement of function. The words or phrases which may be used are:

distributor	producer
publisher	production company

A producer is defined in the *AACR 2* glossary as the "person with final responsibility for the making of a motion picture, including business aspects, management of the production, and the commercial success of the film." This is a much broader definition of this function than the one usually associated with a film producer, who would normally be named in the credits. Generally, a producer will be named in this area only when a production company is not named. The producer, if named here, would be responsible for all of the functions of production normally performed by a company. Some short motion pictures, but relatively few major productions, result from this type of activity.

If a cataloger has chosen to record the name of a publisher, distributor, or releasing agency in the statement of responsibility, that name must be repeated in this area. That name can be given in an abbreviated form if it appears in full in the statement of responsibility. The requirement to record that name here reduces the imperative to record it in the statement of responsibility. It is generally assumed by persons familiar with the film industry that groups responsible for publication and production of a work often have some degree of responsibility for its content.

7.4F DATE OF PUBLICATION, DISTRIBUTION, ETC.

The dates of publication, distribution, and/or release of a motion picture or videorecording should be recorded according to the provisions of Rule 1.4F4. That rule instructs catalogers to record dates associated with the different functions of the various agencies after the name to which the date applies.

The date of the original production of a film or video presentation may be important to the user. Rule 7.4F2 gives the cataloger the option of providing this date. When given, this date must be placed in a note (Rule 7.7B9) rather than in Area 4. The Library of Congress follows this option whenever the difference between the original date of publication is different from the date of publication, distribution, or copyright by more than two years. This date of original publication should, however, be the date of the publication of the work in that form. If the form of the item has changed (i.e., from motion picture to videorecording), that date would be recorded in an edition and history note (Rule 7.7B7).

7.4G PLACE OF MANUFACTURE, NAME OF MANUFACTURER, DATE OF MANUFACTURE

When the publisher of a work is unknown, information about the place and name of the manufacturer should be given, enclosed within parentheses, following the date. Frequently, the use of this rule is unnecessary for motion pictures, but it may be the only information available for some videorecordings.

7.4G2 *Optional Addition*

Optionally, a cataloger can record the place, name, and/or date of manufacture, providing they (1) differ from the place, name, and date of publication, (2) are considered important, and (3) are found on the item. This "optional addition" is not being applied by the Library of Congress and there is little reason for most, if any, multimedia libraries to apply it either.

Emergency shelf [videorecording] / Hemisphere Productions. – New York : Time-Life Video, 1980.

Themes – the day when nothing made sense [videorecording] / Centron Corporation. – Lawrence, KS : Centron Films, 1981.

National parks, playground or paradise? [motion picture] / WQED and National Geographic Society. — Washington, D.C. : National Geographic Society Educational Services, 1981, c1980.

These are the good old days [motion picture] / ITT Continental Baking Company ; [produced by] Blue Marble Company, Inc. — Rye, N.Y. : ITT Continental Baking Company, 1981.

Persuasive techniques [videorecording] / Agency for Instructional Television ; [produced by] Educational Film Center. — Bloomington, Ind. : The Agency, 1980.

Norman physical assessment, a tool for the beginning practitioner [videorecording] / U.S. Dept. of the Army. — Washington, D.C. : The Department, 1977 : Distributed by National Audiovisual Center, 1981. *[Date of production differs from the date of release.]*

7.5 PHYSICAL DESCRIPTION AREA

The physical characteristics of motion pictures and videorecordings must be considered when constructing a complete and accurate physical description. While films and videotapes or videodiscs all record moving images, and usually sound, their physical characteristics are markedly different. Items made originally as motion pictures, issued later in a video format, should be described as videorecordings. In presenting the information requirements for Area 5, rules which are pertinent to both formats will be discussed first, followed by those rules which apply to only motion pictures or videorecordings.

Films

Film is described in terms of its base, the container of the base, its duration, unusual projection requirements, sound characteristics, color, unusual projection speed, and width.

7.5B EXTENT OF ITEM (INCLUDING SPECIFIC MATERIAL DESIGNATION)

Base

The same type of base, cellulose acetate, with a top coat, emulsion, and backing, is found in all modern motion picture film. Thus, the term "film" is sufficient to describe all types of motion pictures. Early motion pictures were made of cellulose nitrate, a highly flammable material no longer used.

Containers

Film of varying widths is housed on, or in, several types of containers— open reels, cartridges, and cassettes. In projection, open reel film passes through a projector and is taken up on another open reel. After viewing, it must be rewound. Film in a closed cartridge is usually housed within a closed loop mechanism, that is, one end of the film is connected to the other and the film plays continuously. It does not go through a rewind process. Film housed in cassettes travels from one reel to another within the cassette. As with audiotapes in cassettes, these films must be rewound and do not play continuously.

The definitions given above are generic definitions of the terms. There are some companies (e.g., Kodak) which package film in enclosed reel-to-reel containers (called cassettes above) which they refer to as cartridges. These cartridges require a specific type of equipment for playback, and, in this case, the name of the type of cartridge, that is, Kodak Supermatic, must be specified in the physical description of the catalog record or in a note. Generally, however, the term "cartridge" implies a continuous loop. Continous loop cartridges, usually housing film which is 8mm wide, come with film of varying length. The cartridges come in different sizes to accommodate different lengths of the film.

The total number of physical units of the film being described, followed by a specific material designation, are the first two elements recorded in this area. The specific material designations for motion pictures are limited to the following phrases:

film cartridge   film loop
film cassette   film reel

As an option, a cataloger may drop the designation "film" from the specific material designation if the GMD "motion picture" has been used. The Library of Congress is not following this option and, for the benefit of its users, most multimedia libraries will probably find it best to follow LC's policy.

7.5B2 [Playing Time]
The 1985 Revision to *AACR 2* deleted the original *AACR 2* rule for recording playing time and replaced it with a new rule. This new rule instructs catalogers to follow the provisions of Rule 1.5B4. That rule, also revised in 1985, provides several ways to record the playing time.

If the time is stated on the item, it should be recorded as given. The old *AACR 2* rule had required that the playing time for a motion picture or videorecording under five minutes in duration had to be recorded in terms of minutes and seconds. The revised rule now allows for recording playing time in minutes and seconds, without any maximum duration limit, provided that the playing time is given that way on the item.

As an option to this rule, a cataloger can give an approximate playing time if no time is stated on the item and cannot be readily ascertained. The Library of Congress does not apply this option. Multimedia libraries may wish to reconsider the LC decision since some information about the time, even a rough approximation, can be of far greater value to the potential user of the material than no time indication at all.

For multipart items, this rule provides another option, that of recording the playing time of each part, if the parts have approximately the same playing time. This time is indicated by stating the uniform time followed by the word "each." The Library of Congress is applying this option on a case-by-case basis. Multimedia libraries will probably wish to either apply this rule selectively as LC does, or in all cases where uniform times exist.

7.5C OTHER PHYSICAL DETAILS

7.5C2 Aspect Ratio and Special Projection Characteristics

Each type of film container, open reel, cassette, or cartridge, requires its own type of projection equipment. Equipment made for one type of container cannot play film housed in another container format.

Projection equipment for cartridges differs in its capability to accommodate cartridges of different sizes. It is necessary to indicate these characteristics in the description of the film so that the catalog record will adequately inform potential users of projection requirements. This information can appear in the Physical Description Area, in a note, or a combination of both areas.

Cartridges manufactured by some companies can only be played back on equipment produced by that company or compatible equipment produced by another firm. Fairchild Camera and Instrument Corporation manufactures cartridges and playback equipment to accommodate its cassettes for films of varying length. A Kodak projector must be used to play back Kodak Supermatic cassette-cartridges. Technicolor, Inc., manufactures equipment to play 8mm cartridges. Several other companies also manufacture equipment compatible with this type of cartridge. Although the characteristics of the software are the major concern of the cataloger, software which requires one type of equipment for playback necessitates that the name of that equipment be mentioned in the catalog record.

If characteristics of the film require special projection requirements, this should be included succinctly in the Physical Description Area according to the provisions of Rule 7.5C2. Other special projection requirements can be specified in a note (Rule 7.7B10h). Although film cartridges are commonly accommodated by equipment produced by several manufacturers, this equipment can accommodate only certain sizes of cartridges (determined by the length of the film held by the cartridge). For this reason, the length of these films should also be recorded in a note (Rule 7.7B10b).

7.5C3 Sound Characteristics

For most motion pictures, sound is integral to the item. One exception to this would be cartridge films accompanied by sound on cassettes. Because the film's form is so standardized, sound characteristics are most often simply indicated in the Physical Description Area as either the presence or absence of sound (e.g., "si." or "sd."). Sound can be recorded on film optically or magnetically. Some projectors accommodate both types of sound tracks; others play back only one. Almost all 8mm films with sound contain a magnetic sound track; while almost all 16mm films have an optical sound track. If the item in hand differs from these standards, that information should be given in a note.

7.5C4 Colour

The cataloger must indicate whether a motion picture is in color (col.) or black and white (b&w). The color indication is limited to these two statements. The rule instructs that sepia prints are considered to be black and white.

7.5C5 Projection Speed

Sound and silent motion pictures are photographed at different speeds — 16 frames per second (fps) for silent films and 24 fps for sound films. If sound is indicated, it is assumed that the film was photographed at the standard speed for sound; likewise, if the film is described as silent, it is assumed that it was photographed at the standard speed for silent films. If this is not the case, the different speed should be noted. Motion pictures made at the speed for silent films can be played back on a projector designed for sound films, but the frames will pass through the projector more rapidly than intended and produce a speeded-up visual image.

7.5D DIMENSIONS

Film also varies in its width. The most common widths of motion pictures in a multimedia collection are 8mm and 16mm. Film is also produced in 35mm, 70mm, and 105mm widths. Generally, the larger the image on the film, the better its projected image. There are two forms of 8mm film, standard and super 8mm. The size of the image on super 8mm is larger than for standard 8mm. Most 8mm film produced today is of the super 8mm variety.

1 film cartridge (28 min.) : sd., col. ; super 8 mm.

1 film loop (3 min., 22 sec.) : si., col. ; standard 8 mm.

1 film reel (22 min.) : sd., col. ; 16 mm.

1 film reel (34 min.) : sd., col. ; 35 mm.

3 film reels (110 min.) : sd., col. ; 70 mm.

Videorecordings

Like film, all videotapes contain a similar base, usually polyester, with a top-coat, a magnetic oxide layer, and a backing. A videodisc has the magnetic properties associated with videotape, but is more similar to a sound recording disc in terms of the characteristics of its base. The technology related to the retrieval of the visual images and sound recorded magnetically on tape and disc is dissimilar.

Videotapes are described in terms of the integral container of the videotape (i.e., cartridge, cassette, or reel). Videodiscs are described in terms of their duration, sound characteristics, color, and playing speed. The dimensions, that is, tape width for videotape and the disc size for videodiscs, are the final elements of the physical description of videorecordings.

Open reel videotape was the first video format developed and also the first collected by libraries. The tape is produced in different widths, ¼-inch, ½-inch, 1-inch, and 2-inch. Most broadcast tape and original professional productions on videotape are done on 2-inch tape, which is recorded in a quadraplex mode. Quadraplex recordings require quadraplex playback equipment. Videotape in widths other than 2-inch uses the helical scan mode of recording. It is assumed that tape other than 2-inch is helical scan and that 2-inch is quadraplex. Libraries which collect master tapes, from which others are duplicated, usually collect 2-inch tape, which can be reproduced in any of the other tape sizes.

The first type of tape collected by libraries, other than those with large collections of master tapes, was the ½-inch reel-to-reel tape. The Electronics Industry Association of Japan, which represents the manufacturers of video equipment, developed a standard, the EIAJ standard, which ensured that most ½-inch videotape could be played back on most videorecorder-players. For ½-inch tape there are two standards, one for regular equipment and one for portable equipment. The only difference between the two is in the size of the reel. The smaller reel, used for portable equipment, can be played back on regular size, standard equipment.

When ¾-inch tape, enclosed in videocassettes, was developed, many libraries began collecting prerecorded tape in this format because of the ease of operation of this equipment. There is a standard (EIAJ) for this type of tape which is called the "U" standard or "U-matic." As with the ½-inch reel-to-reel tape, there is also a different size cassette for the portable equipment. The smaller cassettes for the portable recorders can be played back on both portable recorder-players and standard size recorder-players.

For both ½-inch reel-to-reel and ¾-inch cassette recordings, playback is possible on equipment manufactured by many different companies. With 1-inch reel-to-reel and ½-inch cassettes, this is not the case. Equipment with competing technologies requires different types of tape reels and cassettes. Type "C" tape is used with Sony, Ampex, and NEC 1 equipment. Type "C" tape, with "B" wind, and with the oxide side out is used for Bosch-Fernseh equipment. Few libraries collect 1-inch tape.

The two major types of ½-inch cassette tape are the VHS format and the Beta format. Marketed for the home video market rather than the commercial market, these two types are widely collected and circulated by libraries. Numerous manufacturers produce equipment for use with each of these types, although Sony is usually associated with the Beta format. These tapes should be described in terms of the standard (i.e., VHS or Beta) rather than a specific trade name of the manufacturer of a particular piece of equipment. This is particularly true of VHS, which can be used with Panasonic, RCA, Phillips, Magnavox, or GE equipment as well as equipment manufactured by several other companies. Although VHS cassette tape can be played on the equipment of a variety of manufacturers, VHS and Beta format cassettes are not compatible and require different playback equipment.

Videodisc technology has not attained the popularity anticipated by its developers. One likely reason for its lack of acceptance is that it, like a sound disc, is exclusively a playback medium rather than a recording and playback medium. Its presence in multimedia libraries has been greatly overshadowed by videotape although that may change as newer technology develops.

There are currently two different recording and playback technologies in the videodisc field. One uses a diamond stylus to decode the magnetic signals imbedded on the disc, while the other uses laser technology. The laser technology of DiscoVision was developed by MCA Phillips and is used with Magnavision from Magnavox. RCA SelectaVision uses the stylus technology. Obviously, discs of each type must be used with equipment compatible with that technology. Because no standards have yet been developed, the best way to describe these discs is with the terms applied to them by the producer.

7.5B EXTENT OF ITEM (INCLUDING SPECIFIC MATERIAL DESIGNATION)

For videorecordings, as with motion pictures, the total number of physical units of the item being described is recorded first followed by the appropriate specific material designation. The specific material designations for videorecordings begin with the prefix "video," combined with one of the terms appropriate to describe the container or format—tape, cassette, reel, or disc. The specific material designations for videorecordings are limited to these four terms.

As was the case with motion pictures, as an option, a cataloger may drop the designation "video" from the specific material designation if the GMD "videorecording" has been used. Again, the Library of Congress is not following this option and, for the benefit of its users, most multimedia libraries will probably find it best to also follow LC's policy.

A "trade name or other technical specification" should be added to the specific material designation of a videorecording if: (1) it is necessary to know this information in order to properly use the item, and (2) if the item is only available in that one form. If both of these conditions are not met, information about the "trade name or other technical specification" should be recorded in the Note Area (Rule 7.7B16) instead.

There are situations in which a multimedia library will acquire a videorecording in more than one type of container or format. In these situations, a cataloger can provide a separate description for each item, or a multilevel description. A third alternative available is to create a more generic physical description statement appropriate to all forms of videorecordings. An indication of the different containers or formats available in the library is then recorded in the Note Area (Rule 7.7B16).

In giving this multiple format description, the word "videorecording" is used in the extent of item location rather than a more specific indication of the video format. This description approach is very frequently employed by the Library of Congress. The use of the specific material designation "videorecording" should not be used if the library possesses the work in the same form of container even though the tape size may vary, for example, two videocassettes of the same work, one VHS, the other Beta. In these cases, the appropriate SMD for the specific type of container (e.g., videocassette) is provided. A note (rule 7.7B16) is used to indicate the different standards and sizes, when appropriate.

Work available in multiple types of containers

Physical description	1 videorecording (ca. 28 min.) : sd., col. + 1 teacher's guide + 1 manual.
Note	Issued as cassette (U standard ¾ in. or Beta ½ in. or VHS ½ in.) or reel (EIAJ ½ in. or Type C 1 in. or Quad 2 in.).
Physical description	1 videocassette (21 min.) : sd., col. + 1 study guide.
Note	Issued as U-matic, ¾ in. or Beta 1½ in. or Beta 2 ½ in. or VHS ½ in.

7.5C   OTHER PHYSICAL DETAILS

7.5C3   Sound Characteristics
The presence or absence of sound should be indicated for videorecordings. This information is recorded in the same way as it is for film, that is, "si." or "sd." Video formats can contain more than one channel for sound, and therefore may have more than one soundtrack.

7.5C4   Colour
The presence of color is not controlled by the type of tape stock used, but by the equipment with which the images are recorded on the tape. A color video-recording can be played back on equipment which is not color sensitive and the picture will appear in black and white. The presence or absence of color should be noted. Care should be taken to ensure that a b&w image is the result of the recording process and not due to the limitations of the playback equipment. As with films, only the terms "col." and "b&w" may be used to indicate the color of a work.

7.5C6   Playing Speed
The duration of a videorecording depends upon the length of the tape or the size of the disc and the speed at which it is recorded. Because the playing speed of a videodisc will vary from one manufacturer to another, it is important to record the playing speed in the physical description. The speed of videodiscs should be given in terms of revolutions per minute (rpm).

Most reel-to-reel videotape is recorded at a standard speed which does not have to be described. Most ¾-inch tape is also recorded at the same speed. However, equipment originally manufactured for use with both VHS and Beta ½-inch cassettes used a different speed from the later "extended play" cassettes more common today. Some equipment can accommodate both the regular speed and the extended play speed, while other equipment cannot.

"Extended play" cassettes, very common in the home market, allow from two to six hours of viewing on a standard VHS cassette depending upon the speed at which the recording was made. Generally, greater quality of picture is achieved at the faster speed. This is the recording speed of most commercially produced videocassette programs for the home market. Regardless of the speed at which "extended play" VHS or Beta tape was recorded, it will play at the standard setting of the appropriate videocassette player. Thus, these tape characteristics are not described.

7.5D   DIMENSIONS
The dimensions of a videotape are given in terms of its width (gauge) in inches. For videodiscs, the dimension recorded is that of its diameter in inches. When the specific material designation used to describe videorecordings is in more than one size, no dimensions are given in the Physical Description Area. They are recorded instead in an "other formats available" note along with the other information about the formats.

> 1 videocassette (30 min.) : sd., col. ; ¼ in.

> 1 videocassette (25 min.) : sd., col. ; ½ in.

1 videocassette (Type C-B wind) (20 min.) : sd., col. ; ½ in.

1 videoreel (18 min.) : sd., b&w ; ½ in.

1 videoreel (22 min.) : sd., col. ; 2 in.

1 videoreel (Helical scan) (40 min.) : sd., col. ; 2 in.

1 videodisc (SelectaVision) (35 min.) : sd., col., 1500 rpm ; 10 in.

1 videodisc (MCA DiscoVision) (22 min.) : sd., col., 1800 rpm ; 12 in.

7.6 SERIES AREA

Motion pictures and videorecordings may be issued in series, although the use of series for noneducational motion pictures and videorecordings is not as common as it is for other types of nonprint materials. Series should be described according to the provisions of Rule 1.6. Most series for materials covered by this chapter are not numbered, although they frequently carry some form of indication of their placement within the series.

Often, items covered by this chapter, although not part of a published series in their current form, are parts or segments taken from other types of presentations. This information can be indicated in the Note Area using an edition and history note.

Series statements

(Medicine for the layman)

(Science rock) (Schoolhouse rock)

(Our vanishing wilderness ; no. 1)

(Milton Freedman speaking ; lecture 8)

(Mechanical maintenance training ; module 14)

(The Six wives of Henry VIII ; 2)

(Information processing and the computer ; unit 10) (The Computer as a tool ; module 2)

Notes related to the edition and history of a related series (Rule 7.7B7)

Program 7 in a television series for parents and professionals.

Part of ABC afterschool special series.

7.7 NOTE AREA

Many different types of notes are necessary for the complete description of motion pictures and videorecordings. The following sections highlight notes most frequently used for these materials.

7.7B1 Nature or Form

The wide variety of content characteristics for motion pictures and videorecordings can be indicated using this note. If a motion picture or videorecording is prepared for a different type of presentation, such as a filmed opera or stage play, this should be indicated here.

Film version of staged opera.

News broadcast.

Excerpts from film producer.

Original TV play.

7.7B2 Language

When the language, or languages, used in a work are not evident from other parts of the description, usually the title, a note should be made indicating the language(s) used. Although not all that common, this situation does occur with foreign films where a film has been given an English title but retains the language of the original using subtitles to supply the English dialog.

Although *AACR 2* does not mention closed-captioned works for the hearing impaired, the Library of Congress has issued a rule interpretation to this rule to include them. LC instructs its catalogers to make a note for videorecordings which include closed-captions. That note is to be worded: "Closed-captioned for the hearing impaired."

In English and French.

In English and Spanish with portions subtitled in English.

Russian dialogue with English subtitles.

7.7B3 Source of Title Proper

Although it is relatively rare to have commercial motion pictures or videorecordings which lack a title proper, it is not all that unusual to have variant forms of the title appear on places on different prescribed sources. Notes which identify the source of the title proper used in the description can help clarify and uniquely identify the item in hand. LC frequently uses this note to indicate that a work has been cataloged from a data sheet.

Title at end of film.

Title from container.

Title from instructor's guide.

Title from data sheet.
[Data sheets supplied to the cataloging agency by the publisher.]

7.7B4 Variations in Title;
7.7B5 Parallel Titles and Other Title Information

Frequently, as was indicated above, titles appear in variant forms on different prescribed sources of information, and sometimes, in variant forms within the same prescribed source. These variant titles can be useful in the identification of an item, particularly if an access point is also provided for the variant title. Additional title information omitted from Area 1 (i.e., lengthy subtitles) should also be recorded in a note.

In an interpretation to this rule, the Library of Congress has formalized the decision process for variant titles. LC is to determine whether an additional access point is desired for the title variation based upon Rule 21.2 (Changes in Title Proper). These conditions are:

- a change occurs in the first five words of the title (exclusive of initial articles in the nominative case), or

- the addition, deletion, or change of important words in the title, or

- a change occurs in word order.

If, based on these conditions, a decision is made that an additional access point is necessary, then a variation in title note should be made to justify the use of the added entry. If the decision to make an additional access point is negative, then the variation in title note should not be made.

> "Associated Press special report"
> Original title: Search for the origin of our species.
> *[Two notes used for one item.]*

> Original title: California's coast, the sunset shore.

7.7B6 Statements of Responsibility

Names associated with the content and production of motion pictures and videorecordings (e.g., players, performers, narrators, cast) often may not appear prominently in the chief source of information, and therefore should not be named in the statement of responsibility. These names can, however, be invaluable information for users, particularly those engaged in the study of the art of the medium, and can be recorded in this note. When appropriate, a cast note can be combined with a contents note (Rule 7.7B18).

AACR 2 provides no specific instructions for recording cast and credit information. The Library of Congress, however, has issued an Interpretation which provides additional guidelines on the use of this note. LC indicates that producers, directors, writers, and corporate bodies would not be recorded in this note but would be recorded in the Title and Statement of Responsibility Area. Other individuals involved in the "artistic and technical" production of the work would be listed in this note if they performed one of the following functions:

> photographer, camera, cameraman, cinematographer

> animator

artist, illustrator, graphics

film editor, photo editor, editor

music

consultant, advisor

In listing these individuals, the name is prefaced with the term indicating function. The functions should be listed in the order they appear in the list above. LC further indicates that persons performing the following functions would not be listed in a statement of responsibility note:

assistants or associates

production supervisors or coordinators

project or executive editors

technical advisers or consultants

audio or sound engineers

writers of discussion, program, or teacher's guides

other persons making minor or purely technical contributions

The Library of Congress usually precedes this note, when referring to the contributions of individuals, with the term "Credits." The examples that follow illustrates the use of the statement of responsibility note and the LC Rule Interpretation of it.

Additional information about a person named in the cast or credits can be presented in a summary note. A narrator, interviewer, person interviewed, or other relationship of an individual or group to the presentation can also be named there.

Developed by a consortium of U.S. and Canadian education agencies as part of the Secondary School Television Project.

Funded by the U.S. Office of Education and developed by Sharon Gadberry.

Produced in cooperation with the New Jersey College of Medicine and Dentistry.

Sponsored by the National Petroleum Institute.

Cohosted by Linda Harris and Will Lyman.

Cast notes

Cast: Brad Dourif, Frank Converse, William Daniels, Stephen Elliott, Rue McClanahan.

Cast: Laurie Hendler, Kevin King Cooper, Annrae Walterhouse, Robbie Rist, Tim Reid, Beverly Archer.

Cast: Robert Keeshan (Captain Kangaroo).

Cast: Karlene Crockett (Lisl Gilbert), Rosemary Forsyth (Jean Gilbert), Wayne Heffley (Louis Gilbert).

Credit notes

Credits: Narrator, Philip Schopper ; voices, Helen Rubinstein, John Canemaker.

Credits: Cameraman, William Heffner ; animation, Mark Sawicki ; editors, Stephen Wallen & Thomas Sabin ; music, Richard McCurdy.

Credits: Host, Joseph P. Earley.

Credits: Photographers, Hanania Bear ... [et al.] ; editor, Dan Perry.

Credits: Narrator: Maurice Hart.

7.7B7   Edition and History
Information related to the history of the work, or to the edition, which does not come under another note category can be recorded here. This note can also be used to provide information about a work upon which the one in hand is based.

The Library of Congress has issued a Rule Interpretation which gives additional details about the application of this rule. Whenever a work has been issued in another medium, regardless of whether the medium of the original item is known, and its production/release date is greater than two years from that of the item being cataloged, a note should be made indicating the medium and year of the original item. LC generally uses the following note structure:

Originally produced as [medium] in [year]

or

Originally issued as [medium] in [year]

If the date of production/release of an original master or an earlier medium is unknown, or if the difference in the date is less than two years, LC indicates this in an "other format available" note (Rule 7.7B16).

Based on the cartoons of Gerard Hoffnung.

Based on the book: A matter of time / Roni Schotter.

Segments from the television program Phenomenal world.

Third in a series of fourteen programs originally shown on television.

Revised version of motion picture of the same name issued in 1965.

Updated version of the 1972 motion picture of the same name issued by Films/West.

Edited from the longer version (93 min.) of the same name.

Correlated with the book Behavior of exceptional children.

Shorter version (14 min.) issued under title: A Faculty feeling.

Originally issued as motion picture in 1975.

Originally released 1969.

7.7B9   Publication, Distribution, etc., and Date
Important information related to the item in hand that was not reported in Area 4, or information from there which requires additional explanation, can be given in this note. This note is also used to record information about the date of original production when it differs from the date of publication.
Whenever a foreign film is listed as the originator or emanator, the Library of Congress advises its catalogers not to assume that the work has been made or released in the country of that firm unless it is actually stated on the item. Instead, the foreign nature of the item is indicated in this note using the following structurre:

A foreign [medium] ([Country])

If the work has either a U.S. emanator and a foreign producer or a foreign emanator and a U.S. producer, this note is not made.

First released in Spain.

First released in 1976.

Released in France in 1977.

Made in 1977.
  [Publication date is 1980.]

Also distributed in Canada by National Film Board of Canada.

A foreign film (Italy).

A foreign videorecording (Canada).

7.7B10   Physical Description

If information about the physical characteristics of a motion picture or videorecording cannot be given succinctly in the Physical Description Area or does not fit into the structure mandated for that area, it can be given in the Note Area, provided the information is considered to be important.

Any physical characteristic, that is, sound, length, color, form of print, etc., which: (1) is not typical of the format asa it is described in the physical description, (2) must be known in order to use the item, but which was not stated specifically enough in the Physical Description Area, or (3) would dictate the item's use or storage, should be commented upon in this note.

Motion pictures

Use with Kodak Supermatic projector.

Use with Fairchild film cartridge projector.

Silent film at the speed for sound, 24 fr. per sec.

Magnetic sound track.

Use with standard 8 mm. loop projector.

Videorecordings

EIAJ.

Beta.

U-matic.

VHS.

Type C-B wind cassette.

RCA SelectaVision.

Quadraplex recording.

Sound recorded on Channel 1 only, Channel 2 for student response.

7.7B11   Accompanying Material

Accompanying material can be named and, optionally, described in the Physical Description Area. Any amplification upon the information given there can also be given in this note. This note can be particularly important when dealing with educational material to clarify the nature and location of supporting material.

With 2 instructor's guides, 50 student workbooks, and 12 transparencies.

With script and guide.

Study guide contains script.

With teacher's handbook, lesson plans, 25 activity sheets, and 25 music sheets.

Requires text: How to write for the work of work / Thomas E. Pearsall, Donald H. Cunningham.

7.7B14 Audience

A statement of the intended audience of a work should be given, provided that the indication of the audience is obtained from the item itself, its container, or accompanying textual material. This information may designate the age or grade of users or special classes or types of users. The descriptive statement used by the item is generally preferable over a rephrasing of the statement by the cataloger. Before 1985, Library of Congress generally prefaced this note with the phrase "Intended audience:". Since then, LC has prefaced this note with the word "Audience:".

If no audience information is available on the item or on material associated with the item, a cataloger is prohibited from writing his/her own audience statement. In these cases, the purpose and audience level of the item are often incorporated into a summary note (rule 7.7B17). There are some cases, however, where the audience level is known, although it is not actually stated on the item, the accompanying material, or the container. This most frequently occurs when an audience statement is given in an advertisement or in a publisher's catalog. In these situations, the cataloger could sidestep the restrictions of this rule by simply quoting the statement and giving its source.

Audience: General.

Audience: High school and vocational school students and the general public.

Audience: Physicians, other medical personnel, and advanced medical students.

Audience: Students learning basic patient care.

Audience: Ages 5-10.

7.7B16 Other Formats Available

Under Rule 7.5, the multiple containers and formats used for motion pictures and videorecordings were discussed at length. This note is intended to alert the user about other formats in which the item is available. The Library of Congress will make this note whenever the date of production/release of an original master or an earlier medium is unknown, or when the difference in the dates is less than two years. LC uses the following structure for this note:

Previously produced as [medium] in [year]

or

Previously issued as [medium] in [year]

For other multimedia libraries, the use of this note should probably be limited to information about other formats actually available in the library rather than about formats available for purchase but not held. This latter information is only confusing to the user trying to identify the holdings of a library.

If a library collection contains the same work in different formats, the best way to describe each one is with a separate catalog entry. An alternate method for videorecordings, as described previously in Rule 7.5B, is to give a generic phrase as the specific material designation and more detail about each format in this note.

Physical description	3 videorecordings
Note	Available also as 1 videocassette (22 min.) : sd., col. ; 2 in. or 1 videocassette (22 min.) : sd., col. ; ½ in. or 1 videocassette (22 min.) : sd., col. ; ¾ in. Quadraplex, Beta and U standards.
Physical description	1 videocassette
Note	Issued as U-matic ¾ in. or Beta ½ in.

Again, this method and the multilevel description are potentially confusing to a user and probably should be avoided in preference to a separate entry for each format. It should be cautioned, however, that libraries which purchase many titles in the same format will add significantly to the size of their catalog if the separate entry approach is used. In these cases, the multiple format description is preferable.

7.7B17 Summary

A brief overview, using phrases whenever possible, explaining the subject content, scope, point of view, and nature of the visual and sound accompaniment, is usually necessary for motion pictures and videorecordings unless the item's content is evident from other parts of the description. The importance of this note is due to the fact that these materials cannot be easily browsed by users. Information in the summary can also include the names of persons or groups who have participated prominently in the work in order to describe their relationship to the production. Significant technical or artistic attributes of the production can also be mentioned, if they are deemed important to users.

A summary should avoid interpretation, evaluation, and prescription for use, although an implied audience can be noted. It should also avoid the repetition of information already given elsewhere in the description as well as promotional words or phrases found on the item or its accompanying material.

The use of the traditional formal note structure, headed by the word "Summary" and followed by a colon, enables a user to easily locate this information on the catalog record. This formal summary note style is used by the Library of Congress.

Summary: Shows painter Helen Frankenthaler creating a complete work ; with friends and colleagues in her studio, at home, and at an exhibition of her work. Examines paintings and interviews colleagues and critics.

Summary: Animated characters made of sculpted Plasticine applied over glass create images of life after death. Without narration.

Summary: Interviewer with representative from IBM discusses jobs available to liberal arts graduates in large corporations.

Summary: Uses photomicrography and time-lapse sequences to show research technique of nuclear transplantation. Shows how nuclei are transplanted from donor body cells into activated eggs.

Summary: A documentary showing nurses working in hospitals, in independent practice, on strike and in support groups. Nurses discuss expectation vs. reality, nurses as a political force, collective bargaining, and professionalism.

7.7B18 Contents

Contents notes are not nearly as common an occurrence for motion pictures and videorecordings as they are for other types of nonprint materials. As with other materials, this note is used to record individual works contained in, or parts of, a motion picture or videorecording as well as any statements of responsibility associated with the titles which have not been given in Area 1. In some cases, cast statements are combined with the contents note. This is done for multipart items, where different casts are associated with each item.

When readily available, the duration of the parts is also given in this note. These durations are generally recorded within parentheses, although *AACR 2* does not actually prescribe this structure.

7.7B20 Copy Being Described

This note is useful particularly for videotapes which have been recorded from a master copy but differ in some way from the original. If these differences are not identified in the notes about the physical characteristics, they can be given here. If portions of a production are missing, or if the work has substandard recording quality, this can also be indicated here.

7.8 STANDARD NUMBER AND TERMS OF AVAILABILITY AREA

Any restrictions on the use of the material should be indicated in this area, following the instructions given in Rule 1.8D. That rule calls for recording the price of an item if it is for sale, or a brief statement of other terms under which it is available, if not for sale. In its Interpretation to Rule 1.8D, the Library of Congress instructs its catalogers to give the price of an item only for monographs which are cataloged under Chapters 2 ("Books, Pamphlets and Printed Sheets"), 5 ("Music"), 6 ("Sound Recordings"), 7 (Motion Pictures and Videorecordings"), and 8 ("Graphic Materials") and which were issued during the past three years. In all likelihood, the indication of price serves no useful purpose for catalog users and should probably not be recorded, regardless of LC policy.

Some motion pictures and videorecordings may require some restriction on their use and circulation. Others may be restricted in their circulation to instructional staff or to classroom use. Still others may not circulate outside the library or are unavailable for interlibrary loan. This information, of great importance to the potential user, should be indicated here.

Available to teaching staff only.

Deposit required for use.

Free loan available from distributor.

Not available for distribution in the United States.
[This type of note would more likely be made by a national cataloging agency rather than a local library.]

EXAMPLES: Descriptive Cataloging for Motion Pictures and Videorecordings

Motion Pictures

Roll of thunder, hear my cry [motion picture] / Tomorrow Entertainment, Inc. ; producer, Jean Anne Moore ; director, Jack Smight ; writer, Arthur Heinemann. — New York : Learning Corporation of America, 1979.
3 film reels (110 min.) : sd., col. ; 16 mm. + 1 study guide.

Based on the book of the same name by Mildred D. Taylor.
Cast: Claudia McNeil, Janet McLachian, Robert Christian, Roy Poole, Lark Ruffin, John Collum.
Summary: Set in the poverty-stricken South of 1933, tells the story of a Black family's struggle to hold on to the land they have owned for three generations.

I. Taylor, Mildred D. Roll of thunder, hear my cry. II. Tomorrow Entertainment (Firm). III. Learning Corporation of America.

Main Entry — An adaptation of a work of fiction into motion picture form is entered under the title of the motion picture.
Area 1 — Statements of responsibility are recorded as they appear on the item.
— LC policy of placing directors, producers, and writers in the statement of responsibility rather than placing in a note was followed.

Area 7 — Note to identify the work upon which this motion picture was based. Note allows for the provision of an access point for the original book.
— Cast taken from the item.
Added Entries — Added entry (Name. Title) for the original work.
— LC generally traces corporate bodies recorded in the statement of responsibility and those recorded in the Publication, Distribution, etc., Area.
— "(Firm)" added to the entry for Tomorrow Entertainment to indicate that it is a corporate body.

Techniques of defense [motion picture]. — North Palm Beach, Fla. : Athletic Institute, 1976.
1 film reel (20 min.) : sd., col. ; super 8 mm. — (Basketball ; no. 4)

Summary: Assists in the teaching of basketball by focusing on techniques of defense.

I. Athletic Institute. II. Series.

Comment — One motion picture in a series. The series could have been cataloged as a unit, using the series title as a collective title, with the individual titles recorded in a contents note. Each item in the set was cataloged individually because each was on a separate reel and the library desired more detailed individual descriptions than would be possible with a multipart description. The fact that the library desired to circulate the items individually was also a factor.
Area 5 — Physical description does not require additional information because many types of equipment can accommodate this motion picture format.

Dinky Hocker [motion picture] / Robert Guenette-Paul
Asselin Productions ; director, Tom Blank. — New
York : Learning Corporation of America, 1979.
1 film reel (30 min.) : sd., col. ; 16 mm. + 1
teacher's guide.

Based on the book: Dinky Hocker shoots smack /
M.E. Kerr.
Cast: Wendie Jo Sperber, June Lockhart.
Summary: Story of an adolescent girl who overeats
and whose mother is too involved with helping strang-
ers to recognize her daughter's needs.

I. Kerr, M.E. Dinky Hocker shoots smack. II. Robert
Guenette-Paul Asselin Productions. III. Learning
Corporation of America.

Area 1	— Responsibility for the work attributed to the produc-tion company. Note that the added entry will bring the film and the book together bibliographically even though they will not be together on the shelves.
Area 7	— Separately named author of the film guide is not named in note in accordance with LC's policy not to record the names of "writers of discussion, program, or teacher's guides" in a note.
	— Motion picture designed for adolescents, with a guide intended for teachers. No audience note made because the audience level is not stated on the item or its accompanying material.
	— Summary note implies the intended audience.
Added Entries	— Added entry (Name. Title) for the original book.

Water birds [motion picture]. — Mahwah, N.J. : Troll
Associates, 1972.
1 film loop (4 min.) : si., col. ; super 8 mm. + 1
study guide.

Audience: Elementary through junior high grades.
Summary: Various species of ducks, geese, and swans
photographed in natural habitat.

I. Troll Associates.

Comment	— Single concept film loop which can be used in several types of super 8mm loop projectors.
Area 5	— Short films in cartridges are described as film loops, longer continuous loop films in cartridges are described as film cartridges.
	— When no sound is present, "si." must be indicated.

Area 7   —Audience stated on the item.
              —Summary taken from information on the guide.

Hayward, C.O.
     The beginning [motion picture] : a film / by C.O.
Hayward. — [Santa Monica, Calif.] : Stephen
Bosustow Productions, 1971.
     1 film reel (5 min.) : sd., col. ; 16 mm.

     Title on beginning frames: A Wiggleman tale.
     Audience: Elementary grades and up.
     Summary: A parable with animated figures in which a
butterfly touches a person who is inspired to be
different.

     I. Stephen Bosustow Productions. II. Title.
     III. Title: A Wiggleman tale.

Main Entry   —Main entry under the person considered principally
               responsible for the work.
Area 1   —LC policy calls for the treatment of phrases like "a
               film" as "other title information" rather than as part
               of the statement of responsibility.
Area 4   —Place of publication was not indicated on the work
               or its container. It was located in a reference source.
Area 7   —Title of the film, verified in the publisher's catalog,
               appears at the end of the film. A descriptive and in-
               troductory variant title appears at the beginning of
               the motion picture.
Added Entries—Access point provided for the variant title.

Cosmic zoom [motion picture] / produced by the National
     Film Board of Canada. — New York ; Contemporary
     Films, McGraw-Hill Films [distributor], 1970.
     1 film reel (8 min.) : sd., col. ; 16 mm.

     Based on the book: Cosmic view / Keis Boeke.
     Credits: Drawings, Eva Szasz ; animation camera,
Raymond Dumas, Wayne Trickett, James Wilson ;
actuality camera, Tony Ianelo.
     Audience: Elementary grades through college.
     Summary: Relates, in a wordless journey, the unseen
microcosmic universe within the human body to the
limitless universe of space. Uses camera zoom device.

     I. Boeke, Keis. Cosmic view. II. National Film
Board of Canada. III. Contemporary Films/McGraw
Hill.

(Explanation is on page 138.)

Area 4   — U.S. distributor recorded as stated on the item. Statement of function was added.

Area 7   — Credits considered important because of the nature of the film technique used.

                    — Summary mentions filming technique used and indicates that the motion picture is not narrated.

Added Entries — *AACR 2* heading for Contemporary Films.

McLaren, Norman, 1914-
    Two bagatelles [motion picture] / by Norman
McLaren and Grant Monro. — [Montreal] : National
Film Board of Canada, 1951.
    1 film reel (2 min. 22 sec.) : sd., col. ; 16 mm.

    Summary: Two examples of pixillation accompanied
by different music.
    Contents: On the lawn — In the backyard.

    I. Monro, Grant. II. National Film Board of
Canada. III. Title. IV. Title: On the lawn. V. In
the backyard.

Main Entry   — Entry under the first person named in statement of responsibility.

Area 1   — The collective title appears on the film.

Area 5   — The rule requiring that motion pictures or video-recordings under five minutes have their duration described in terms of minutes and seconds was revised in 1985. Under the revision this specific requirement no longer exists. Rule 1.5B4 does require, however, that the duration be recorded as stated on the item.

Area 7   — Contents note for the separately titled parts.

Added Entries — Added entries for the other person mentioned in the statement of responsibility.

                    — Access points provided for the titles of the parts.

Uncle Sam Magoo [motion picture] / United Productions
of America. — Mt. Prospect, Ill. : Mar/Chuck Film
Industries, [197-]
1 film reel (28 min.) : sd., col. ; 16 mm.

Credits: Music, Walter Scharf.
Made in 1969.
Longer version (52 min.) also issued.
Summary: Cartoon character Mr. Magoo outlines
America's history from the founding of the New World
to the landing on the moon.

I. United Productions of America. II. Mar/Chuck
Film Industries.

Area 4　　　— Slash in the name of distributor is not preceded or
　　　　　　followed by a space in order not to duplicate ISBD
　　　　　　punctuation.
Area 5　　　— Year of publication uncertain, decade certain.
Area 7　　　— Note indicates that the date the motion picture was
　　　　　　made is different from the date of publication.
　　　　　　— Note indicating other formats available. Most multi-
　　　　　　media libraries would only make this note if the
　　　　　　other version was also available in the library.

The Steadfast tin soldier [motion picture] / Benchmark
Films, SHB Films. — Briarcliff Manor, N.Y. : Benchmark Films, 1985.
1 film reel (9 min.) : sd., col. ; 16 mm. + 1 teacher's
guide. — (Fairy tale series)

U.S. version of the motion picture released in Austria
under the title: Der Standhafte Zinnsoldat.
Audience: Kindergarten through intermediate grades.
Summary: A puppet film presentation presenting the
Hans Christian Andersen Fairy tale about a one-legged
toy tin soldier who falls in love with a paper doll
ballerina.

I. Andersen, H.C. (Hans Christian), 1805-1875.
Standhaftige tinsoldat. II. Benchmark Films. III. SHB
Films. IV. Standhafte Zinnsoldat (Motion picture)

Area 7　　　— Release history of the work.
　　　　　　— Summary note includes an indication of the source
　　　　　　of the story.

(Explanation continues on page 140.)

Added Entries —Access point for the work upon which this motion
picture was based. Libraries which do not have users
who would be familiar with, or need, the title in the
original language, may wish to deviate from the
AACR 2 uniform title form of the heading for the
original work and use instead the English-language
title.
—Access point for the Austrian motion picture. Many
multimedia libraries would probably have little, if
any, need for this point of access and could eliminate it.
—"(Motion picture)" is not used as a GMD, but is instead an addition to the title to specifically identify
this title as that of the motion picture.

The Voice of Cape Code [motion picture] / National Park
Service, Division of Audiovisual Arts ; [produced by]
Peace River Films ; producer, director, writer, Neil
Goodman. — Washington, D.C. : The Division :
Distributed by National Audiovisual Center, 1984.
1 film reel (12 min.) : sd., col. ; 16 mm.

Credits: Photography, Neil Goodman ; narrator,
William Lyman.
Audience: General.
Summary: Deals with the events that occurred in the
life of Gugielmo Marconi, the person and inventor,
who sent the first trans-Atlantic radio transmission.

I. United States. National Park Service. Division of
Audiovisual Arts. II. Peace River Films. III. National
Audiovisual Center.

Area 1	—Statement of function added.
	—Multiple functions indicated for the person.
Area 4	—Shortened name used for the publisher previously mentioned in Area 1.
	—Distributor recorded.
Area 7	—One function of the person previously mentioned in the statement of responsibility is given in a note. According to LC's guidelines, usually the photography function does not constitute involvement in the overall production of the item. This function could have been combined in Area 1 with those functions involving overall production responsibility.
Added Entries	—Distributor is used as an access point because of its importance as a retrieval point for users.

Videorecordings

Younger, Irving.
Everything you wanted to know about hearsay but were afraid to ask. Part I [videorecording] / lecturer, Irving Younger. — [Chicago] : American Bar Association, 1976.
1 videocassette (51 min.) : sd., col. ; ¾ in.

Lecture presented at the American Bar Association Conference, Section of Litigation in Atlanta, Georgia in 1976.
U-matic.

I. American Bar Association Conference (1976 : Atlanta, Ga.). II. Title.

Main Entry	— Entry under the lecturer responsible for the content of the item.
Area 4	— Place established from reference sources.
Area 7	— Note indicating the relationship of the work to the conference provides justification for an access point under the name of the conference.
	— Recording standard for this videorecording.

The New copyright law [videorecording] : issues and answers / Appalachian Education Satellite Project. — [Lexington, Ky. : University of Kentucky : distributed by AESP, 1978]
2 videocassettes (90 min.) : sd., col. ; ¾ in.

Includes segments of American Library Association teleconference on copyright with Barbara Ringer, Register of Copyrights.
U-matic.
Summary: A panel discussion about fair use, educational copying, and legal responsibilities of educators.

I. Appalachian Education Satellite Project.
II. American Library Association.

Area 4	— Group named in the statement of responsibility is also the distributor of the work. Another organization produced the item.
Area 7	— First note indicates additional responsibility for part of the content.
	— Standard for this videorecording.
Added Entries	— Added entries provided for organizations making significant contributions to the work.

The Light of experience [videorecording] / British
   Broadcasting Corporation ; writer and narrator,
   Kenneth Clark. — New York : Time-Life Multimedia,
   1971.
      1 videocassette (52 min.) : sd., col. ; ¾ in. + 1
   discussion guide. — (Civilization series ; no. 8)

   U-matic.
   Previously issued as motion picture in 1970.
   Summary: Surveys the development of Western
civilization during the seventeenth century. Includes
works of Dutch painters and shows the change in
thought that replaced divine authority with experience,
experimentation, and observation.

   I. Clark, Kenneth, 1903-   II. British Broadcasting
Corporation. III. Series.

Main Entry   — Entry under title because of the mixed responsibility
                of individuals to the work despite the fact that one
                person was both the writer and narrator.
Area 1   — Narration function included in the statement of
                responsibility even though the LC Rule Interpreta-
                tion indicates that narrator is not normally a func-
                tion which involves overall responsibility for a
                work. LC does allow for liberal application of its
                guidelines, however. In this case, it was desired to
                keep the entire responsibility together.
Added Entries — Added entry provided for the writer of the work be-
                cause of the probable close association of him with
                the work in the minds of many users.

Non-verbal communication [videorecording]. — Santa
   Monica, Calif. : Salenger Educational Media, 1980.
      1 videocassette (14 min.) : sd., col. ; ¾ in. + 1 book
   + 1 leader's guide + 20 worksheets.

   Made in 1979, a rev. version of a videorecording first
issued in 1978 under the same title.
   U-matic.
   Accompanying book is: The silent messages / Albert
Mehrabian.
   Summary: Psychologist Dr. Albert Mehrabian points
out that an awareness of non-verbal messages enhances
the ability to communicate.

   I. Mehrabian, Albert. II. Mehrabian, Albert. The
silent messages. III. Salenger Educational Media
(Firm)

Area 5	— If desired, all of the accompanying material information could have been given in a note.
Area 7	— Comprehensive note records all the information about the history and edition of the work.
	— Title and statement of responsibility of the accompanying book recorded.
Added Entries	— Added entry for the lecturer.
	— Added entry (Name. Title) for the accompanying book even though the author of the book is also the lecturer and an access point. This is done because of indexing and filing requirements of online and manual catalogs.
	— "(Firm)" added to the entry for Salenger Educational Media to indicate that it is a corporate body.

Towser and the water rats [videorecording] / Journal
Films presentation ; produced by King Rollo Films,
Ltd. ; writer, Tony Ross. — Evanston, Ill. : Journal
Films, 1985, c1982.
　　1 videocassette (5 min.) : sd., col. ; ½ in. + 1
teacher's guide.

　　Based on the book of the same name by Tony Ross.
　　Credits: Animator, Tony Ross.
　　First released in England in 1982.
　　VHS.
　　Audience: Kindergarten.
　　Summary: An animated Towser story on bargaining,
in which Towser outsmarts two water rats who want to
buy his house.

　　I. Ross, Tony. II. Ross, Tony. Towser and the water
rats. III. Journal Films, Incorporated. IV. King Rollo
Films, Limited.

Area 1	— Multiple statements of responsibility.
Area 4	— Date of U.S. release differs from that of the copyright date.
Area 7	— Note indicates work upon which the videorecording is based.
	— Edition and history note indicates the actual age of the work.
	— Videocassette standard indicated.
Added Entries	— Entry provided for both the person responsible for the writing and the animation. Even though it is the same person, a second access point (Name. Title) is made for the work upon which the videorecording is based.

(Explanation continues on page 144.)

– Journal Films, Incorporated is the *AACR 2* heading
for that firm. LC would have used "Journal Films,
Inc.", LC's *AACR 2* compatible heading for the
firm.

The Victory garden. Program 10, Harvest of things to
come [videorecording] / WGBH. — Deerfield, Ill. :
MTI Teleprograms, 1983.
1 videocassette (30 min.) : sd., col. ; ½ in.

Hosted by Bob Thomson.
Originally broadcast on PBS.
Issued as Veta or VHS.
Summary: Begins with the planting of everlastings
and gourds. Viewers get to see plants in full bloom as
well as harvest scallions, peas, beets, and lettuce; steak
and sucket tomatoes, hill potatoes, and leeks. Also takes
a look at clematis, hosts, spires, and forsythia.

I. Thomson, Bob. II. WGBH (Television station :
Boston, Mass.) III. MTI Teleprograms Incorporated.
IV. Title: Harvest of things to come.

Comment   – Catalog record for one program in a series. This
work could also have been cataloged as a multipart
item with a contents note giving the titles of each
episode. The shortcoming to that approach would be
that the summary note would have to be more
general to cover the entire series rather than each
episode.

Area 1   – Title proper includes the title of a section.
     – GMD follows the title of the section.

Area 7   – Statement of responsibility for a person not considered to have responsibility for the overall production of the work.
     – History of the videoproduction.
     – Indication of videocassette standards available in the
library. Separate catalog records could also have
been made for each standard instead of a combined
description. This would create a great deal of duplication, however, if a library frequently purchases
videocassettes for a work in multiple standards, e.g.,
in Beta and VHS.

Added Entries – Access point for the host – a person many users
would associate with the program.
     – *AACR 2* heading for a television station.
     – Title access point provided for the title of the section.

Employment agencies and services [videorecording] /
    Mississippi Authority for Educational Television. —
    New York : Cambridge Book Co., 1978.
      1 videocassette (15 min.) : sd., col. + 1 user's guide
    + 1 student videotext. — (Just around the corner.
    Series 2, Jobs and employment opportunities)

      Audience: Adults.
      Issued as U-matic ¾ in. or Beta ½ in. or VHS ½ in.
      Summary: Using the experiences of an unemployed
husband who visits a government employment agency,
explains how private and government employee agencies
operate, what services they offer, and how to tell the
difference among want ads placed by these job sources.

      I. Mississippi Authority for Educational Television.
    II. Cambridge Book Company. III. Series.

Comment   —Demonstrates LC's approach to cataloging multiple
    videoformats on one catalog record. Ideally, librar-
    ies which use this approach would only indicate in a
    note the formats or standards they actually hold. For
    multiple formats, the term "videorecording" would
    have been used as the SMD rather than "videocas-
    sette." An alternative to this type of cataloging would
    be to create separate records for each format or size.

Area 5   —No dimensions are given because the videocassettes
    are in more than one size.
    —Multiple accompanying materials.

Area 6   —Series and subseries.

Area 7   —Videocassette standards and dimensions indicated.

Added Entries—Access point for the series title proper. Subseries
    would have a reference leading users to the series title
    proper.

6
Description of Graphic Materials

8.0 GENERAL RULES

8.0A SCOPE

This chapter covers the description of all types of graphic materials, some of which are intended for projection. The rules in this chapter are appropriate for individual graphic items, graphic packages which contain many images intended to be viewed or displayed sequentially (e.g., the images on a filmstrip), and sets of graphic materials published as a unit, such as a set of filmstrips. Films, videotapes, microforms, and microscope slides are covered elsewhere in *AACR 2*, although slides on transparent film intended for projection are covered by this chapter. Maps which are published in a graphic format can be cataloged according to the rules in Chapter 3 ("Cartographic Materials") or they can be described in terms of the physical characteristics of the graphic format. A library which has a separate map section or department will probably catalog all maps, regardless of format, as maps. Notes could then be used to record the physical characteristics of the format. If maps are integrated into the general collection, the cataloger may decide to catalog the item as a graphic format according to this chapter, using notes to describe the characteristics of the map.

This chapter covers a large number of diverse types of materials, some of which are educational in content and some of which are not. For materials not published for educational purposes, or those produced locally and perhaps not formally published, the determination of bibliographic information can be particularly difficult.

An additional problem is identifying the most useful unit for the description of multipart items. For example, a group of slides or transparencies, whether published or locally produced, could be described separately as individual units or collectively as a group. The decision should be based on the intellectual unity of the material and on the needs of the users and can also be influenced by the way the materials are published and packaged. In most cases graphic items will, however, be cataloged as a unit. For example, a set of four or five filmstrips would usually be handled as a unit. Likewise, a slide presentation with a theme or subject focus would also be cataloged as a unit.

Another problem involves identifying the predominant item to be cataloged. Is a sound filmstrip to be cataloged as a sound recording with accompanying graphics material or as a graphic item with accompanying sound? Generally, whenever sound is necessary for, or a complement to, the graphic material, the material is considered to be a graphic rather than a sound item. The assumption is that the intellectual burden of the content is contained in the graphic material with only accompanying information or artistic enhancement presented in the sound accompaniment. Therefore, graphic materials accompanied by sound, such as sound filmstrips and slide-tape presentations, where sound is intended to be used in the presentation of the material as narrative and/or musical accompaniment, should be cataloged according to the rules in this chapter. When graphic materials are associated with sound which is intended to be used separately from the graphic material, the items should be cataloged as a kit. See the definition of "kit" in the *AACR 2* glossary. Some forms of graphic materials may have sound that is "integral," that is, physically inseparable from the graphic material. The treatment for this type of sound is rather different from that accorded nonintegral sound described above.

In 1982, the Library of Congress published *Graphic Materials: Rules for Describing Original Items and Historical Collections.* Compiled by Elisabeth W. Betz of the Prints and Photographs Division, this work is intended to provide additional guidance beyond that provided by *AACR 2* Chapter 8 for the cataloging of original, historical, and archival graphic materials. Although these guidelines are designed to conform to the "general structure and theory" of *AACR 2*, there are significant differences between some of the guidelines and the *AACR 2* text. One of these differences involves the use of the GMD "graphic," a term which appears in the List 1 used by British libraries, rather than the List 2 graphic GMDs used by North American libraries. The numbering structure of these guidelines is also not compatible with the rule numbering of *AACR 2*. A library with a sizable special collection of archival graphic materials may wish to consider the application of these rules. Libraries which integrate their bibliographic records for graphics with those of other materials will probably want to follow *AACR 2* generally as much as possible when the LC guidelines differ from *AACR 2*.

8.0B SOURCES OF INFORMATION

8.0B1 Chief Source of Information

The chief source of information is the item itself, including any permanently affixed labels and container which are integral parts of the item (i.e., physically inseparable from it). The chief source of information for a graphic item which has separate physical parts is the container itself, which, even though not an integral part of the item, provides a collective title; the individual items do not.

When information is not available from the chief source of information, it can be taken from:

- a container which is not an integral part of the item
- accompanying textual material
- any other sources.

These sources should be consulted in this order of preference.

For a collection of graphic materials, the entire collection serves as the chief source of information.

8.0B2   Prescribed Sources of Information

For each area of the description there are different prescribed source(s) from which information can be taken without having to enclose it in square brackets. For the Title and Statement of Responsibility Area, the chief source of information serves as the prescribed source of information. For some of the areas, such as Edition, Series, etc., the chief source of information is among several acceptable prescribed sources although it is the preferred source. Prefer the prescribed sources in the order in which they are given in the rules in cases where the different sources provide conflicting information. Other areas of the description (i.e., Physical Description, Notes, Standard Number) allow the information to be derived from any source.

In all but a few cases, information required by the chosen level of description can be taken from any source provided that the information is placed within square brackets. Additionally, catalogers are always free to record information in a ‘note without the need of brackets.

In some cases, the accompanying material is the only unifying element for a graphic production as a whole. Parts of multipart graphic items may be published or produced at different times and/or may be produced by different groups or individuals. These items may be brought together as a finished package when the accompanying material is published. In these cases, the accompanying material, and not the container, is the unifying element and should be used as chief source of information.

8.1   TITLE AND STATEMENT OF RESPONSIBILITY AREA

8.1B   TITLE PROPER

Record the title proper as instructed in Rule 1.1B. The prescribed source of information is the chief source of information, that is, the item itself and an integral container or a container which provides a collective title for a multipart item. The following example illustrates the latter situation.

| Title frame (first filmstrip of the set) | Washington, D.C.

The City Freedom Built |
|---|---|
| Container | WASHINGTON

Five Filmstrip Adventures in full color and sound

NATIONAL GEOGRAPHIC SOCIETY
Encyclopaedia Britannica Educational Corporation |

Catalog record   Washington [filmstrip] / National Geographic
Society, Encyclopaedia Britannica Educational
Corporation. –

According to Rule 1.1B7, when a graphic item or collection of items lacks a title
on the chief source of information, the cataloger must either obtain a title from
somewhere else on the item or from an outside source or must create a title for it.
The example below illustrates a case of the use of a supplied title.

Title provided   [Beethoven listening to a cassette player]
by the cataloger   [transparency]. –

In addition to placing the title within square brackets, another rule (8.7B3)
instructs the cataloger to provide a note identifying the source of the title proper
if it was derived from other than the chief source. In the case of the example
above, this note would be written as:

Title supplied by cataloger.

8.1C *OPTIONAL ADDITION.* GENERAL MATERIAL DESIGNATION

The general material designation follows the title proper. The GMD, always
recorded in singular form and lowercase, must be taken from one of the
following terms:

art original	picture
chart	slide
filmstrip	technical drawing
flash card	transparency

8.1D PARALLEL TITLES

Parallel titles are recorded following the title proper and the GMD according
to the instructions given in Rule 1.1D. A parallel title is preceded by a space,
equals sign, space. For level two descriptions, the cataloger is instructed to record
the first parallel title. If a subsequent parallel title is in English it is also recorded.
Generally, the use of parallel titles is not very common for graphic materials.

Parallel title   The Bullfrog [transparency] = Rana catesbiana. –

8.1E OTHER TITLE INFORMATION

Other title information, usually in the form of a subtitle, is recorded as
instructed by Rule 1.1E. Other title information is preceded by a space, colon,
space. Note that the position of the other title information follows the GMD.
This is different from that used in *AACR 1* Revised Chapter 12 where other title
information was given before the GMD.

Other title   Gun control [filmstrip] : a target for controversy. –
information

Czarist Russia [filmstrip] : the Russian revolution /
written by Stephen Larabee ; produced by John Dent
and Cal Industries for Educational Enrichment
Materials. –

8.1F STATEMENTS OF RESPONSIBILITY

In *AACR 2*, catalogers have a decision to make whether to record statements of responsibility in this area, in a statement of responsibility note, or to ignore the statement entirely. This problem is a particularly difficult one when dealing with graphic materials because often numerous individuals are mentioned on the item as having some involvement in its production. In its Interpretation to Rule 8.1F1, the Library of Congress indicated that statements of responsibility are generally made for persons who have had some degree of "overall" responsibility for the item. Generally, LC considers producers, directors, and writers to have had some degree of overall responsibility. For slides and transparencies, this overall responsibility also extends to authors, editors, and compilers. Persons who do not meet this level of responsibility would either be mentioned in a statement of responsibility note or not mentioned at all. LC encourages its catalogers to be "liberal" in making exceptions in the general policy to allow for the inclusion of others who have made an important, albeit only a partial, contribution.

Statements of responsibility are recorded as instructed in Rule 1.1F, that is, if they appear prominently in the chief source(s) of information. In most cases, this excludes information found only in accompanying material, unless that material is the unifying element. It would also exclude information found in sources outside the item. When recording a statement of responsibility, include the entire statement of responsibility, that is, phrases indicating the relationship between the title and the person or corporate body, rather than just the name if the relationship is not clear.

Title frame	ECOLOGY OF HAWAII
	Script and Photography by Ernest S. Booth
	Produced by OUTDOOR PICTURES Anacortes, Washington
	© 1974 Outdoor Pictures
Catalog record	Ecology of Hawaii [filmstrip] / script and photography by Ernest S. Booth ; produced by Outdoor Pictures. —

If the relationship between the title and statement of responsibility is not clear and no statement exists on the item, a short word or phrase, enclosed in square brackets, explaining the relationship should be added by the cataloger.

8.1G ITEMS WITHOUT A COLLECTIVE TITLE

For graphic items that lack a collective title, the titles of the individual parts should be recorded according to the provisions of Rule 1.1G. Each title is separated by a full stop. Statements of responsibility are recorded following the individual title with which they are associated. The GMD is recorded in brackets following the statement of responsibility of the last item.

Frame preceding title frame of 1st work	weston woods presents
Title frame of lst work (A copy of the book's cover)	THE HAPPY DAY By RUTH KRAUSS Pictures by MARC SIMONT © COPYRIGHT 1949 BY RUTH KRAUSS AND MARC SIMONT
Next to end frame of 1st work	From the Book by RUTH KRAUSS Pictures by MARC SIMONT HARPER & ROW, PUBLISHERS © 1949 of the book by Ruth Krauss © 1949 of the pictures by Marc Simont
Frame preceding title frame of 2nd work	weston woods presents
Title frame of 2nd work (A copy of the book's cover)	Where does the butterfly go when it rains by May Garelick WITH PICTURES BY Leonard Weisgard © COPYRIGHT 1961 MAY GARELICK AND LEONARD WEISGARD
Next to end frame of 2nd work	From the Book by May Garelick with Pictures by Leonard Weisgard Published by Young Scott Books TEXT © MCMLXI BY MAY GARELICK PICTURES © MCMLXI BY LEONARD WEISGARD
Catalog record	The happy day / from the book by Ruth Krauss ; pictures by Marc Simont. Where does the butterfly go when it rains / from the book by May Garelick ; with pictures by Leonard Weisgard [filmstrip]. —

The preceding example also illustrates a problem created by the organization of *AACR 2*. This problem concerns the statement "weston woods presents" in the example. Is this type of statement preceding a title to be considered a part of the title or a form of statement of responsibility?

In *AACR 1*, a single chapter treated both motion pictures and filmstrips while a different chapter addressed the description requirements of pictures. *AACR 2* rearranged this order, placing all moving pictures (motion pictures and videotapes) in one chapter and all graphic materials, whether intended for projection or not, in another chapter. Unfortunately, many of the characteristics possessed by motion pictures and videotapes are also possessed by filmstrips and slides. Although Chapter 7 may treat these characteristics in a satisfactory manner for motion pictures and videorecordings, the same characteristics might not even be addressed by Chapter 8. The Library of Congress has attempted to resolve some of the more serious implications of this chapter arrangement by applying many of its Interpretations for Chapter 7 to Chapter 8. In other situations, although LC may not have applied the Interpretation to both chapters, the Interpretation to a rule in Chapter 7 may work perfectly well for a Chapter 8 rule.

This problem regarding Chapters 7 and 8 applies to the previous example. In an Interpretation to Rule 7.1B1, the Library of Congress addressed this exact situation for motion pictures and videorecordings but did not issue a similar Interpretation for Chapter 8. In its Interpretation, LC instructs that credits which precede or follow the title are not to be considered part of the title proper unless the credit is within the title. Based upon this Interpretation, the cataloger of the filmstrip in question can easily borrow or extrapolate from the Chapter 7 Interpretation and ignore "weston woods presents" as part of the title.

Multipart graphic items which lack both a collective title and titles for the individual parts must have a title supplied from an outside source or one created by the cataloger. This supplied title should be appropriate for the entire unit.

Collective title supplied from publisher's catalog	[The Cat in famous paintings] [slide]. —
Associated note	Title from publisher's catalog.

8.2 EDITION AREA

8.2B EDITION STATEMENT
This rule refers the cataloger to Rule 1.2B when recording information about the edition. Generally, graphic materials, and especially filmstrips and slides, do not possess edition statements with the frequency that they are encountered in other formats such as books and machine-readable data files. Instead, when graphic materials are issued in revised versions, the title is usually also changed without any indication that the work is a later edition. This results in the revised work being cataloged under the new title. Statements relating to its earlier form are recorded in a note (Rule 8.7B7).

Care should be exercised when dealing with edition statements which appear on accompanying materials. It is not an infrequent practice for a producer of graphic material to update or revise the accompanying material but leave the graphic material unchanged. In these situations, differences in copyright dates between the item and its accompanying material may serve as a clue that the revision has not been made to the graphic item itself. A note (Rule 8.7B11), quoting the revision statement from the accompanying material, is one way to indicate this "revised" condition, particularly when the extent of the revision is in doubt.

Rule 8.2B3 is an "optional addition" rule which allows the inclusion of information, in square brackets, concerning the edition of a graphic item when that item lacks an edition statement. This option is not used by the Library of Congress and should probably not be adopted by other libraries. These supplied statements can create misleading information about editions and lead to the citing of "ghost" editions. This type of edition information is best recorded in a note.

The packaging of graphic materials in different combinations is a common practice with nonprint publishers. These relationships are often complicated and can be more fully explained in a note than in the body of the description. When one part of a multipart item, such as one filmstrip in a set of four, has been published separately under its own title or a previous title, this information should be given in a note. The inclusion of this information then justifies its inclusion as an access point in the catalog.

Edition related information recorded in a note

Edited from the 1975 American Hospital Association slide set entitled This way to reality.

Rev. version of the 1979 filmstrip of the same title.

Rev. version of the transparency issued in 1972.

Second ed. of: Full circle.

Updated and rev. version of: Values, goals, decisions. New York : Butterick Publishing, 1976. (Lifestyles − options for living).

8.4 PUBLICATION, DISTRIBUTION, ETC., AREA

The prescribed sources of information for this area include the chief source of information, the container, and accompanying material. Several places and a variety of names are likely to be given in these sources. Names are also frequently given in varying forms in other sources of information. Prefer the form of the name found in the prescribed sources based upon the order of precedence for chief sources of information listed in Rule 8.0B2.

The 1985 *Revisions* to *AACR 2* deleted Rule 8.4A2 (Art Originals, Unpublished photographs, etc.) and Rule 8.4A3 (Collections of Graphic Materials). Instructions for these materials are now covered under Rules 8.4C, 8.4D, and 8.4F as revised.

8.4B GENERAL RULE

Instructions regarding the recording of information in this area are found in Rule 1.4B. When describing a graphic item which is a reproduction of another graphic or of an item in another format, such as a photograph of a three-dimensional item, give the publication, distribution, etc., details of the reproduction in this area. Information about the original, if it appears on the item or in accompanying material, can be given in a note under Rule 8.7B7 or Rule 8.7B9.

Reproduction of a photo in another format	Join the midnight sun set in Alaska [picture] / photograph by Frank Whaley. — [S.l.] : Air Alaska, c1970. 1 poster : col. ; 90x60 cm. Copy of a time-lapse photograph of the Arctic sun taken between 11:00 A.M. and 1:00 A.M.

8.4C   PLACE OF PUBLICATION, DISTRIBUTION, ETC.

The 1985 Revision to Rule 8.4C1 instructs that the place of publication, distribution, etc., of a published graphic is recorded according to the provisions of Rule 1.4C1. The 1985 Revisions also provided a new rule (8.4C2) which states that the place of publication, distribution, etc., should not be recorded for unpublished graphic items or collections of these items. This provision also applies to collections of graphic materials which contain published materials if these were not published as a collection.

8.4D   NAME OF PUBLISHER, DISTRIBUTOR, ETC.

This rule has been revised in a manner similar to that of Rule 8.4C above. The name of a publisher, distributor, etc., of a published graphic item is recorded according to the instructions in Rule 1.4D. According to the new Rule 8.4D2, no publisher, distributor, etc., should be recorded for unpublished graphic items and collections.

Instructions for recording multiple publishers, distributors, etc., are now provided under Rule 1.4D5. Rule 1.4B8, which previously covered this situation, was cancelled by the 1983 Revisions. When an item has more than one publisher, distributor, etc., the name and corresponding place of the first is recorded. Other publishers, distributors, etc., and their associated places are also given in the following situations:

- when the entities are linked in one statement

- when the first named entity is a distributor or releasing agency and a later named entity is the publisher

- when a later named entity is "clearly distinguished" as principal publisher, distributor, etc., by topography or layout

- when the first named entity is not in the country of the cataloging agency and a later named entity is in that country.

As an option, the cataloger may add the name and, when appropriate, the place of the distributor when the first named entity is the publisher.

8.4E *OPTIONAL ADDITION.* STATEMENT OF FUNCTION OF PUBLISHER, DISTRIBUTOR, ETC.

This rule follows the provisions of Rule 1.4E1. A word or phrase designating the function of those named as publisher, distributor, etc., can be added, in square brackets, to the name or names at the option of the cataloger. This option should be used in cases where a phrase, indicating the function, (1) is not available from the item, (2) is not recorded, or (3) in cases where the function is not clear from the context of the information given in the body of the entry.

The word or phrases to be used are:

distributor	producer
publisher	production company

See the *AACR 2* glossary for the definition of "producer" and "production company." The Library of Congress is applying this option on a "case-by-case" basis.

Statement of Function	Diagnosis and treatment planning in endodontics [slide] : pulpal pathosis / Medical University of South Carolina, College of Dental Medicine, Department of Endodontics. — Charleston, S.C. : The Dept. ; Washington, D.C. : National Audio-visual Center [distributor], 1978.

8.5 PHYSICAL DESCRIPTION AREA

8.5B EXTENT OF ITEM (INCLUDING SPECIFIC MATERIAL DESIGNATION)

The total number of physical units of the graphic item being described, followed by a specific material designation, are the first two elements in this area. For multipart items, a specific material designation which covers all of the graphics items should be used. Although a GMD must be chosen from the standard terms found in Rule 1.1C1, a variety of terms can be used for the specific material designation. A list of specific material designations terms is given in Rule 8.5B1. This list includes some terms which are also used as general material designations and some terms which are not GMDs. The specific material designations are apportioned among the GMDs by the Library of Congress as follows:

Chart	**Picture**	**Slide**
Chart	Art print	Slide
Flip chart	Art reproduction	Stereograph
Wall chart	Photograph	**Technical drawing**
Filmstrip	Picture	Technical drawing
Filmslip	Postcard	**Transparency**
Filmstrip	Poster	Transparency
Flashcard	Radiograph	
Flash card	Study print	

If the terms in this list are not adequate to identify the item in question, a more specific term can be used at the option of the cataloger. The Library of Congress is applying this option.

The intended use of an item is one factor to be considered in determining the specific material designation to be used. For example, a poster, which would be assigned the generic term "picture" as the GMD, may be a reproduction of a photograph. Its intended use as a poster would indicate that it should be assigned the specific material designation "poster" rather than either "picture" or "photograph." Study prints may be reproductions of art originals, but their designed use for teaching purposes would suggest that the specific material designation "study print" be used. Thus, many graphic materials will have one term as their GMD with another term appearing as the specific material designation even though the GMD term is also an acceptable specific material designation.

Rule 8.5B2, as originally published in *AACR 2*, was deleted and replaced by the 1985 Revisions. The revised Rule 8.5B2 restates the original rule in a more concise manner. It still requires that a designation of the number of frames or double frames should be added to the specific material designation for filmstrips and filmslips. For stereographs, the number of double frames is added to the designation.

Very frequently, the frames of filmstrips and filmslips are not numbered. In these situations, the cataloger must count the number of frames.

Unnumbered frames   1 filmstrip ([47] fr.) : col. ; 35 mm.

The revision to the original rule removes the instructions which limited the necessity of recording unnumbered frames which are too numerous to count and also removes the instructions related to recording the number of separately numbered title frames.

The Library of Congress has provided guidelines for the counting procedure in an interpretation it issued to the original version of the rule. LC indicated that there are no items which have too many frames to count. Counting begins with the first content frame and ends with the last content frame. Noncontent frames included between the first and last content frame are included in the count. The total number of frames is recorded within square brackets. *AACR 2* does not define the phrase "content frame" although *AACR 1* Chapter 12 Revised did include such a definition. In the absence of a current definition catalogers may wish to utilize the earlier one as does the Library of Congress. These earlier rules defined a "content frame" as

> a filmstrip frame which presents subject matter, rather than title, credits, etc. (If titles, credits, etc., are superimposed on a frame which presents subject matter, the frame is considered as a content frame.)

In general this definition is satisfactory except for those cases in which title frames appear after the start of the content frames. In these cases, the cataloger can choose to ignore the internal title frames or include them in the total. Additionally, when counting frames, the Library of Congress ignores minor optional content frames. There are the frames, frequently used to provide a review or quiz about the filmstrip's content, which sometimes follow the end of the presentation.

According to Rule 8.5B5, when the parts of a multipart filmslip, filmstrip, stereograph, flip chart, or transparency have either exactly or approximately the same number of elements, they can be recorded in terms of the number possessed by each or approximately the number possessed by each.

Same number of components	6 filmstrips (52 fr. each)
Approximate number of components	5 filmstrips (ca. 40 fr. each)

Note that in the latter case, the number is not enclosed in brackets even though the number is supplied by the cataloger. This follows a pattern which appears in other chapters (e.g., Rule 2.5B7) of not using square brackets when the context of the statement (e.g., "ca.") already indicates that the number is an approximation.

Other extensions of Rule 8.5B deal with the designation of the number of sheets possessed by a flip chart (Rule 8.5B3) and the number of overlays associated with transparencies. This rule also called for an indication of whether the transparency overlays are attached.

8.5C OTHER PHYSICAL DETAILS

Because this chapter covers many different types of graphics having dissimilar details, the rules for recording "other physical details" are given in alphabetical order by specific material designation. In cases where a designation more specific than those listed in the rules has been used, follow the general instructions for the most relevant specific material designation. Terms used in the description of "other physical details" are not standardized. They are best taken from information appearing on the item or from its accompanying material.

Virtually all graphic formats have an instruction that some indication of color should be recorded. For some formats, such as filmstrips and filmslips, the choice of terms to use is limited to "b&w" or "col." For most other items, additional terms can also be used to indicate color. This is indicated by the use of "etc." in the instruction to use "col., b&w, etc."

8.5C3 Art Reproductions

In addition to the color, the method of reproduction is also supplied.

8.5C4 Filmstrips and Filmslips

Sound is indicated as a part of "other physical details" only when it is an integral part of the item, that is, the sound is recorded on the film itself. This type of sound recording for filmstrips is rare and not represented in most library collections. In almost all cases, the sound accompaniment for filmstrips is described as accompanying material under Rule 8.5E rather than as "other physical details."

8.5C7 Photographs

When the photograph is a transparency not designed for projection or a negative, this must be indicated. The cataloger has the option of also recording the process used to create the photograph.

8.5C11   Radiographs

No "other physical details" are recorded for radiographs.

8.5C12   Slides

Only one or two systems exist to record and playback sound integral to slides (i.e., the sound recorded on the slide mount). Because these systems are not compatible, the name of the system is included as a part of the "other physical details."

8.5C15   Technical Drawings

When the drawing is a reproduction, the method of reproduction is recorded. No color indication is recorded.

8.5D   DIMENSIONS

A general instruction to record both the height and width of graphic materials in centimeters is given in Rule 8.5D1. There are several caveats and exceptions, however, to this general rule. Filmstrips and filmslips have only the width given and it is given in millimeters. For stereographs, no dimensions are recorded. For slides, the dimensions are recorded only when they are other than 5x5 cm (i.e., 2x2 in.). Although different types of cameras and film produce standard slides with different aperture sizes, all of these slides can be viewed using equipment which projects, or allows for the viewing of transparencies, mounted in a standard size mount. Other sizes for slides include 1-3/16x1-3/16-inch slides produced with 110 film, 2¼x2¾-inch slides produced with 120 or 620 film, and 3¼x4-inch lantern slides. For these latter sizes, both dimensions must be recorded in using metric measurement. When recording the height and width of art originals, art prints, art reproductions, and transparencies, the frame or mount is excluded from the measurement. For folded technical drawings and wall charts, in addition to recording the height and width of the extended item, the dimensions of the item when folded are also given.

8.5E   ACCOMPANYING MATERIAL

Graphic materials are often accompanied by one or more other materials in graphic and/or nongraphic formats. Most often these accompanying materials are either sound or textual materials. In chapter 2 of this text, four methods for recording information about accompanying material were presented under Rule 1.5E1. These four methods allowed accompanying material to be recorded:

a.   in a separate entry

b.   in a multilevel description according to Chapter 13.

c.   in a note according to 1.7B11 and 8.7B11.

d.   at the end of the physical description.

A separate entry for each item in a package (method a.) is generally desirable only when the parts are cataloged, classified, and housed separately by necessity. Multilevel description (method b.) is not only more complicated for the cataloger, but, more important, it can also be very confusing to the user. Method d.

provides an opportunity to include further description of accompanying material in the physical description and is the method most commonly used for items which accompany graphic materials. In most cases, method d. alone, or a combination of methods c. and d., produces a unified record for the item that clearly presents all of the information needed by the user.

When method d. is used, Rule 8.5E1 provides that the name of the material, that is, a specific material designation or other name of the material, be recorded as the last element of the physical description preceded by a space " + " space. When the item has multiple accompanying materials the space " + " space precedes each item. For textual material, the name of the type of item (e.g., booklet, study guide, script, etc.), not its title, is recorded. This name should be taken from the item whenever available. Although not specifically prescribed by the rule, this part of the accompanying materials statement includes the number of items held, such as one teacher's manual, twenty-seven student guides, whenever this is grammatically possible.

Optionally, the cataloger can additionally record the physical description (extent of item, other physical details and dimensions) of some, or all, of the accompanying materials. The physical description of the accompanying material is enclosed in parentheses following the specific material designation for the accompanying material. The order of the elements of the physical description is identical to that used in recording the physical description for that material format. The mnemonic numbering structure of the *AACR 2* rules allows the cataloger to consult the appropriate chapter for the format of the accompanying material — extent under .5B, other physical details under .5C, and dimensions under .5D. Thus, in recording the physical description of an accompanying sound recording, the cataloger would follow the requirements of Rule 6.5 (Sound Recordings. Physical Description Area). The Library of Congress is applying this option of adding the physical details on a case-by-case basis. It is applying it, however, for virtually all nonintegral sound accompaniment.

The equipment requirements of sound recordings make a complete physical description most useful. More important, the duration of the sound accompaniment, also provided in the physical description, is the primary determinant of the amount of time required to use the graphic item. If several types of accompanying materials are included with a graphic item, a combination of complete physical descriptions for those requiring equipment and only specific material designation statements for those items not requiring equipment is often a good approach.

Single graphic items

1 filmstrip (48 fr.) : col. ; 35 mm.

1 art original : woodcut on paper ; 20x42 cm.

1 transparency drawing : b&w ; 60x40 cm.

Multipart items without accompanying material

4 filmstrips (ca. 45 fr. each) : b&w ; 35 mm.

2 posters : col. ; 53x36 cm.

80 slides : col.
*[Size of the slides is not given because these slides are the standard
size (2x2 in.)]*

**Multipart items with accompanying material without
optional physical description**

4 filmstrips : col. ; 35 mm. + 1 sound disc.

4 filmstrips : col. ; 35 mm. + 4 sound cassettes + 1 teacher's guide.

120 slides : col. + 2 sound cassettes + 2 sound discs + 1 script.

**Multipart items with accompanying material with
optional physical description**

5 filmstrips : col. ; 35 mm. + 5 sound discs (ca. 90 min. : analog,
33⅓ rpm ; 12 in.) + 1 teacher's guide.
*[Physical description for the teacher's guide not provided because the
information was not considered significant for the work. Sound
channels are not given because they are not stated explicitly.]*

6 filmstrips : col. ; 35 mm. + 3 sound cassettes (86 min. : analog) +
1 study guide (132 p. : ill. ; 27 cm.)
*[Speed of the cassette not provided because 1⅞ ips is considered
the standard speed of cassettes.]*

160 slides : col. + 2 sound cassettes (30 min. : analog)
*[Track information provided because it differs from the standard
(4 tracks) for a cassette.]*

8.6 SERIES AREA

Publishers of multimedia materials often use what might be called a
"pseudo-series" as a marketing device. A single work may be listed as part of
several groupings by a publisher in order to have it listed under several areas of
interest to potential buyers. In determining whether a series relationship exists for
a graphic item, a cataloger should follow the definition given in *AACR 2*. Characteristics possessed by items in a true series include the following:

• they are related by bearing both their own title and a collective title.

• there may or may not be numbering within the series.

• they are issued in sequence.

Unless the series fits requirements of the definition, the "series" information
should not be recorded here. It can, however, be recorded as a note (Rule
8.7B12).

**One filmstrip in a set of 5 cataloged separately with
set title recorded as the series**

1 filmstrip (53 fr.) : col. ; 35 mm. + 1 sound cassette (9 min. : analog).
— (Let's learn the basics)

Unnumbered series consisting of sets of filmstrips

6 filmstrips : col. ; 35 mm. + 3 sound cassettes (86 min. : analog) +
1 teacher's guide. — (SRA/CBS News filmstrip series)

Numbered series

8 study prints : col. ; 33x46 cm. + 1 sound disc. — (Basic science
series ; PSSP-100)

**Single item in a set cataloged separately. First series is title
of the sets, second series is the series for the individual sets.**

1 filmstrip (87 fr.) : col. ; 35 mm. + 1 sound cassette + 1 program
guide + 1 overview guide. — (Optics ; pt. 4) (Physics : fundamental
concepts)

8.7 NOTE AREA

8.7B2 Language
When the language or languages used for a work are not evident from the
title, a note should be made indicating them. Although not all that common, this
situation does occur when captions or scripts are in two languages while the title is
only given in one. In recording multiple languages, the Library of Congress lists
the predominant language first, with other languages listed in alphabetical order.
If no language predominates, all are listed in alphabetical order.

Captions in English and French.

Narration guide in English and Spanish.

Sound accompaniment in English, German and Russian.

With teacher's manual in English and French.

8.7B3 Source of Title Proper
When a title proper is chosen from a source of information other than the
chief source, a note is made to indicate its source. A unifying element, such as a
container which is not integral to the item or an accompanying item which is used
for all the items, is often the best source of title information for multipart items.
This note is frequently required to indicate that the cataloger supplied the title.
LC uses it most often to indicate that a work was cataloged from a data sheet.

Title from study guide.

Title supplied from publisher's catalog.

Title from data sheet.
[Data sheets supplied to the cataloging agency by the publisher.]

Title supplied by cataloger.

8.7B4 Variations in Title

Often, the title associated with a graphic package varies from one source to another. One would generally note these variations if they are considered significant and if a user is likely to identify the item by a title other than the one selected as the title proper. In an Interpretation to this rule, the Library of Congress has formalized this decision process. LC indicates that the first step in the process of determining whether a variation in title note should be made is the decision as to whether an additional access point is desired for that title variation. This determination is based upon the conditions given in Rule 21.2 (Changes in Titles Proper). These conditions are:

- a change occurs in the first five words of the title (exclusive of initial articles in the nominative case), or

- there is addition, deletion, or change of important words in the title, or

- a change occurs in word order.

If, based on these conditions, a decision is made that an additional access point is necessary, then a variation in title note should be made to justify the use of the added entry. If the decision to make an additional access point is negative, then the variation in title note should not be made.

Title proper	An American asset [filmstrip]. —
Variation in title note	Title on container: Coal, an American asset [filmstrip]. —
Title proper	The Automotive cooling system explained [filmstrip] : water-cooled type. —
Variation in title note	Title on container: Cooling system.

8.7B6 Statements of Responsibility

Names associated with the content and production of graphic items often may not appear prominently in the chief source of information and, therefore, should not be named in the statement of responsibility. These names can, however, be recorded in a note.

AACR 2 provides no specific instructions for recording cast and credit information. The Library of Congress, however, has issued an Interpretation which provides additional guidelines on the use of this note. LC indicates that producers, directors, writers, and corporate bodies would not be recorded in this note but would be recorded in the Title and Statement of Responsibility Area. Other individuals involved in the "artistic and technical" production of the work would be listed in this note if they performed one of the following functions:

photographer, camera, cameraman, cinematographer

animator

artist, illustrator, graphics

film editor, photo editor, editor

music

consultant, advisor

In listing these individuals, the name is prefaced with the term indicating function. The functions should be listed in the order they appear in the list above. LC further indicates that persons performing the following functions would not be listed in a statement of responsibility note:

assistants or associates

production supervisors or coordinators

project or executive editors

technical advisers or consultants

audio or sound engineers

writers of discussion, program, or teacher's guides

other persons making minor or purely technical contributions

The Library of Congress usually precedes this note, when referring to the contributions of individuals, with the term "Credits." The following examples illustrate the use of the statement of responsibility note and the LC Rule Interpretation to it.

Credits: Photographer, James Crissey ; graphics, Donald Williams ; educational consultant, Donald Heaney.

Credits: Art, Judy Almendariz ; editor, Sheryl Niemann ; consultants, Ronald E. Reed, Paul Bloomquist.

Credits: Narrator, Barrett Clark ; voices, Doug Mathewson, Gloria Rascoe, Sonny Sharrock.

Credits: Consultants, Anne E. Nesbit, Donna L. Osness.

Created under the guidance of the U.S. Sewing Products Division of the Singer Company.

  Filmed in cooperation with Hillcrest Kidney Disease Treatment Center, Tulsa, Okla.

8.7B7 Edition and History

  The history of an item, as well as names and titles associated with a work in another format, are recorded in this note. The reissue of an item, particularly as part of a different set or series, should be noted along with any title or content change.

  The Library of Congress has issued a Rule Interpretation which provides additional details about the use of this rule. Whenever a work has been issued in another medium, regardless of whether the medium of the original item is known, and its production/release date is greater than two years from that of the item being cataloged, a note should be made indicating the medium and year of the original item. LC generally uses the following note structure:

Originally produced as [medium] in [year]

Originally issued as [medium] in [year]

  If the date of production/release of an original master or an earlier medium is unknown, or if the difference in the date is less than two years, LC indicates this in an "other format available" note (Rule 7.7B16). The note structure is then changed to:

Previously produced as [medium] in [year]

Previously issued as [medium] in [year]

  Based on: A golden threat / by Ken Butti and John Perlin.

  Based on the textbook series Western man and the modern world.

  Originally issued as filmstrip in 1978.

  Previously issued as motion picture in 1983.

  Picture from Charles Kuralt's On the road series filmed in 1976.
   [Filmstrip using stills from a production in another format.]

  Taken from Dr. Carl Sagan's television series of the same name.

  Rev. version of the 1973 filmstrip of the same title.

  Rev. version of: Cutaneous clues to systemic disease. 1972.

  Original in The Louvre, Paris.

  Detail of original painting in Folger Library.

8.7B8 Characteristics of Original of Art Reproduction, Poster, Postcard, etc.

This note was deleted by the 1982 Revisions. Notes relating to the original of a work are now covered by Rule 8.7B22 also issued by the 1982 Revisions.

8.7B9 Publication, Distribution, etc., and Date

Important information related to the item in hand that was not reported in Area 4, or which requires additional explanation, can be given in this note. This note is also used to record information about the date of original production when it differs from the date of publication.

Whenever a foreign firm is listed as the originator or emanator, the Library of Congress advises its catalogers not to assume that the work has been made or released in the country of that firm unless it is actually stated on the item. Instead, the foreign nature of the item is indicated in this note using the following structure:

$$\text{A foreign [medium] ([Country])}$$

if the work has either a U.S. emanator and a foreign producer or a foreign emanator and a U.S. producer, this note is not made.

8.7B10 Physical Description

Important details not given in the Physical Description Area are recorded in this note. It is particularly important to note characteristics which will affect the item's use.

Art reproduction

Mounted and framed, measures 73x59 cm. framed.

Frame: gold wood.

Filmstrips

With captions.

In container 32x43x4 cm.

Pictures

In portfolio (72 cm.).

Slides

Issued in a loose-leaf notebook.

In two carousel trays.

Transparency set

In plastic mounts, 23x30 cm. in container, 24x32x4 cm.

8.7B11 Accompanying Material

Notes about accompanying materials are needed whenever methods c. or d. in Rule 1.5E1 are used. Method c. requires that information regarding the accompanying material be given in this note rather than in the Physical Description Area. When using method d., some information about the accompanying material may be included in the physical description while other information is recorded in this note.

Here, as with the physical description note, it is particularly important to note information which will have a bearing upon the type of equipment required for the use of the accompanying material. Perhaps the most common use of this note is to comment upon the playback characteristics of the sound accompaniment. The wording that the Library of Congress uses most frequently is:

Sound accompaniment for manual operation only.

Sound accompaniment for automatic operation only.

Sound accompaniment compatible for manual and automatic operation.

Other ways in which this note might be worded include:

Sound cassette with automatic advance.

Sound cassette side 1 with automatic advance, side 2 without signal.

Sound cassette side 1 with automatic advance, side 2 with audible advance signal.

Sound disc side 1 with automatic advance, side 2 with audible advance signal.

For use with Viewmaster projector.

Sound cassette (30 min. : analog, 2 track, mono.).

Sound disc (12 min. : 45 rpm, mono. ; 7 in.)

Instructions for use on container.

Study guide on cover of sound disc.

Teacher's guide (12 p. : col. ; 18 cm.).

Teacher's guide includes bibliographies.

8.7B14 Audience

If an intended audience is identified on the item, its accompanying material, or its container, this should be noted. This information may designate an age or grade of users, or special classes or types of users. A descriptive phrase taken from the item is generally preferable over a rephrasing of the statement by the cataloger. Before 1985, the Library of Congress generally prefaced this note with the phrase "Intended audience:". Since then, LC has prefaced this note with the word "Audience:".

If no audience information is available on the item or with material associated with the item, the cataloger is prohibited from writing his or her own audience statement. In these cases, the purpose and audience level of the item are often incorporated into a summary note (Rule 8.7B17). There are some cases, however, in which the audience level is known although it is not actually stated on the item, the accompanying material, or the container. This most frequently occurs when an audience statement is given in an advertisement or in a publisher's catalog. In these cases, the cataloger could sidestep the restrictions of this rule by simply quoting the statement and giving its source.

Audience: College students and adults.

Audience: For parents of handicapped children.

Audience: For paralegal personnel.

Audience: Physicians, other medical personnel, and advanced medical students.

Audience: Primary grades.

8.7B16   Other Formats Available
This note is intended to alert the user to other formats in which the item is available. Its use should be limited to information about other formats actually available in the library rather than about formats available but not held. Because this information can easily be overlooked by the user, a separate entry in the catalog for each form of the item actually held by the library is preferable to giving the information in this note. The role of the Library of Congress as a national library and as a source of cataloging data for a wide range of libraries makes its use of this note for material it does not hold justifiable.

Graphic items with sound accompaniment are often published with the option to select the format of sound accompaniment desired. For example, slide sets frequently are offered with either disc or cassette sound accompaniment. Sound filmstrip sets also offer the same option. In addition to the format option, there are other options available in terms of the form of frame or slide advance used, that is, manual or automatic.

Cataloging prepared by the Library of Congress reflects its policy of providing physical description and note information which reflects all variations of the optional accompanying sound offered by the publisher. LC makes this note whenever the date of production/release of an original master or an earlier medium is unknown or when the difference in the dates is less than two years. Libraries using LC cataloging need to alter LC's cataloging to provide physical description and notes statements appropriate to the item in hand. Again, because LC's method may be confusing to the user, a separate catalog entry for each format in the library is a preferable cataloging approach. If the "other format" note approach is used, it should indicate that an alternate format is available in the collection and should give sufficient detail about the nature of that format. In a Rule Interpretation, LC instructs its catalogers to begin this note with the term "Issued."

Issued also as filmstrip.

Issued also as slide set.

Issued also as slide set and videorecording.

Issued also as 16 mm. filmstrip in cartridge and as slide set.

Issued also with sound accompaniment on disc.

Issued also in b&w.

Issued also in a French version.

Another format available with enhanced physical description

Issued also as 1 filmstrip (45 fr.) : col. ; 35 mm. + 1 sound cassette (15 min. : analog, 2 track, mono.). Sound accompaniment compatible for manual or automatic advance.

Issued also with 1 sound cassette (30 min. : analog, 2 track, mono.). Sound accompaniment compatible for manual and automatic operation.

8.7B17   Summary
A summary note enables the user to gain a general idea of the subject content, scope, and point of view of the presentation. This note is particularly important in dealing with multimedia formats which cannot easily be browsed by the user, such as slide sets and filmstrips. The note should be a brief statement, using phrases whenever possible, describing what the user will see and experience. Significant technical or artistic attributes can also be mentioned as well as the visual treatment and the type of sound used. The statement should be objective, nonevaluative, and should avoid interpretation.

The summary note should avoid the repetition of information already given elsewhere in the description. Thus, it is common to refrain from using a summary note when items in a set have their individual titles recorded in a contents note. It should be remembered, however, that although contents notes are often descriptive of the topics covered, a summary statement may provide information about the way in which the media address the topic.

The use of the traditional formal note structure, headed by the word "Summary" and followed by a colon, enables a user to easily locate the information on the catalog record. This formal summary note style is used by the Library of Congress.

Chart

Summary: Illustrates 12 cell types with 40 labels.

Filmstrip

Summary: Three cartoon episodes conceived and narrated by Art Buchwald. English comedians Flanders and Swann, and Bill Cosby demonstrate typical struggles between adolescents and their parents.

Summary: Visits the home of kings, and for many years the seat of the French government. Shows how the rooms are decorated for various periods and relives events which took place there.

Flash card

Summary: Each card contains a topic heading and questions on one side and answers on the other.

Graphics package

Summary: Items divided into 12 displays with visuals and captions for each.

Postcard

Summary: Shows front and side view of the building.

Slide set

Summary: Uses art, music, and photography to discuss need for planning the future with technology. Illustrates ways technology may affect the family, religion, education, the arts, and the environment.

8.7B18 Contents
Contents notes are necessary for multipart graphic materials with individually titled parts. In this note, each named part can include both a title and, if appropriate, a statement of responsibility. In addition, the cataloger may add the extent (e.g., frames, slides, etc.) of the individual part. This information is recorded in parentheses following the title or statement of responsibility, if there is one. The Library of Congress has issued a Rule Interpretation which adds, after the extent of the part, the durations of the sound accompaniment, if they vary significantly from one part to another. These elements are separated by a comma. If no extent of the part needs to be recorded, the duration of the accompanying sound can be recorded by itself within parentheses.

Filmstrip set with collective title

Contents: Early hunters and gatherers − Early planters of the southwest − Ancient cliff dwellers and apartment house builders − The mound builders.

Contents: Introducing the library (43 fr.) − Using the card catalog (45 fr.) − Using reference works (43 fr.) − Reports and research (44 fr.).

Contents: Communities are alike and different (71 fr., 9 min.) — Communities have goods and services (57 fr., 8 min., 4 sec.) — Government and law in the community (60 fr., 9 min., 55 sec.) — How communities change (59 fr., 9 min., 25 sec.).

Slide set

Contents: pt. I (76 slides) — pt. II (80 slides).

Slide set with collective title

Contents: pt. A. Planning, design, costs — pt. B. Bedding, safety, environment.

8.7B19   Numbers
Few graphic materials are assigned ISBNs or ISSNs. However, other numbers, usually assigned by the publisher from its ordering system, are associated with nonprint materials. Multipart items often carry numbers for their individual parts as well as for the composite package. The package number should always be recorded. The numbers for individual items should be recorded when a package number is not assigned. If the package has a number, it is not necessary, but nevertheless useful, to record the numbers of individual parts. Numbers recorded in the note should be associated with the part(s) to which they refer.

Sound filmstrip set

Filmstrip: 174.

Sound cassette: 174 C.

Study prints with sound disc

Picture story study prints: SP104.

Sound disc: TSP 104 RR.

Postcard

"119528"

Single filmstrip in a set cataloged separately

Filmstrip no. 14166.

Sound slide set

258.

8.722 Notes Relating to Original

Notes related to the original of a reproduced art work are recorded in this location. This note was created by the 1985 Revisions and replaces Rule 8.7B8 (Characteristics of Original of Art Reproduction, Poster, Postcard, etc.). The bibliographic information is recorded in the order of the areas of description using normal ISBD punctuation (except that a space, dash, space is not used to separate each description area). The example provided in the Revisions begins the note with the phrase "Reproduction of:".

EXAMPLES: Descriptive Cataloging for Graphic Materials

Art original

> Hassam, Childe, 1958-1935.
>   [Street corner with carriage and crowd] [art original] /
> Childe Hassam. — 1888.
>   1 art original : oil on cigar box cover ; 20x30 cm.
>
>   Title supplied by cataloger.
>   Size when framed: 41x34 cm.
>   University of Kentucky property no.: B730339.
>   Accession no.: 79.28.

Area 1	— An original oil with supplied title.
	— Object is signed.
Area 4	— Date of creation. Place and publisher information is inappropriate for an art original, unpublished photograph, or other unpublished graphic materials.
Area 5	— Framed size is given because it differs significantly from the size of the object being described.
Area 7	— Source of supplied title.
	— Numbers needed for identification within collection.
Added Entries	— Supplied titles are not traced.

Art print

> Cézanne, Paul, 1839-1906.
>   The blue vase [picture] / by Paul Cézanne. — [New
> York] : Abrams, [19--]
>   1 art print : col. ; 63x49 cm.
>
>   Original in the Louvre Museum, Paris.
>
>   I. Title.

Main Entry	— A reproduction of an art work is entered under the artist of the original.

(Explanation continues on page 172.)

Area 4   — Place determined from reference sources.
                        — Date undeterminable.

Area 5   — Process for reproducing the item is unknown. If known, it would have preceded the color indication.
                        — Size does not include the frame or mount.

Chart

Periodic chart of the elements [chart]. — Rev. ed. — Los Angeles : Chemical Services, 1978, c1969.
    1 chart : double sides, b&w ; 22x28 cm.

Contents: Side 1. Chart of the elements based on carbon-12 — Side 2. Chemical valence and planetary electrons / I. Shapiro.

Main Entry   — Lacking a statement of responsibility for whole item, the entry is under title.

Area 2   — Edition statement was found on the item.

Area 5   — Type of chart is not specific, resulting in the use of only the term "chart" as the specific material designation.

Area 7   — Contents note made for the titled parts.

Single filmstrip with sound accompaniment

Perspectives and challenges [filmstrip] : a national program for library and information services / presented by the National Commission on Libraries and Information Science ; [produced by] Image Innovations. — Washington, D.C. : The Commission, 1978.
    1 filmstrip (156 fr.) : col. ; 35 mm. + 1 sound cassette (25 min. : analog) + 1 guide.

Sound accompaniment compatible for manual or automatic operation.
Summary: Structured around library professionals at Statewide Library Planning Committee meeting. Presents aspects of proposed national program of NCLIS.

I. United States. National Commission on Libraries and Information Science.

Area 1	— Although somewhat lengthy, the entire title proper is given and not abridged.
	— Statement of responsibility appears prominently on the item.
	— The statement showing the relationship of the production company does not appear on a prescribed source.
Area 4	— Shortened form of the name of the publisher is given because that name has already been used previously in the description.
Area 5	— Speed of the cassette tape is not recorded because it is standard, that is, 1⅞ ips. This is an approved revision to *AACR 2*.
	— Analog indication added as instructed by the *AACR 2* revisions.
	— Tracking and number of channels are not given because they were not readily available or stated explicitly respectively.
	— Two types of accompanying material are present. Only the one requiring equipment has additional physical description supplied.

Filmstrip set

Bibliographic information on item

Box container front	WASHINGTON Five Filmstrip Adventures in full color and sound NATIONAL GEOGRAPHIC SOCIETY Encyclopaedia Britannica Educational Corporation
Title frames first filmstrip	Washington, D.C. The City Freedom Built
	The National Geographic Society and the Encyclopaedia Britannica Educational Corporation present
	from the worldwide resources of the National Geographic
	The City Freedom Built © 1968 by the National Georgraphic Society and Encyclopaedia Britannica Educational Corporation
First filmstrip end frames	The City Freedom Built Producer David S. Boyer An educational service from The National Geographic Society School Services Division Ralph Gray, Chief

Filmstrip set

> Washington [filmstrip] / National Geographic Society and Encyclopaedia Britannica Educational Corporation ; producer, David S. Boyer. — [Chicago] : Encyclopaedia Britannica Educational Corp., c1968.
>> 5 filmstrips : col. ; 35 mm. + 5 sound discs (analog, 33⅓ rpm ; 12 in.)
>
>> Sound accompaniment compatible for manual or automatic operation.
>> Each disc cover contains script.
>> Contents: The city freedom built (83 fr.) — The United States Capitol (94 fr.) — The White House (84 fr.) — The Supreme Court (95 fr.) — Shrines and monuments (88 fr.).
>>> 6420.
>
>> I. National Geographic Society (U.S.) II. Encyclopaedia Britannica Educational Corporation.

Main Entry	— Entered under title. Corporate body (National Geographic Society) does not qualify for main entry under Rule 21.1B.
Area 1	— Statement of responsibility is given for the corporate bodies because they are considered to be prominent based on the typography on the box combined with the statement on the end frames.
	— Producer was named in the responsibility based upon a Library of Congress Rule Interpretation to Rule 7.1F1 which indicates that LC usually records producers, directors, and writers in a statement of responsibility.
Area 4	— Place determined from reference sources.
Area 5	— Physical description of the accompanying material is described in detail.
	— Speed not given because it is the standard speed for a cassette.
	— Duration omitted because it was not readily available.
Area 7	— Note on the sound accompaniment indicates the type of equipment required.
	— No summary note is necessary because of the information supplied in the contents note. A summary note, however, could be given.
	— Number of frames of the individual parts, indicated in the contents note, gives an indication of length of production.

—The number assigned to the item by the publisher is given as the last note. The Library of Congress generally does not record this type of number for these materials. This number can be supplied whether or not a standard number is recorded in Area 8.

An American sampler [filmstrip] / produced by CBS News and Joshua Tree Productions. — Chicago : Science Research Associates, c1974.
6 filmstrips : col. ; 35 mm. + 3 sound cassettes (86 min. : analog) + 1 teacher's guide. — (SRA/CBS News filmstrip series)

Narrator: Charles Kuralt.
Based on: Charles Kuralt's On the road series for CBS News.
Sound cassettes with audible signals.
Audience: Intermediate and secondary grades.
Summary: An anthology of human interest stories and a structured examination of the country's life styles.
Contents: America : variety and individualism (79 fr.) — America celebrates tradition (68 fr.) — America : changing and unchanged (97 fr.) — Americans and their land (70 fr.) — America on the go (72 fr.) — Americans and a job well done (63 fr.).
No. 3-11000.

I. Kuralt, Charles, 1934-   II. CBS News.
III. Science Research Associates. IV. Series.

Area 1	—Collective title appears on container and filmstrips.
	—Statement of responsibility also appears on both sources.
Area 4	—Science Research Associates is both the publisher and distributor.
Area 5	—Accompanying material is described in detail.
	—Speed not given because it is the standard speed for a cassette.
Area 6	—Unnumbered series is recorded.
Area 7	—Lacking information on the cassettes themselves or in the guide, the nature of the sound was determined by listening to the cassettes.
	—Summary taken from the guide.

(Explanation continues on page 176.)

—Contents listed with the number of frames for each part. If all the parts were of the same length, this information could have been recorded in the physical description. Although normally the Library of Congress does not record subtitles in contents notes, it is necessary in this case to differentiate between identical titles proper.

Added Entries — Added entries for all information which might be used by library patron in attempting to locate the item.

—A publisher can be used as an access point if it is considered useful to catalog users.

Flash card set

Steiner, Wilfred J.
American history I [flash card] : discovery to Civil War / by Wilfred J. Steiner. — Springfield, Ohio : Visual Education Association, [197-?]
1000 flash cards : col. ; 4x9 cm. + 1 booklet.

Booklet contains "Table of contents," "Alphabetical index," "Major topic headings."
Audience: High school and college.
Summary: Side 1 of each card contains a topic heading and one or more questions. Side 2 contains the answers.
VE507.

I. Title.

Main Entry — Main entry under the prominently named author.
Area 1 — Number is included as part of title proper.
—GMD precedes the other title information.
Area 4 — Decade certain. Date derived from information appearing on the cards; no other date information given on the item.
Area 7 — Intended audience on the item as given.
—Accompanying material details provided.
—Summary needed.
—Publisher's number is included as the last note.
Added Entries — An access point could have been provided for Visual Education Association.

Flip chart

    Campbell, Anneke.
        Your pregnancy year [chart] : a day-by-day guide to
pregnancy and birth / by Anneke Campbell. — 1st
ed. — Garden City, N.Y. : Doubleday, c1979.
        1 flip chart (13 sheets) : col. ; 28x41 cm.

        Summary: On the left of each page is a description
of progress of pregnancy. On the right, in calendar, is
space for user's pregnancy record.
        ISBN 0-385-14323-0

        I. Title.

Main Entry	—Entry under the person responsible for the content of the item.
Area 1	—Other title information follows the GMD.
Area 5	—Number of sheets is indicated in the physical description.
Area 7	—Summary needed.
Area 8	—Standard number recorded.

Postcard

    Law Building, University of Kentucky, Lexington
[picture]. — Louisville, Ky. : Postal Color Corp.,
[196-]
        1 postcard : col. ; 9x14 cm.

        Summary: Front view of building completed in 1965.
119528.

Area 1	—Title taken from the item.
Area 4	—Decade certain.
Area 7	—Summary useful.
	—Publisher's number included as the last note.

Poster

> Alpha.
>> Photo of monkey jungle, Miami, Fla. [picture] / by
> Alpha. — Niles, Ill. : Argus Communications, c1976.
>> 1 poster : col. ; 53x36 cm.
>
>> Summary: An orangutan pointing with caption,
> "Don't follow me, I'm lost."
>> Poster 2333.
>
>> I. Title. II. Title: Don't follow me, I'm lost.

Area 1	— Title and statement of responsibility taken from information on back of poster.
	— The caption is not the title.
Area 7	— The graphic content is the basis of the summary.
Added Entries	— If there could be doubt in a user's mind whether the caption on the document is the title, an added entry for the caption would be appropriate.

Poster display package

> [The American Revolution] [picture] / People's
>> Bicentennial Commission. — Washington, D.C. : The
> Commission, [1976?]
>> 76 posters : b&w ; 22x28 cm. + 1 booklet.
>
>> Title supplied by cataloger.
>> Booklet, entitled The patriot's handbook : a syllabus
> and study guide to the American Revolution, includes a
> bibliography following each of its 14 sections.
>> Summary: Fourteen poster displays depicting the
> American Revolution through illustrations, captions,
> and text.
>
>> I. People's Bicentennial Commission.

Main Entry	— Entry under title. The corporate body does not come under the provisions of Rule 21.1B2 for the use of a corporate body as a main entry.
Area 1	— Title is supplied because the package lacks a collective title.
	— Statement of responsibility found prominently on booklet, the unifying element.
Area 4	— Shortened form of publisher's name is used. A more complete form was given previously in the description.

—Probable date for material published by a group formed to celebrate the Bicentennial.
Added Entries—Added entry for the group responsible for the work.

Slide set with sound accompaniment

How to live with your parents and survive [slide]. — White Plains, N.Y. : Center for Humanities, c1975.
    80 slides : col. + 1 sound disc + 2 sound cassettes + 1 teacher's guide.

Identical sound accompaniment provided in three forms. Duration is 14 min. Sound accompaniment compatible for manual and automatic operation.
    Guide contains script, credits, and references.
    Summary: Three cartoon episodes conceived and narrated by Art Buchwald. English comedians Flanders and Swann, and Bill Cosby demonstrate typical struggles between adolescents and their parents.
    007.

    I. Center for Humanities.

Area 5   —Physical description of this set, with identical sound in different formats, does not make use of the option to record details of the accompanying material in the physical description.
Area 7   —Notes are used to explain the nature of the sound accompaniment.
Added Entries—Added entry provided for a publisher useful as an access point for library patrons.

**Slide set with sound accompaniment and
additional cassette**

> Musical instruments of the baroque and early classical
> eras [kit] / Division of Musical Instruments, National
> Museum of History and Technology. — Washington,
> D.C. : Distributed by the Smithsonian Institution,
> Office of Printing and Photographic Services, c1978.
> 58 slides col.
> 2 sound cassettes (60 min.) : analog.
> 1 guide (22 p.) ; 20 cm.
>
> Prepared by Helen R. Hollis with assistance from
> James M. Weaver ; consultants: Mark Lindley, Anne
> Melton Kimsey.
> First cassette contains narration and musical examples
> to accompany slides and has audible signals for manual
> advance. Second cassette contains two baroque musical
> works.
> Summary: Shows musical instruments in the
> Smithsonian Institution and works of art which illus-
> trade similar instruments played during period covered.
>
> I. National Museum of History and Technology.
> Division of Musical Instruments.

Main Entry	— Entry under title. The corporate body does not come under the provisions of Rule 21.1B2 for the use of a corporate body as a main entry.
Area 1	— Statements of responsibility taken from item.
	— GMD is [kit] because the package contains a film-strip with sound accompaniment and another cassette to be used separately.
Area 4	— Distribution statement from the item.
Area 5	— Physical description is done according to method b. of Rule 1.10C2.
	— No size for the slides because their size is standard, 5x5 cm (i.e., 2x2 in.).
	— Speed of the cassette is not recorded because it is standard for a cassette.
Area 7	— Names are placed in a statement of responsibility note rather than in body of entry because of their affiliation with the responsible organization.
Added Entries	— Provided for the corporate body name in the statement of responsibility. Not entered directly under the name of the subordinate body, the Division, because the word division fits (Rule 24.13, Type 1).

Stereograph

>The Wizard of Oz [slide]. — New York : GAF Corp., c1957.
>
>3 stereograph reels (Viewmaster) (7 pairs of fr.) : col. + 1 story booklet. — (Classic tales)
>
>Based on the book of the same title by L. Frank Baum.
>Contents: reel 1. Land of Oz — reel 2. The Emerald city — reel 3. The Wizard's secret.
>Packet no. B361.
>
>I. Baum, L. Frank (Lyman Frank), 1856-1919. The wonderful Wizard of Oz.

Area 1	— "Slide" is the appropriate GMD for stereographs.
Area 5	— Technical specifications or a trade name should be added to the specific material designation for a stereograph (Rule 8.5B1).
	— 1985 revision to the example to Rule 8.5C13 creates this statement about the multiple frames rather than the statement "(7 double frames)" given in the original *AACR 2* text.
	— No dimensions should be recorded for a stereograph.
	— Edition and History Note. This will justify an added entry for the document upon which this work was based.
Added Entries	— Added entry was provided for the book from which this material was taken because the entry element for the book was significantly different from that of the stereograph. If the entry elements were the same, an added entry might not have been made. Regardless of the similarity of the titles, this access point would be very useful for a library which has separate catalogs for print and nonprint materials. The added entry card for the title of the book could be placed in the catalog for printed materials to inform users of a related document in a nonprint format.
	— The added entry is entered under the author because the author would be the main entry of the book. The title used in the added entry is the uniform title of the work. Libraries not using uniform titles would have used the title "The Wizard of Oz" following the name of the author.
	— Series is not important or distinctive enough to be traced.

Study prints with sound accompaniment

> Common birds. Group I [picture]. — Chicago : Produced
> and distributed by SVE, c1963.
> > 8 study prints : col. ; 33x36 cm. + 1 sound disc (28
> > min. : analog, 33⅓ rpm ; 12 in.). — (Basic science
> > series ; PSSP-100)
>
> > Contents: Great horned owl — Cardinal — Blue
> > jay — Redwing blackbird — Mourning dove — Brown
> > thrasher — Robin — Hairy woodpecker.
> > Sp 104.
>
> > I. Society for Visual Education.

Area 1	—Title proper includes the title of a part.
Area 4	—Publisher's name as it appears on the item.
Area 6	—Series with number.
Area 7	—Contents are unnumbered on item.
Added Entries	—Added entry for the full form of the publisher's name. Because it is known by both forms, the catalog should contain a reference from SVE to the full form of the name.

Transparency

> Formation of a volcano [transparency]. — Maplewood,
> N.J. : Hammond, [197-?]
> > 1 transparency (3 overlays) : col. ; 22x25 cm. + 1
> > teacher's manual. — (Hammond earth science
> > transparency series)
>
> > Summary: Illustrates the active, dormant, and extinct
> > stages in the life of a volcano.
> > 8558.
>
> > I. Hammond Incorporated. II. Series.

Added Entries	—Incorporated is included in the heading to show the corporate nature of the name. If it had not been part of the name, the word (Firm) would have been added to indicate that it is a corporate body.

7
Description of Computer Files

AACR 2 CHAPTER 9 [REVISED]: COMPUTER FILES

9.0 GENERAL RULES

9.0A SCOPE

This chapter covers the description of all types of files, both published and unpublished, that are "encoded for manipulation" by computers. These computer files include those designed for mainframe and minicomputers as well as those intended for use with microcomputers. Files covered can be either data or program files. Excluded are electronic games and other devices that are not computers but which do use encoded instructions and/or data in their operation. Games of this sort are covered by the provisions of *AACR 2* Chapter 10 ("Three-Dimensional Artefacts and Realia").

When *AACR 2* was published in 1978, computer files were a new and somewhat unusual item in most libraries. That year, coincidentally, also saw the introduction of microcomputers into the general marketplace, an event that rapidly had an impact upon the collections of multimedia libraries. *AACR 2* Chapter 9 introduced something new to cataloging codes—a chapter which addressed the descriptive cataloging requirements of machine-readable data files. Although that chapter was a major step forward in providing for the description of this material, it was best applied to software associated with mainframes and minicomputers. As libraries began to apply its rules to microcomputer software, it became readily apparent that the chapter was insufficient in detail to cover the descriptive needs of these items. Thus, in 1984 a first step was taken to meet this need through the publication of *Guidelines for Using AACR 2 Chapter 9 for Cataloging Microcomputer Software*. The statements in the *Guidelines* were not actual rules, but, as the title indicates, were intended to facilitate the use of the existing Chapter 9 for this new type of software.

In 1987, a draft revision of *AACR 2* Chapter 9 was published. These rules were approved by the Joint Steering Committee for the Revision of the Anglo-American Cataloguing Rules (JSCAACR). Although the rules are not in a final form (that will appear in a consolidated *AACR 2* in 1988), they are accurate in terms of the approach to the concept of describing computer files, although their final form "will probably contain changes in detail." These rules form the basis of this chapter of this text. They are presented here because they represent the "state-of-the-art" for the cataloging of computer files. This chapter will refer to parallel Library of Congress Rule Interpretations to rules in the Revised Chapter 9 because, to date, no Rule Interpretations have been issued specifically for that chapter.

9.0B SOURCES OF INFORMATION

9.0B1 Chief Sources of Information
The chief sources of information for all types of computer files are the title screen or screens. In those cases where a work is divided into multiple physical units, a unifying container or "permanently affixed" label is the chief source if it provides a collective title, and the information in the items, or the labels on the parts, do not. When no title screen is present, the information should be derived from other "formally presented" statements given internally. Overall, this statement identifying the chief source of information is a great deal clearer than that given in the original Chapter 9.

There will be times when required information is not available from the chief source of information. The issue of availability of information is somewhat different in this chapter from that encountered in other chapters for nonprint materials. Nonavailability includes those situations in which the information is not actually provided internally and those cases where a cataloger cannot gain access to the internal information because of a lack of appropriate hardware or firmware to read the information. It should be noted that information mentioned internally in a file frequently will not be reported on the associated labels and printed documentation. This is particularly true for names, dates, and edition statements. Other information may be very different when a computer file has been revised but not its printed materials. Thus, catalog records developed from an examination of the internal record may vary significantly from records developed from only an examination of the external labels, accompanying materials, and any associated container.

The mere availability of a computer to use when cataloging a file does not ensure that the information contained in the file will be used to its fullest. Catalogers must be familiar with the features of particular machines, their operating systems, and the program itself, in order to call all useful information into view. Merely "booting" a computer disk is not sufficient. A case in point would be a Macintosh program. A cataloger might know how to use "pull down" commands and also be aware that there is an information window available from the desktop display. This knowledge would still not produce the desired information because the cataloger would actually have to execute the program in order to use the "About ..." display on the Apple menu. Without executing the program, the "About ..." display would only give information about the "Finder" component of the system and not information about the program itself.

When information is not available from the chief source of information, it can be taken from:

- the physical carrier or its labels (The term label means any label added by the publisher that is permanently affixed to the item itself. This excludes labels or statements added to the container.)

- documentation provided with the item (This includes both printed and machine-readable documentation.)

- the container issued by the publisher, distributor, etc.

These sources should be consulted in the above order. If the information from these sources varies in fullness, the source with the most complete information should be used regardless of its position in the order of precedence. If the chief source of information and these other sources do not provide the needed information, a cataloger may use:

- published descriptions of the item

- other sources

Information derived from a published description of an item is preferred over information derived from "other sources."

9.0B2 Prescribed Sources of Information
For each area of the description, there are different prescribed source(s) from which information can be taken without having to enclose it in square brackets. For the Title and Statement of Responsibility Area, the chief source of information; the carrier; its labels; information issued by the publisher, distributor, etc.; and the container serve as the prescribed sources of information. These same sources are also the prescribed sources of information for the Edition Area; the Publication, Distribution, etc., Area; and the Series Area. Other areas of the description (File Characteristics, Physical Description, Notes, and Standard Number) may have their information derived from any source.

In all but a few cases, information required by the chosen level of description can be taken from any source provided that the information is placed within square brackets. Additionally, catalogers are always free to record information in a note without the need of brackets.

9.1 TITLE AND STATEMENT OF RESPONSIBILITY AREA

9.1B TITLE PROPER
The title proper should be recorded as instructed in Rule 1.1B. Unlike the rules in other chapters for description, this chapter specifically calls for indicating the source of the title in a note (Rule 9.7B3). Other chapters only call for the use of this note when the source used to derive the title proper is other than the chief source of information. The reason for this different approach is the necessity of using multiple sources of information for Area 11 and because the use of a chief source may be limited by the availability of equipment.

The names of files and data sets should only be used as the title proper if they are the only title on the chief source of information. If these types of title are considered important and there is also a title proper present on the chief source, the file or data set name may be given in a note (Rule 9.7B4).

Rule 9.1B3 instructs catalogers to supply a title, following the provisions of Rule 1.1B7, if no source can provide a title. This title should be enclosed in square brackets (Rule 9.7B3), which indicates that the title has been supplied by the cataloger.

9.1C *OPTIONAL ADDITION.* GENERAL MATERIAL DESIGNATION

The general material designation follows the title proper. The GMD used for this type of material has changed from what was originally used in *AACR 2*. The GMD prescribed by Revised Chapter 9 is "computer file" rather than "machine-readable data file" as called for in the original rules. Parallel titles, "other title information," and their associated punctuation follow the GMD.

9.1D PARALLEL TITLES

Parallel titles (i.e., titles proper which appear in more than one language or script) are not very common to computer files. When they occur, they are recorded following the title proper and the GMD according to the instructions given in Rule 1.1D. A parallel title is preceded by a space, equals sign, space. For level two descriptions, catalogers must record the first parallel title. If a subsequent parallel title is in English, it must also be recorded.

9.1E OTHER TITLE INFORMATION

Other title information, including subtitles, is recorded following the GMD. Rule 1.1E is the operative rule for recording this information. In many cases, subtitles associated with published computer files serve the purpose of defining the nature or scope of the work. Frequently these subtitles will, in fact, carry the total burden of a descriptive title with the title proper serving as an "eye catching" or "cute" marketing title. If desired, catalogers may record "other title information" in a note (Rule 9.5B5) rather than in this area. This does reduce the bulk of the body of the description and thus improves its readability.

MacProof [computer file] : spelling, style and grammar checker

Diabetes [computer file] : programs to teach adjustment of insulin to patients with diabetes

Super*cat [computer file] : cataloging your library and using the data

SYSTAT [computer file] : the system for statistics

OMNIS 2 [computer file] : information manager

True BASIC [computer file] : the structured language for the future

9.1F STATEMENTS OF RESPONSIBILITY

Statements of responsibility are recorded as instructed by Rule 1.1F. When recording a statement of responsibility, include the entire statement of responsibility, that is, phrases indicating the relationship between the title and the person or corporate body, rather than just the name, if the relationship is not clear.

Notes related to the statement of responsibility are discussed under Rule 9.7B6. Rule 9.1F1 specifically instructs that collaborators, sponsors, etc., as well as persons and corporate bodies related to the production of the file should be named in this note rather than in the statement of responsibility. Under the earlier rules, programmers were seldom placed in the statement of responsibility.

This was because programmers seldom were responsible for the intellectual content of programs designed for mainframe computers and minicomputers. This situation is very different with microcomputer software, where the programmer may play the key or only role in the creation of the intellectual content of the file.

If the relationship between a title and statement of responsibility is not clear, and no statement exists on the item, a short word or phrase explaining the relationship, enclosed in square brackets, should be added by the cataloger.

There will be many cases where no name of a person or corporate body is directly associated with a computer file. In some of these situations, however, a person or corporate body will be named in the copyright statement. These statements should not be used as the basis for a statement of responsibility. Copyright statements are merely indications of the holder of legal rights to the work. Although there will be many cases in which the entity named is actually responsible for the work, in other cases the entity may have played no role in its creation.

9.1G ITEMS WITHOUT A COLLECTIVE TITLE
It is not uncommon to find computer software containing several individually titled computer files. When these multiple files lack a collective title, the titles should be recorded as instructed in Rule 1.1G. That rule allows for several different methods of recording the information for these titles.

If the work has one (Rule 1.1G1) or several titles (Rule 1.1G4) which predominate, they should be given in this area with the other titles given in a note (Rule 9.7B18). For some multiple-part software, one file will predominate and be supported by one or several secondary programs. In many of these cases, this method of description, often considered unsatisfactory for other types of materials, may prove very satisfactory for computer files. These predominant files can often be identified based upon the emphasis placed upon a particular title or titles by the publisher.

Rule 1.1G2, as revised, allows for the description of these works as either a unit or with separate descriptions when no one part predominates. In the latter situation, the individual descriptions should be linked with a "with" note. When described as a unit, the titles of the individual works are listed in the order in which they are stated on the chief source of information. These titles are separated by a space, semicolon, space. If the computer files are by different persons or corporate bodies, the appropriate parallel titles, other title information, and statements of responsibility associated with the individual work should follow the title proper of that work. In these cases, the last element associated with each title is followed by a full stop and two spaces. Although Rule 9.1G refers catalogers to Rule 1.1G, which allows for several methods of describing these types of works, the examples given in the revised text use only the unit description approach given in Rule 1.1G2. This is also the form of description being used by the Library of Congress for other types of nonprint materials.

SuperC [computer file] / by Donald M. Ludlow and Randy Black. —

MicroSpeedRead [computer file] / developed by Gail Benchener, Rose Wassman and Jim Lucas and the editorial staff of Holt, Rinehart and Winston. —

M-ss-ng l-nks [computer file : microencyclopedia / by Carol Chomsky and Judah L. Schwartz. —

Job cost [computer file] / BPI Systems, Inc. —

ATI training power for SuperCalc [computer file] / developed by American Training International. —

Batella de palabras! [computer file] / by Gessler Educational Software ; adapted by Mary Ann Mogot. —

9.2 EDITION AREA

The status of the edition statement for computer files is considerably different from its role for most other nonprint material. The edition statement, often called a version, level, or release, informs the user about the state of a file's content. This information can be very important to a user of an applications program because the capabilities of a program may vary significantly from one version to another.

Information about the source of a named reissue or edition of a computer file should be recorded in a note (Rule 9.7B7) if it is not the same as that used to derive the title proper. When in doubt about whether a statement is actually an edition statement or not, Rule 9.2B2 calls for the cataloger to use the presence of such words as "edition," "issue," "version," "release," "level," "update," or their foreign equivalents, as evidence that it is. Care should be taken to ensure that the edition statement being recorded pertains to the computer file being cataloged. In some instances, version, release, etc., information may pertain to the operating system being used rather than to the file being cataloged. Edition statements given only in the accompanying material should only be recorded as edition statements if it is certain that the statement also applies to the computer file. If this is in doubt, this information should be given in a note rather than in this area.

9.2B3 Optional Addition

Catalogers have the option of adding an edition statement if the work is known to contain "significant" changes from previous editions of the computer file. This statement, enclosed within square brackets, should be given in the language of the title proper. Computer files which contain only minor changes, however, should not be considered to be new editions (Rule 9.2B4). Although no Library of Congress Rule Interpretations have been issued for this option, in the other chapters for descriptions which have a parallel rule, LC has indicated that it does not use this option. It would probably be a good idea for multimedia libraries to apply this LC policy for computer files too.

Release 4.1C. —

Version 3.0. —

Version R1. —

Version 2.0. Special large version. —

V[ersion] 2.02. —

[Version] 1.3. –

Blue level ed. –

Scholastic ed. –

9.3   FILE CHARACTERISTICS AREA

This area, unused in the original Chapter 9 and in most other chapters for the description of nonprint materials, is used for the first time in this revision to record information about the characteristics of the file.

9.3B1   Designation

The designation of a computer file indicates the type of file that it is. File designation information need only be supplied when it is known. Previously, this information was given as part of the extent of file element in the Physical Description Area. In giving the file designation, the indication should be limited to one of the following phrases:

computer data

computer program(s)

computer data and program(s)

As an option to this rule, catalogers can delete the word "computer" from these statements if the GMD has been used. As was the case with the edition statement, although no LC policy has been given for this option in Chapter 9, its policy in other chapters for nonprint material in this situation is not to implement the option. It is recommended that a similar policy be followed in this chapter.

9.3B2   Number of Records, Statements, etc.

When a file designation has been supplied, and if the information is "readily available," the number, or approximate number, of files that constitute the work can be given within parentheses. An arabic numeral(s) should precede the word "file" or "files." Following this information, other details about the files can be given within the parentheses. Instructions for recording these details are given in the subrules to Rule 9.3B2.

The determination of the number of files can be very difficult, if not impossible, for some computer software items. In determining the number of files, the use of a directory or catalog of files is not totally satisfactory. For some computers (e.g., Apple II) the catalog listing provided by the operating system provides a general indication of the type of file contained, that is, binary, text, etc. That information is not always sufficient to distinguish between data and program files. For other computer operating systems (e.g., PC DOS or MS DOS) the file names are assigned by the programmer and do not necessarily indicate the type of file involved unless the programmer elected to assign a file name that did so. For Macintosh, the Desktop display does indicate whether the document is a program or a data file. However, this information is not totally satisfactory, because there may be files which are visible in the directory display. Thus, it is recommended that the phrase "readily available" be used in its most narrow sense (i.e., the program should directly state the number of files present. This statement would most likely appear in the program documentation. For those libraries that do wish to provide this information more frequently, it is recommended that they not go beyond the directory listing to establish the number of files. A note can be made later (Rule 9.7B8) which indicates that the information supplied in this area may not be exact. In the end, it should be remembered that for the majority of users of computer files held by multimedia libraries, the number of files is not really of much, if any, interest.

Neither of the subrules given below specifically prescribes a format for recording the size of a file. The examples for these rules, however, consistently use a full numeric form (e.g., 1250, 7260), rather than an abbreviated form (e.g., 12.5K, 72.6K), even though the abbreviated form is used later in the system requirements note examples. The examples in this text use the form indicated in the Revised Chapter 9. It is recommended, however, that libraries consider using the abbreviated form throughout the description unless a specific instruction or interpretation is issued later which contradicts this recommendation. Use of the abbreviated form can significantly reduce the size of this part of the record when the sizes of multiple files are given.

9.3B2a   Data

If the work contains computer data, the number or approximate number of records and/or bytes may be given. If this information follows the indication of the number of files, it should be preceded by a space, colon, space. If no indication of the number of files is given, the number of records should be indicated within parentheses. Depending upon the nature of the data file, knowledge of the number of records may be of great, little, or no importance. Catalogers should consider recording this information only when it is clearly stated. This policy could be based upon the assumption that, for those data files where the number of records is considered important, the publisher will have supplied that information in a location considered "readily available."

9.3B2b   Programs

If the work is a computer program, the number or approximate number of program statements and/or bytes may be given. This information, like that for "data" above, should be placed within parentheses. If this information follows the indication of the number of files, it should be preceded by a space, colon, space.

9.3B3c   Multipart files

If a multipart item has multiple files of one type (i.e., data or program), give the number or approximate number of records of statements in each. Record this information within parentheses following the indication of the number of files, preceded by a space, colon, space. Information about the byte size of the files may also be recorded here.

If a multipart item consists of both data and program files, the number, or approximate number, of both types of files and their byte sizes may be given. This information is recorded in parentheses. The rule instructs that in those cases where information about multipart files cannot be given in a concise manner, it should not be given here but recorded instead in a note (Rule 9.7B8).

Computer data (1 file : 390 records, 93,000 bytes). —

Computer data (1 file : ca. 400 records). —

Computer data (629 records). —

Computer program (1 file : 219 statements). —

Computer program (89 statements). —

Computer data (2 files : 98, 125 records). —

Computer program (2 files : ca. 100 statements each). —

Computer data (1 file : 652 records, 188,000 bytes) and programs (1 file : 167 statements, 97 bytes). —

9.4 PUBLICATION, DISTRIBUTION, ETC., AREA

9.4C PLACE OF PUBLICATION, DISTRIBUTION, ETC.
The place of publication, distribution, etc., for a published computer file should be recorded as instructed in Rule 1.4C. For computer files which are not published work, no place of publication, distribution, etc., should be given. Instead, the place of publication, distribution, etc., should be left blank rather than recording "s.l." in square brackets. The latter would have indicated that the place is unknown, whereas a place of publication is simply inappropriate for something that has not been published.

9.4D NAME OF PUBLISHER, DISTRIBUTOR, ETC.
The name of the publisher, distributor, etc., of a published computer file should be recorded as instructed in Rule 1.4D. As was the case with the place of publication, no name of a publisher, distributor, etc., should be given for an unpublished computer file, nor should "s.n." be recorded.

9.4E OPTIONAL ADDITION. STATEMENT OF FUNCTION OF PUBLISHER, DISTRIBUTOR, ETC.
There may be cases where it is necessary to record the names of several corporate bodies in this location. The use of this option to record a statement of function can help to clarify the information for the user. It is recommended that it always be used in cases where the function is not clear. Although no Library of Congress decision has been announced on the use of this option, LC's policy in other chapters for nonprint materials is to exercise this option selectively, although not necessarily uniformly. For major companies, the indication of function may not be necessary, while for less well known companies, it may be essential.

9.4F DATE OF PUBLICATION, DISTRIBUTION, ETC.
The dates of publication, distribution, etc., for published computer files should be given according to the instructions in Rule 1.4F. For many computer

files, the most frequently encountered date will be a copyright date rather than date of publication. Care should be exercised to ensure that the date being recorded actually matches the version indicated in the Edition Area. Some manufacturers will simply record a new version onto a disk which previously held the old version without changing any of the documentation or the permanently affixed label. Whenever possible, it is best to obtain the date from the internal computer file itself rather than from labels attached to the software or from its accompanying material.

In addition to the dates of publication, distribution, and copyright, other dates associated with a computer file should be given in a note (Rule 9.7B7). These dates will often have some relationship to the data on a file rather than to the date of the computer program.

For unpublished computer files, the date the file was produced should be recorded. The specific instructions for the provision of this date are given in Rule 1.4F9.

9.5 PHYSICAL DESCRIPTION AREA

This physical description has changed considerably with this revision of Chapter 9. Some of the information previously recorded here in *AACR 2* and in the 1984 *Guidelines* to Chapter 9 have been moved to the File Characteristics Area (Area 3) and the system requirements note. Other elements, retained in this revision, have had either the nature of what is recorded changed or the manner in which it is recorded. No physical description is given for remote access files.

9.5B EXTENT OF ITEM (INCLUDING SPECIFIC MATERIAL DESIGNATION)

The total number of physical units containing the computer file, followed by a specific material designation, are the first two elements in this area. At this time, the specific material designations for computer files are generally limited to the following phrases:

computer cartridge	computer disk
computer cassette	computer reel

If known, a cataloger can add to the specific material designation the specific type of physical medium being used for storage (e.g., chip, tape, optical laser, etc.). Trade names or similar information should not be given here, but rather in a note (9.7B1b).

Due to the rapid changes occurring in computer storage technology, this rule allows catalogers to add new specific material designators as they are needed. In creating these new designators, the rule does advise the use of a concise form of the name for the physical carrier qualified by the word "computer."

As an option, a cataloger may drop the designation "computer" from the specific material designation if the GMD "computer file" has been used. As is the case with other options, LC's practice towards this option in other chapters for nonprint material, that is, not to apply this option, may be applied here also.

9.5C OTHER PHYSICAL DETAILS

9.5C1 [Sound and/or color]

If a computer file produces sound, an indication of this should be given following the extent of file information. Similarly, if the computer file uses a color display, this should also be indicated. The abbreviations "sd." and "col." should be used respectively to record this information. The information given here should reflect the capabilities of the file and not the capabilities of the display equipment available in the library. Specific hardware and firmware required to produce sound or color should not be given in this part of the description but should be given instead in a note (Rule 9.7B1b).

9.5C2 *Optionally.* [Disk characteristics]

As an option, information about the physical characteristics of the computer disk upon which a file resides can be given if that information is considered important and is "readily available." This information is confined to the number of sides used, the density of the recording, and the sectoring. In the 1984 *Guidelines*, the disk characteristics information was recorded in a note (9.7B15. System Requirements and Disk Characteristics). There are cases where recording this disk information can be essential to users of the file; in other cases the information can be totally unimportant. It is recommended that this option be exercised with respect to the number of sides and the density of the recording whenever a particular make of computer comes in configurations which use different disks with varying characteristics. In cases such as this, one model of that computer may use single-sided, single-density disks, while another model uses double-sided, double-density disks. It is probably unreasonable to assume that users would be able to identify the different disk characteristics based only upon an identification of the model or models of the required computer. The sectoring used for computer software issued over the last few years is relatively consistent for disks for the same computer using the same number of sides and density. Generally, a cataloger need only record the sectoring information when there is a particular reason to suspect that it is other than that which the user would expect.

9.5D DIMENSIONS

The dimensions that are given for the physical carrier of computer files vary by the type of physical carrier used. For computer disks, the diameter of the disk is given in inches, rounding to the next quarter inch. Computer cartridges are measured in inches rounded to the next quarter inch. When measuring cartridges, the length of the cassette edge that is inserted into the drive is the aspect to be measured. The dimensions of a computer cassette are given only if they are different from those of a standard cassette (3⅞x2½ inches). This standard size is the same as that of a sound cassette. When a cassette's dimensions are recorded, they are given in terms of inches to the next ⅛th inch.

9.5E ACCOMPANYING MATERIALS

The name of accompanying material should be recorded according to the provisions of Rule 1.5E. For computer files, the accompanying material will most often be some form of printed documentation although there will be some instances in which the accompanying material may be other computer software.

As an option to the general rule, the physical description of that material may also be supplied. This option should generally be applied if the size of the material is considered significant. When a physical description of the accompanying material is not given and it is desired to give details about it, or details that are not considered part of the physical description, that information should be given in a note (Rule 9.7B11).

A relatively common feature of software documentation is the use of looseleaf binding or irregular paging. The frequency of the use of looseleaf binding is based upon the need to update the documentation when a new version is issued without having to reprint the entire document. When accompanying material is in looseleaf form and the cataloger believes that it is intended to receive additions or revisions, it should be designated as "1 v. (loose-leaf)" rather than a specific number of pages or leaves. Irregular pagination can appear in many forms but most commonly involves a combination of the chapter or section number with the page number (e.g., 1-1 to 1-36, 2-1 to 2-12, 3-1 to 3-14, etc.). When irregular paging occurs, the provisions of Rule 2.5Ba or 2.5Bc should be applied. The first rule allows for an indication of the total number of pages in the work while the latter merely indicates the number of volumes involved and the fact that the paging is irregular. While it is more work to use the former method, it is generally useful to know the size of accompanying documentation. This size can serve as an indicator of detail and quality in some cases (for example, one would question the quality of the documentation for a database management program that was less than thirty pages in length).

1 computer disk : col., sd., single sided, single density ; 5¼ in.

1 computer disk : double sided, double density ; 3½ in.

1 computer disk : double sided, high density ; 5¼ in.

1 computer disk : col., double sided, double density ; 5¼ in. + 1 teacher's guide + 1 backup disk.

1 computer disk : col., single sided, single density ; 5¼ in. + 1 teacher's guide + 3 spirit masters + 3 posters.

2 computer disks : sd., single sided, double density ; 3½ in. + 1 user's guide (1 v. (loose-leaf) : ill. ; 24 cm.)

9.6   SERIES AREA

Computer files may be issued in series, although the use of series for this type of material is less frequent than it is for some other types of nonprint material, except for educational software packages. Series should be described according to the provisions of Rule 1.6.

(Chelsea science simulations)

(Early games series)

(Master type series)

(MECC home software library)

(Microbiz)

(Scholastic wizard)

9.7 NOTE AREA

9.7B1 Nature and Scope and System Requirements

This note is a considerable expansion over its previous form in *AACR 2* as well as an expansion upon its use in other chapters for the description of nonprint materials. Rule 9.7B1a represents the original rule in *AACR 2*, while Rules 9.7B1b and 9.7B1c introduce new data elements into this note's coverage.

9.7B1a Nature and scope

In this location catalogers should record information about the nature or scope of the computer file if either is not apparent from the title or other parts of the description, particularly the summary and contents notes. This note can be particularly important for computer files because of the use of nondescriptive titles for many commercially produced application programs.

Database management system.

Font editor.

Game.

Word processor.

Integrated spreadsheet, graphics and charting program.

Collection of type fonts.

Demonstration disk.

Digitized MacPaint pictures

9.7B1b System requirements

Hardware, software, and firmware requirements for the use of a computer file should be specified if the information is readily available. Under the *Guidelines* to Chapter 9, some of this information was recorded in the Physical Description Area and some in a note under Rule 9.7B15 (System Requirements and Disk Characteristics). This rule instructs that the note should begin with the phrase "System Requirements:" followed by one or more of the requirements, each preceded by a semicolon. The types of requirements which should be listed, and their prescribed order, are

• computer (make and model) on which the computer file was designed to be run

• minimum memory requirement

- additional software requirements including any required programming language

- specifics on any required or recommended peripherals

In giving system requirements, catalogers should be cautious of giving requirements which, although they may be given as a part of the file's documentation, are obvious from either the physical characteristics of the item, its related computer, or the nature of the program. If all requirements are given, the size of this note can increase significantly without adding any useful information for the catalog user. Examples of some unnecessary system requirement statements would be indicating that a printer is necessary when describing a word processing program or indicating that a one-disk drive is needed when the item being cataloged is a computer disk. Likewise, when only one-disk drive is required and the make and model or the computer for which the program is intended comes equipped with one drive, making this statement would be unnecessary. It would be important, however, to indicate that two drives are required if the computer can be configured with only one drive. Generally, when in doubt about whether to give a particular requirement or not, it is better to err on the side of giving too much rather than risk recording too little and missing a key system requirement.

Although frequently a listing of system requirements is given near the beginning of the file's documentation, there will be cases in which a cataloger will have to search throughout the documentation in order to get a complete listing of requirements. In some instances, it may be necessary to add additional system requirements known to the cataloger but unstated in the documentation. Because of the rapidly changing and complex nature of computer technology, there may be instances in which a cataloger may actually need to record requirement statements the meaning of which are unknown to the cataloger. In these situations it is best to word the requirement exactly as stated.

System requirements: Commodore 64; 64K RAM; 1 disk drive; color monitor.

System requirements: IBM PC/XT, AT or compatible; 256K RAM; PC DOS or MS DOS 2.0 or higher; word processing program or text editor capable of generating and editing ASCII text files; monochrome adapter for 80 column display; 2 360K or 1.2M disk drives or 1 disk drive and 1 hard disk.

System requirements: IBM PC and compatibles; 384 or 512K RAM (preferred); 1 disk drive; 1 monochrome display, 1 printer adapter or color/graphics monitor adapter; 1 color or b&w monitor; 2nd disk drive (optional); 8088 coprocessor (optional).

System requirements: Apple II Plus; 48K RAM; DOS 3.3.

System requirements: Macintosh, Macintosh XL, MacPlus; 128K RAM; MacDraw, MacDraft, Penman, Microsoft Chart, Microsoft Excel, Mac 3-D, Jazz or other graphics programs; X-Y plotter.

System requirements: Macintosh; 512K RAM; 1 external disk drive; Apple Modem 300 or 1200 or Hayes Smartmodem (optional); Imagewriter printer (optional).

System requirements: IBM PC, PCjr, XT or AT; 64K RAM (PC, XT, AT), 128K RAM (PCjr); IBM Color/Graphics monitor adapter (PC, XT); color television or color composite, b&w, or RGB monitor; 1 disk drive; 1 or 2 joysticks (optional); Microsoft mouse (optional); IBM Game Control Adapter Card (PC, XT) (optional).

System requirements: Apple II, II Plus, IIe, IIc or Franklin ACE 1000; 48K RAM; 1 disk drive.

9.7B1c Mode of access
In those cases where a computer file is only available through remote access, the mode of access should be indicated in this note. Unlike the system requirements note, there are no specific formatting requirements for this note.

Available only through DIALOG.

Available only through the University's Computer Center using dial access.

9.7B2 Language and Script
When the language or script of either the spoken or written content of a computer file is not evident from the rest of the description, this note should be used to indicate either one or both of them. Unlike this rule in the original Chapter 9, no specific mention is made of using this note to record information about the type of characters (e.g., ASCII) that make up the file. That information is now recorded under Rule 9.7B8 (File Characteristics). This rule does specifically preclude recording the name of the programming language used. Requirements for a specific programming language needed to run a program are recorded under Rule 9.7B1b.

User's guide in English and Spanish.

Script in English and French.

9.7B3 Source of Title Proper
The source of the title proper for a computer file must always be indicated. This differs from the use of this note in the original Chapter 9, where it was only required if the title was derived from other than the file itself. It also differs from its use in other chapters for nonprint material where the note is made only when the title is not taken from the chief source of information.

Title from disk label.

Title from documentation.

Title from menu screen.

Title from publisher's catalog.

Title from title screen.

Title supplied by cataloger.

9.7B4   Variations in Title;
9.7B5   Parallel Titles and Other Title Information

Frequently, different parts of a computer file will have variant forms of the title. One should generally note these variations if they are considered significant, particularly if it is likely that a user will identify the file by a title other than the one selected as the title proper. This occurrence of title variations is relatively common for microcomputer software. One reason for these variations may be the fact that software publishers range in size from large publishing corporations with a significant publishing history to virtual "cottage industry" operations with no previous experience in any form of publishing. This lack of experience may affect the concern for consistency in providing information elements considered to have major importance in the identification of books and similar materials. Because of the presence of variant titles, some of which may be given in very prominent locations, catalogers must be especially conscious of title variations under which users may know a particular computer file.

The LC Interpretation for the variation in title rule in other chapters for nonprint materials established a policy which formalized the decision-making process. LC indicates that the first step is to determine whether an additional access point is desired for that title variation. This determination should be based upon the conditions given in Rule 21.2 (Changes in Titles Proper). These conditions follow:

- a change occurs in the first five words of the title (exclusive of initial articles in the nominative case)

- the addition, deletion, or change of important words in the title

- a change occurs in word order

If, based on these conditions, a decision is made that an additional access point is necessary, then a variation in title note should be made to justify the use of the added entry. If the decision to make an additional access point is negative, then LC indicates that the title note should not be made.

As an option to Rule 9.7B4, a cataloger can also record a file name or a data set name, when it differs from the title proper, unless the name is a local data set name. Generally, it is recommended that this option not be followed unless an access point is also made for the file or data set name, because there is reason to suspect that a user might attempt to gain access to the work by that name rather than the title proper. The names of local data sets are recorded using Rule 9.7B20.

Title on disk label: Chief of detectives.

Title on disk label: Microsoft flight simulator for IBM PC and PCjr.

Title on disk label: Theory formation : reflections and patterns.

Title on disk label and guide: Nutri-venture.

Subtitle on disk label: A bibliographic program.

Subtitle on disk label, guide and container: The typing instruction game.

At head of user manual title: WE CAN — Wholesome Effective Computer Applications Network.

Cover title on manual: dBase III for your 16-bit PC.

On user's manual cover: Degrees of reading power.

Title on spine of manual: Guide to operations personal computer XT.

9.7B6 Statements of Responsibility
This note is used to record the names of persons or corporate bodies, not previously mentioned in the description, who have "prepared or contributed" in some way to the production of a computer file and who are considered to be important to the work. These contributions can include collaboration, sponsorship, etc. In recording these statements of responsibility, catalogers should be aware that the functions associated with computer files (e.g., programmer, system designer, analyst, etc.) may differ significantly from those encountered for other types of nonprint materials. Some individuals may only be associated with the production of accompanying documentation. There are often a considerable number of persons with varying responsibilities associated with the production of a computer file who, although mentioned on the work and vital to its existence, are not essential to the identification of the work and would be unknown to users. Thus, libraries may wish to consider implementing a policy similar to that given above for title variant notes in which only those individuals considered important enough to the identification of the work, that is, those represented by access points, will be mentioned in either Area 1 or this note.

At head of title on disk: CBS Software presents.

Program authors: Sam Edwards, Charles Leu, Brad Crain.

Program written by Dan Ross.

Author of user's guide: Jonathan Harland Briggs.

Manual by Virginia Estabrook and Deborah Russell.

TEXbook [sic] by Donald E. Knuth.

Copyright by Bruce A. Artwick ; produced by Microsoft Corporation.

Copyrighted by the Regents of the University of California.

9.7B7 Edition and History

This note is used to provide a variety of information points related in some way to the edition or history of the computer file. These information points include

- the source of the edition statement given in Area 2 if that source is not the same as the one used for the title proper;

- indications of important "minor changes" in an edition. (These "minor changes" can include the correction of misspelled data, rearrangement of content, differences in the output format, display medium, or physical characteristics of the storage medium);

- the history of the item;

- information on the edition being described;

- citations to works upon which the computer file's content depends;

- date of the content of the file;

- date of data collection; and

- dates associated with accompanying material that are different from the dates of the computer file. These dates should only be provided, however, if the accompanying material has not been cataloged as a separate item.

Vol. 1 is version 1.2. Vol. 2 is version 1.5.

Calorie magic is version 5.16; documentation is version 1.04.

"English language version."

"Updated version."

At head of title: New improved.

"Created 05 Sep 86."

Created 1985, revised 1987.

User's manual has date: c1986.

Disk label and manual: c1984; title page of manual: c1985.

Adapted from: Word attack / by Richard Eckert and Janice Davidson.

Adapted from: Speedway : a race to improve speed with number facts.

Based on the television program Star trek.

Correlated to Ginn '82 basal series.

Revision of: Superscribe.

Data from Jan. 1, 1981-Dec. 31, 1985.

Source of data: 1984 U.S. statistical abstract.

9.7B8   File Characteristics

Additional information about the characteristics of the file that was not recorded in Area 3 may be given here. This note can be particularly useful because of the restrictions that Area 3 imposes on the type of file information that can be recorded there, as it allows considerable flexibility. Some information normally recorded in Area 3 may be given here when it is felt that the information could be given more succinctly here than in that area. Specifically, the rule refers to recording numbers associated with multiple part items (e.g., records, statements, etc.) when those numbers are considered to be important. This note was originally used in *AACR 2* to record information about the program version or level. That information is now given in the Edition Area.

HFS file structure.

File size varies.

File size: 52, 226, 134, 98, 347 records.

Files contain up to 65,525 records that can have 32 fields of up to 254 characters with a maximum of 1000 characters per record.

9.7B9   Publication, Distribution, etc.

Important publication, distribution, etc., information that was not reported in Area 4 can be given in this note.

9.7B10   Physical Description

Important details not given in the Physical Description Area are recorded here. For computer files available by remote access this rule introduces an additional requirement. It calls for recording physical details when they are "readily available" and also considered important. Previously, this note was used to record information about both the physical description of the computer file and a description of the file. In this revised Chapter 9, the file description information is given in another note (Rule 9.7B8).

Housed in case 27x22 cm.

In container, 19x19x4 cm.

9.7B11   Accompanying Material

Notes about accompanying materials are needed whenever methods c. or d. of Rule 1.5E are used. Method c. requires that information regarding the accompanying material be given in this note rather than in the Physical Description Area. When using method d., some information about the accompanying material may be included in the physical description while other information is recorded here.

> User's manual on disk.

> User's manual (33 p.) can be printed from file on disk.

> User's manual: 2nd ed.

> Reference manual is 5th ed. (Oct. 1986).

> User's guide published by McGraw-Hill.

9.7B14   Audience

Information about the intellectual level of, or the audience for, a computer file may be given in this note provided that the information is taken from the item, its container, or any accompanying material. Information derived from the item may be derived either from in or on the item.

If no audience information is available from these sources the cataloger is prohibited from writing his or her own audience statement. There are some cases, however, in which the audience level is known, although it is not actually stated on the required sources. This most frequently occurs when an audience statement is given in an advertisement or in a publisher's catalog. In these situations, the purpose and audience level of the item may be incorporated into a summary note (Rule 9.7B17) or a cataloger may sidestep the restrictions of this rule without using a summary note by simply quoting the statement and giving its source.

> Audience: Elementary students.

> Audience: Junior and senior high school students.

> Audience: Grades Pre-K to 6.

> Audience: Skill level, grades 3-8; reading level, grades 2-5.

> Audience: Accountants.

> Audience: Medical professionals.

> For use by 1 or 2 children (ages 5-8).

> Most programs are for grades 4-6 and remedially for grades 7-12.

9.7B16 Other Formats

This note is intended to alert users to other formats in which the item is available and to identify other machine-readable versions of the file. Its use should generally be limited to information about other formats and computer versions actually available in the library rather than others available but not held. Because this information can easily be overlooked by the user, a separate entry in the catalog for each form of the item actually held by the library is preferable to giving this information in this note. This note can also be used to indicate other systems upon which the program held will run that may not have been given in the system requirements note.

Versions also available for the Apple Macintosh.

Also available on 3½ in. disks.

Also available in microfiche.

Also runs on the Lisa (i.e., Macintosh XL) computer.

Also runs on IBM PCjr with DOS 2.1 and BASIC cartridge.

9.7B17 Summary

A summary note enables the user to gain a general idea of the content and purpose of the computer file. It should be provided whenever this information is considered important and has not been given by another part of the description (e.g., title, nature and scope note, contents note, etc.). The summary statement should be both objective and nonevaluative and avoid repetition of information already given elsewhere in the description. The use of a traditional format note structure, headed by the word "Summary," followed by a colon, enables the user to easily locate this information on the catalog record. This formal summary note structure is used by the Library of Congress for other types of nonprint materials.

Summary: Players create and explore unknown galaxies using stars they discover to complete exploratory expeditions.

Summary: Programs and data allow students to experience "live" demonstrations of faulty analyses based on spurious correlations.

Summary: Interactive statistical package for the social sciences. Capabilities include crosstabulations, analysis of variance, multiple regression. Allows interactive or batch processing.

Summary: Program for typesetting written documents and arranging how things will appear on the printed page. Useful where professional appearance is important or when the document includes mathematical formulae. Does not include the text editor required for creation of documents.

Summary: Programming aid for the IBM PC. Works with Fortran, Cobol, C, Assembler and other programming languages.

Summary: Designed to be used by adults or adolescents with impaired or inadequate comprehension of written or spoken English. Intended to be applied in conjunction with therapy supervised by speech/language pathologists, grading specialists, teachers of English as a second language, or other qualified personnel.

Summary: Allows graphic images completed on a graphics program to be converted to hardcopy output with a peripheral X-Y plotter. 39 plotters are supported. Programs allow scaling from 12:1 to 1:32, rotation of image and capability of using up to 30 pens for color.

9.7B18 Contents

A contents note should be used to list the individual parts of a multipart computer file. This is generally done using a formal note structure, preceding the listing of the parts with the word "Contents" followed by a colon. Each of the parts is separated by a space, long dash, space. Additional information about the contents of a file can be given in an informal note.

Contents: Number line — Estimate — Heartbeat — Boo hoo — Shopping.

Contents: Crime and deviance in North America showcase — Family and socialization in North America showcase — Aspects of social change in Europe and Latin America showcase — Combo 1000.

Contents: Authoring & utilities system — Student system.

Contents: Disk 1. TEX — Disk 2. TFM files — Disk 3. INITEX, Preload, plain, tex, hyphen. tex — Disk 4. Utility programs.

Contents: Disk C. Custom file — Disk R. REFWP file.

Includes a demo disk and sample data disk.

Includes four lessons for each concept.

Includes a calculator, notepad, appointment book, autodialer and ASCII table.

Accompanying disk includes clip art.

Student guide includes bibliographies.

9.7B19 Numbers Borne by the Item

Important numbers, usually assigned by the publisher, can be given in this note. A key word in this rule is the word "important." While many computer files will have numbers associated with them, these numbers are generally not essential to the identification of the item and could be excluded from the description at the discretion of the cataloger.

It should be noted that commercially published microcomputer software can be assigned an ISBN. This note should not be used to record either ISBNs or ISSNs; instead, they should be listed under Rule 9.8. It also should not be used to record numbers unique to the library's copy (e.g., serial numbers). If considered important, these numbers should be given in a "copy being described" note.

20034.

Disk 1286.

PSIBM 1294.

014-096-054; 014-096-055.

No. 81496.

Disks #752-753.

On manual: 6137856.

9.7B21 "With" Notes
When individually titled files in a collection are given separate descriptions, this note is used to link the parts. The files should be listed in their order of occurrence on the item. Although not specifically required by the rule, this note traditionally begins with the word "with."

With: MacTools.

With: PCTalk.

With: Switcher / Andy Hertzfeld.

With: Perception (v. 14, no. 2, 1985).

With: Sudden death / Curtis P. Clogston.

9.8 STANDARD NUMBER AND TERMS OF AVAILABILITY AREA

9.8B STANDARD NUMBER
Commercially produced microcomputer files are issued with ISBNs. When present, this number should be recorded in this location following the provisions of Rule 1.8B. If the ISBN is not for the computer file itself, the relationship of the number to the part should be given in a parenthetical statement. It is not unusual to encounter microcomputer software that has one ISBN for the computer files and separate ISBNs for each of the accompanying materials. In these situations, the ISBN of the computer file should be given first.

ISBN 0-0380-170-9

ISBN 0-87524-003-0 (reference manual)

ISBN 0-13-452-152-8 (teacher master)

ISBN 0-87-524-145-X (user's guide)

ISBN 0-8989-3200-9 (container)

9.8D *OPTIONAL ADDITION.* TERMS OF AVAILABILITY

Any restrictions on the use of the computer file should be indicated here, following the instructions given in Rule 1.6D. That rule calls for recording the price of an item if it is for sale, or a brief statement of other terms under which it is available if not for sale. In all likelihood, the indication of price serves no useful purpose for catalog users and should probably not be recorded. The terms under which an item is available, however, may be very important to a potential user.

Copy protected.

Copy protected. For use on only one library computer at a time.

Key-disk copy protection. Requires master disk and copy for use.

This computer file is protected under U.S. copyright laws and is not available for duplication.

Shareware.

Write protected.

Deposit required for use.

Available for use in library only.

Library's copy a "demo" version. Printing capability is disabled.

EXAMPLES: Descriptive Cataloging for Computer Files

> Clock [computer file]. — Computer program. —
> Dimondale, Mich. : Hartley Courseware, c1982.
> 1 computer disk : single sided, single density, soft
> sectored ; 5¼ in. + 1 teacher's guide (15 p. : ill. ;
> 22 cm.)
>
> System requirements: Apple II Plus; 48K RAM;
> DOS 3.2 or 3.3; Applesoft in ROM; 1 disk drive.
> Title from title screen.
> Audience: Grades 2-5.
> Summary: Students move the hands of a clock to
> convert from digital time and words to clock time and
> also from clock time to digital time.
> Includes 1 tutorial and 3 practice modes, 5 levels of
> difficulty and student management file (on disk).
> 01-01.
>
> I. Hartley Courseware, Inc.

Main Entry	—Entry under title because no person or corporate body was identified as being principally responsible for the work.
Area 1	—GMD reflects the change from "machine-readable data file" to "computer file."
	—No statement of responsibility appears in or on the item or its accompanying material.
Area 3	—Indicates that the computer file is a computer program, not computer data.
	—No information was available on number of files or the size of the files.
Area 5	—The option was implemented to indicate the number of sides, the recording density, and the sectoring of the disk. This information was "readily available" on the disk.
	—The option was followed of providing a physical description for the accompanying material.
Area 7	—Although this program will probably run on other models of the Apple II computer, the system requirements given here are those stated in the accompanying documentation. Catalogers should be wary of attempting to add to the system requirements to include newer models of computers because some newer models of computers will not run all programs designed for earlier models and because no list will be complete, considering the number of new models that are created for some computers.

(Explanation continues on page 208.)

           —System requirements stated here include all of those given in the teacher's guide, even though in some cases they would appear to state the obvious, such as the need for a disk drive. A cataloger could elect to eliminate these obvious requirement statements.

           —Rule 9.8B3 requires that the source of title always be given.

           —Audience statement was taken from the accompanying material.

           —Summary note indicates the purpose of the program.

           —Informal contents note indicates a number of additional files that comprise this program.

           —Numbering on the item recorded as given. This number is given here mainly for illustrative purposes. Many libraries would not consider this type of number as "important" and thus would not record it.

Added Entries —Access point provided for the publisher. In many cases, the publisher will be as well known to the user as the name of the program. Given the limited number of other name access points for this type of material, it is often useful to provide access through the publisher's name.

Reflex [computer file] : the analyst. — Computer data and programs. — Scotts Valley, Calif. : Borland/ Analytica, c1985.
    3 computer disks : double sided, double density ; 5¼ in. + 1 user's guide (478 p. in various pagings : ill. ; 23 cm.)

    System requirements: IBM PC, XT, AT or fully compatible IBM PC computers; 384K RAM; PC DOS 2.0 or higher; 2 disk drives or 1 disk drive and a hard disk drive; IBM Color Graphics Adapter or a Hercules Monochrome Graphics Card or equivalent; monitor capable of high resolution graphics; mouse (optional).
    Title from disk labels.
    Manual has subtitle: The analytic database system.
    Data files generated using Lotus 1-2-3, Symphony, dBase II and III, and PFS File can be translated for use as can DIF and ASCII text files.
    Issued also for the Macintosh under the title: Reflex for the Mac.
    Includes tutorial.
    Contents: System disk — Report and utilities disk — Help disk.
    ISBN 0-87524-145-X (user's guide)

    I. Borland/Analytica, Inc.

Area 3	—Indication given that the disk contains both computer data and computer programs. No information was available on the number of files or their size.
Area 5	—User's guide has irregular paging. The structure of the pagination statement was taken from Rule 2.5B8a. This type of paging quite frequently occurs in documentation, particularly looseleaf documentation, accompanying computer files. This is done to allow for the revision of a section or chapter of the documentation without having to reprint and repage the entire document.
Area 7	—No nature of the item note is supplied because other parts of the description, i.e., the other title information variant note, indicate that it is a database management program. If this was a relational database and the other parts of the description did not indicate this, then either a nature of the item note or a summary note would have been used.
	—System requirements note includes a statement about an "optional" requirement. Nothing in Rule 9.7B1b specifically calls for the inclusion or exclusion of this information.
	—Variant subtitle note.
	—Note made to indicate other programs which can produce data for use with this program.
	—Title of this program designed for another computer is given because this library had the computer file in that other form. Although the Macintosh program is cataloged separately, this note directs Macintosh users to the correct catalog record for their computer. This note would not have been made had the title been the same or if the library did not own the other form of the program.
	—No ISBN was given for the computer file but there is one for the user's guide.

Microsoft excel [computer file] : complete spreadsheet
with business graphics and database management. –
Version 1.03. – Computer data (6 files : 138,600
bytes) and programs (2 files : 412,500 bytes). –
Bellevue, WA : Microsoft, c1986.

1 computer disk : double sided, double density ;
3½ in. + 1 user's guide (1 v. (loose-leaf) : ill. ; 24
cm.) + 1 arrays guide (v, 297 p. : ill. ; 27 cm.) + 1
quick reference guide + 1 Switcher guide.

System requirements: Macintosh; 512K RAM; 1 800K
disk drive (internal or external), 2nd disk drive
(recommended).
Title from "Get Info" window.
HFS file structure.
Disk label, Arrays and Switcher guides have date:
c1985.
Arrays guide has title: Arrays, functions and macros.
Switcher guide has title: Using Switcher with Microsoft
applications.
Compatible for use with Microsoft Word.
Includes help functions, Excel/Word document, and
Switcher program.
Also includes System files including Finder 5.3 and
desk accessories (230,400 bytes).
065-096-006.
This program is also available on the hard disk drive
on the Library's computer no. 3.

I. Microsoft Corporation. II. Title: Excel.

Area 1	– Subtitle is very much a nature of the item statement. This information could have been recorded in an "other title information" note (Rule 9.7B5). That would have reduced the size of the body of the catalog record and would have improved its readability.
Area 2	– Version indicated.
Area 3	– Number of files and the file sizes are given. This information was readily available from the "Get Info" windows for each data file and program.
Area 5	– The option to record the disk characteristics is more important to implement here because this disk form (i.e., double sided) could not be read on all types of Macintosh computers. The system requirement does state this indirectly, however, by requiring an 800K disk drive, which means that it is a double-sided drive.

— Physical description of the user's guide was given as "loose-leaf" rather than with page numbers as instructed in Rule 2.5B9. This was done because the guide is designed to receive page changes as new versions of the file are issued.

— No physical description was given for the Switcher guide because its size was considered insignificant.

Area 7   — System requirements given in the user's guide were added to by the cataloger to provide for greater conciseness and clarity.

— Note gives a variant date on some of the parts. This note combines information for the item itself and its accompanying material. This was done to save space. The difference in the dates probably indicates that these parts were not revised with Version 1.03, which has the date "c1986."

— File structure indicated. The file structure was given in the user's guide.

— Titles for two of the accompanying documentation works are given. These works were not cataloged separately although they could have been.

— Informal contents note indicates special features not apparent from the rest of the description.

— Second informal contents note lists some program elements nearly always present on a Macintosh application disk. Rather than complicate the body of the catalog record by giving this information in Area 3, it is given in this location. The version is mentioned because it has a bearing on features available with this program. File size was given because it was readily available.

— Numbers appearing on the disk label. This is not an ISBN.

Area 8   — Availability statement informs users of an additional way this program can be accessed.

Added Entries — Access provided for a shortened form of the title proper. This shortened title is frequently used for this computer file.

Rosenberg, Victor, 1942-
　　Pro-cite [computer file] / created by Victor
Rosenberg, Peter Rycus and Cyrus Ghalambor. —
Version 1.2. — Computer program. — Ann Arbor,
Mich. : Personal Bibliographic Software, c1986.
　　2 computer disks : double sided, double density ;
5¼ in. + 1 user's manual (1 v. (loose-leaf) : ill. ; 23
cm.)

　　System requirements: IBM PC, XT, AT or 100%
IBM compatible computers; 256K RAM; DOS 2.0 or
higher; printer (recommended).
　　Title from title screen.
　　User's manual written and adapted by Gretchen
Whitney.
　　An update of the Professional bibliographic system.
　　Also issued for the Macintosh under the title:
Personal bibliographic system.
　　Summary: Database management program for
inputting, punctuating and formatting bibliographies
and reading lists. When used with the Biblio-link
programs, online bibliographic databases can be
accessed, downloaded and converted into formatted
citations.
　　Includes tutorial.
　　Contents: Program disk — Utility disk.

　　I. Rycus, Peter. II. Ghalambor, Cyrus.
III. Rosenberg, Victor, 1942-　　　Professional
bibliographic system. IV. Personal Bibliographic
Software, Inc. V. Title. VI. Title: Personal bibliographic
system.

Main Entry　　—Entry under the first named person responsible for
the content of the item. Principles for the determination of the choice of access points are the same as
they are for other types of nonprint materials, except
sound recordings which have their own rules. In
many cases, the contributions of persons to the creation of a computer file are such that main entry is
under title because the contributions are considered
too diffuse to assign the main entry to one individual. In this situation, however, it was decided that
this work was one of shared responsibility of three
individuals with no person indicated as principal
author. In this case, main entry is made under the
first person named in the statement of responsibility.
It is recognized that entry under a person in many
cases results in the provision of the chief access point
under a name most likely unknown to users. Some

libraries may wish to deviate from *AACR 2* in cases such as this and make all main entries for computer files under the title, although this really isn't necessary as long as access points are made for the title and probably for the publisher — names more likely to be known by catalog users.

Area 1   — Statement of responsibility as given in the item.

Area 7   — Statement of responsibility for the user's manual should be given in a note rather than in Area 1.

— Earlier version under a different title is identified.

— Summary gives the nature of the program as well as its association with other computer files.

— Title of each disk given in a formal contents note.

Added Entries — Access point provided for the other two persons who contributed to the entire work.

— No access point is given for the author of the user's manual.

— Name. Title access point provided for the Macintosh version so users who attempt to locate the PC-DOS version under the title of the Macintosh version will be given the PC-DOS catalog record as well as that for the Macintosh. This saves the user a step in the search process.

— Access also provided under the name of the earlier version of the computer file for users who only have a citation to that version.

Gato [computer file] : WWII Gato-class submarine simulation / Spectrum Holobyte ; James Rhodes, Bill Scott and Sean Hill [programmers]. — Version 1.3 / by Mindbender. — Computer program. — Boulder, Colo. : Spectrum Holobyte, c1985.
     1 computer disk : sd., single sided, double density ; 3½ in. + 1 guide (40 p. ; 22 cm.)

     System requirements: Macintosh; 128K RAM.
     Title from title screen.
     Artwork by Mark Dunn.
     Version statement from "About Gato" window on the Apple menu.
     Version statement from the disk label.
     Disk label has date: c1983.
     Versions also available for IBM and Apple II computers.
     Provides 10 different missions at 5 levels of difficulty.

     I. Spectrum Holobyte, Inc.

(Explanations are on page 214.)

Main Entry   — Entry under the title because of diffuse responsibility.

Area 1   — "Other title information" indicates the nature of the item.

— Addition made to the persons named in the statement of responsibility to indicate their function. These individuals could have been named instead in a statement of responsibility note depending upon the importance attached to their contribution.

Area 2   — Statement of responsibility for the version is given.

Area 5   — Sound feature of this file is indicated before the disk characteristics.

Area 7   — Nature or scope of the item note was not given because the other title information adequately indicated the nature of the item.

— No additional details beyond the name of the computer and the minimum memory requirements were given because all of the other system requirements (e.g., a mouse, a disk drive) are standard for this computer. Although it was known that this program is written in Consulair C it was not considered necessary for the user to know this, because there are no hardware or software requirements to support this programming language.

— Creator of the artwork is given in this note rather than in the statement of responsibility because he was listed in a less prominent location than were the company and the programmers.

— As required, the source of the version statement was given, because its source was different from that used to derive the title proper.

— Difference in the date on the label of the disk and the date in the internal file is indicated. The date on the label reflects the date of the previous version. Version 1.3 was probably copied onto labeled disks originally prepared for the earlier version.

— Other formats in which this program is available are indicated. Normally this note would not be given. If the library owned this computer file in other formats they would have separate catalog records.

— Although a summary note could have been provided, it was considered unnecessary because of the information presented in other parts of the description.

— Informal contents note gives a more complete indication of the features of the game. This information could also have been given as a part of a summary note.

Added Entries — No access points were provided for the names of the programmers or the creator of the new version because they were considered unimportant to the retrieval of the catalog record by users of the library (i.e., they are names highly unlikely to be known by catalog users).

Decimal skills [computer file] / author, Contemporary Perspectives. — Computer program. — Springfield, MA : Milton Bradley, c1982.
1 computer disk : single sided, single density ; 5¼ in. + 1 guide + 20 worksheets + 20 tests.

System requirements: Apple II or II Plus computer; 48K RAM; DOS 3.3; Applesoft BASIC.
Title from disk label.
In container: 23x30x3 cm.
Guide also for use with Division skills and Mixed numbers.
Worksheets and tests are reproducible.
Audience: Upper elementary and junior high school grades.
Summary: Utilizes a speed-drill format to develop skills in addition, subtraction, multiplication and division. Also develops subskills in using place values, names and numbers, comparing and ordering.
Includes pretests, classes and student record sheets and student record manager (on disk).
7878.

I. Contemporary Perspectives, Incorporated. II. Milton Bradley Company.

Main Entry — Entry under title because the corporate body given as the author does not satisfy the conditions of Rule 21.1B2 for its use as the main entry.

Area 7 — Unlike in Chapter 10, the size of a container cannot be given in the Physical Description Area. In order to inform users about the size of the item they are seeking, the size of the container may be given in a note.
— Note indicates that the guide accompanying this computer file is also used for two other files. This note is particularly important if a library owns the other two files and only has one copy of the guide.
— Reproducibility of the worksheets and tests indicated.
— Audience statement taken from the guide.

(Explanation continues on page 216.)

— Informal contents note indicates that some of the items in it are located on the disk rather than as separate pieces.

— Number appearing on the disk.

— Both corporate bodies involved with the work are used as access points.

ZyIndex [computer file]. — Standard version 2.02. — Computer data and programs. — Chicago : ZyLab Corp., c1985.

   2 computer disks ; 5¼ in. + 1 user's guide (1 v. (loose-leaf) ; 23 cm.)

   System requirements: IBM PC, XT, AT, 100% IBM compatible computers and some MS-DOS computers; 256K RAM; MS or PC DOS 2.0 or higher; 2 floppy disk drives or 1 floppy disk drive and 1 hard disk drive.

   Title from title screen.

   "Qubie version"—disk labels.

   User's manual: 2nd ed.

   Summary: Indexes files created by WordPerfect, WordStar and many other word processing programs and pure ASCII files.

   Includes tutorial.

   I. ZyLab Corporation.

Area 2	— "Standard" is a part of this version statement because there are two other types of versions.
Area 7	— System requirement note indicates multiple hardware configurations.
	— Another version statement also appears on the item. The source of the information is given for this quotation because it was not derived from the preferred chief source of information used for the other version statement.
	— Indication that the user's manual has an edition statement that is not used for the computer files.
	— Summary note indicates the purpose of the program and the data formats with which it will work.

WordPerfect [computer file]. — Computer data
and programs — Version 4.2. — Orem, Utah :
WordPerfect Corp., c1986.
5 computer disks : col., double sided, double
density ; 5¼ in. + 1 user's manual (1 v. (loose-leaf) :
23 cm.) + 1 installation guide + 1 printer booklet +
1 quick reference card + 1 keyboard template.

Word processor.
System requirements: IBM PC, XT, AT or fully IBM
compatible computers; 256K RAM; PC DOS 2.0 or
higher; 2 disk drives or 1 disk drive and 1 hard disk
drive.
Title from title screen.
Stamped on label: Administrative school copy.
"SSIS Software," an earlier name of the WordPerfect
Corp., appears on the manual.
Includes tutorial.
Contents: WordPerfect — Speller — Thesaurus —
Printer — Learning.

I. WordPerfect Corporation. II. Title: Word perfect.

Area 3 — Number of files was known although not their size.
No distinction could be made between the program
files and the data files so the number of files was not
listed.
Area 5 — Color capability of the program was indicated.
— Each element of documentation was listed separately
in the accompanying materials statement.
— Template for a keyboard is considered to be accompanying material.
Area 7 — Nature of the item note was made because word
processing is only implied in the title proper and in
other parts of the description. Its inclusion was a
subjective decision on the part of the cataloger.
— Alternative drive options are indicated. These were
specifically stated in the documentation.
— Note made to account for what appears to be the
name of another corporate body on the manual.
— Titles of the multiple diskettes given in a formal contents note.
Added Entries — Access point provided for the publisher even though
its name is very similar to the title. This was done to
provide for the different filing locations for
corporate headings and titles in some divided
catalogs and for separate indexes in microform and
online public access catalogs.

(Explanation continues on page 218.)

—No access point provided for the other name of the publisher that appeared on the manual. A reference would be made instead.

—Access provided for the two-word variant of the title to assist users who are not aware that this is one word.

Showmaker software [computer file] : screen capture program / by Sayett Technology. — Version 1.00. — Computer programs. — Rochester, N.Y. : Sayett Technology, 1986.

1 computer disk : col., double sided, double density ; 5¼ in. + 1 user's manual + 1 Datashow manual.

System requirements: IBM PC or IBM plug-compatible computer; 256K RAM; PC or MS DOS 2.0 or higher; IBM color graphics adapter; IBM enhanced graphics adapter or other 100% compatible adapter; 2 disk drives or 1 disk drive and 1 hard disk drive.

Title from title screen.

One user's manual has title: Operator's manual for Kodak Datashow system.

Summary: Provides for the capture of CRT screen images, their combination for a presentation and their control and viewing using the Kodak Datashow system.

I. Sayett Technology. II. Title: Kodak Datashow system.

Area 1	—"Other title information" follows the GMD.
Area 7	—System requirements include one for a specific brand of color adapter.
	—One piece of accompanying material has a title different from that of the computer file. That title is indicated in a note.
	—Summary note indicates the system with which the computer program works.
Added Entries	—Access point provided for the name of the related computer program. Thus a library which owns this related program will have, filed under the name of this program, a catalog listing for that program as well as a listing of all the programs the library owns which are related to this program.

Wigginton, Randy.
MacWrite [computer file] : the Macintosh word
processor / written by Randy Wigginton, Ed Ruder and
Don Breuner. MacPaint / Bill Atkinson. — Computer
programs (2 files : 70,000, 60,000 bytes). — Cupertino,
Calif. : Apple Computer, c1985.
1 computer disk : single sided, double density ; 3½
in. + 1 MacWrite user's manual + 1 MacPaint user's
manual.

Second program is a drawing program.
System requirements: Macintosh; 128K RAM.
Titles from "About MacWrite" and "About
MacPaint" screens on the Apple menu.
MacWrite user's manual written by Lynnea
Johnson. c1983. 143 p. : ill. ; 23 cm. MacPaint user's
manual written by Carol Kaehler, c1983. 32 p. : ill. ;
23 cm.
MacWrite, Version 4.5. MacPaint, Version 1.5.
Date on disk label: c1984.
Also includes System files including Finder 4.1 and
desk accessories (223,000 bytes), Minifinder, Taleisin
font and additional program documentation on disk.
690-5009A.

I. Ruder, Ed. II. Bruener, Don. III. Atkinson, Bill.
MacPaint. IV. Apple Computer, Inc. V. Title.

Comment	— Two programs on one disk cataloged as a unit.
Main Entry	— Entry under the first named of three authors. Based upon the information given, this was considered to be a work of shared responsibility where principal responsibility was not indicated.
Area 1	— Separate title and statements of responsibility were created for each program.
Area 2	— No edition statement was provided because each program had a different version number. Instead, to provide clarity, this information was recorded in the edition and history note.
Area 3	— Type of file is indicated in the plural because more than one program is being described.
	— Both the number of files and their sizes are given.
Area 7	— Nature of the second program is indicated. This was not done for the first program in this note because its nature is evident from the "other title information" statement.
	— Different versions indicated.

(Explanation continues on page 220.)

— Statements of responsibility and associated dates are given for the accompanying documentation.
— Dates in the individual programs differ from the date on the disk label.
— Informal contents note indicates additional programs which are included on the disk but which are not described in any further detail on the record. No further description is provided because these programs in various forms are present on most programs for this computer. Unless their presence was considered unusual, mention of them could also be eliminated.

Added Entries— Access provided for the appropriate form of entry for the second program — Name. Title.
— Access also provided for the other persons who shared responsibility for this work, as called for in *AACR 2*. It is realized, however, that these two access points are probably totally useless to most, if not all, potential users.

Wigginton, Randy.
　　MacWrite [computer file] : The Macintosh word processor / written by Randy Wigginton, Ed Ruder and Don Breuner. — Version 4.5. — Computer program (1 file : 70,000 bytes). — Cupertino, Calif. : Apple Computer, c1985.
　　1 computer disk : single sided, double density ; 3½ in. + 1 user's manual (143 p. : ill. ; 23 cm.)

　　System requirements: Macintosh; 128K RAM.
　　Title from "About MacWrite" window on the Apple menu.
　　MacWrite user's manual written by Lynnea Johnson. c1983.
　　Date on the disk label: c1984.
　　Also includes System files including Finder 4.1 and desk accessories (223,000 bytes), Minifinder, Taleisin font and additional program documentation on disk. 690-5009A.
　　With: MacPaint / Bill Atkinson.

　　I. Ruger, Ed. II. Bruener, Don. III. Apple Computer, Inc. IV. Title.

Comment　　　— One of the two computer programs from the previous example cataloged separately.
Area 2　　　　— Version information can be stated directly.

Area 5   — Physical description information for the accompanying material can now be given more clearly in this area.

Area 7   — "With" note used to indicate the other program on this disk.

Added Entries — No access point provided for the other program on this disk. It will have its own catalog record instead.

SmoothTalker [computer file]. — Releae 2.0. —
Computer data (5 files : 52,879 bytes) : and program (1 file : 44,989 bytes). — Long Beach, Calif. : First Byte, c1985.
    1 computer disk : sd., single sided, double density ;
3½ in. + 1 user's manual.

    Speech synthesis program.
    System requirements: Macintosh; 128K RAM.
    Title from the "About SmoothTalker" window on the Apple menu.
    User's manual on disk.
    Summary: Provides audio output for text data from MacWrite and a variety of other Macintosh programs. User can control the volume, pitch, speed, tone and sex of the voice.
    Also includes System files including Finder 4.1 and desk accessories (230,400 bytes).

    I. First Byte (Firm) II. Title: Smooth Talker.

Area 2   — Term "release" is used on the item rather than the more commonly used word "version."

Area 5   — Sound capability of this program indicated.

Area 7   — No system requirement is given for a speaker because a speaker is always provided with the required computer.
                — Note indicates the location of the user's manual.
                — Summary note indicates the capability of the program including user-controlled options.

Added Entries — Access provided for the two-word variant of the title to assist users who are not aware that this is one word.

Da Vinci interiors [computer file] / by Image Bank
Software. — Computer data (21 files : 395,000
bytes). — Lowell, Mass. : Hayden Software, c1984.
1 computer disk : single sided, double density ;
3½ in. + 1 guide (36 p. : ill. ; 23 cm.)

System requirements: Macintosh; 128K RAM; system
folder; MacPaint; Imagewriter printer.
Title from "About Da Vinci" window.
Da Vinci series developed by Davis Adamson and
James Stokoe.
Related programs: Da Vinci exteriors; Da Vinci
landscapes.
Summary: Scale drawings (1:4 and 1:8) of images used
to plan a room layout. Images can be moved and altered
in size using MacPaint.
Includes house and office sample layouts.

I. Image Bank Software, Inc. II. Hayden Software,
Inc. III. Atkinson, Bill. MacPaint.

Comment	— Data files only.
Main Entry	— Entry under title because the corporate body named in the statement of responsibility does not qualify for main entry under the requirements of Rule 21.1B2.
Area 1	— Statement of responsibility for the program. This is a different corporate body from the one given as the publisher.
Area 6	— Although a statement of responsibility is made for the developers of the series no formal series title is given with the work.
Area 7	— No nature of the item note is required because of the information given in the summary note.
	— System requirements include an indication of the software needed to work with these data files as well as a specific printer.
	— Statement of responsibility for the "series developers."
	— Note made to identify related data files in this "series."
Added Entries	— Access points provided for the company responsible for the item and the publisher because either could likely be known by catalog users seeking the item.
	— Access point also provided for the computer program needed to use the data files. This provides a link in the catalog which gives users an indication of all data files the library holds that use that program. Entry is made under the form appropriate for that work — Name. Title.

Galaxy math games [computer file] / program design,
Jerome I. Weintraub ; programmer Apple II, Paul
Foster. — Computer program (7 files). — New York :
Random House, c1982.
   7 computer disks : single sided, single density ;
5¼ in. + 1 booklet + 1 guide + 1 chart. —
(Mathematics)

   System requirements: Apple II Plus; 48K RAM; DOS
3.2 or 3.3.
   Title from disk labels.
   Title on binder: Galaxy math facts.
   The original Galaxy math facts game was expanded
to include 6 additional programs.
   In 3-ring binder (29 cm.).
   Contents: Galaxy math facts game (grades 1-6) —
Place values (grades 2-6) — Fractions I (grades 3-7) —
Fractions II (grades 3-7) — Rounding and estimating
(grades 4-7) — Decimals (grades 5-8) — Integers
(grades 6-9).
   ISBN 0-394-09337-2 (Facts game). — ISBN
0-394-09868-4 (Place values). — ISBN 0-394-09869-2
(Fractions I). — ISBN 0-394-09870-6 (Decimals). —
ISBN 0-394-09871-4 (Integers). — ISBN 0-394-09872-2
(Estimating). — ISBN 0-394-09873-0 (Fractions II). —
ISBN 0-394-09336-4 (guide). — ISBN 0-394-09831-5
(chart)

   I. Random House (Firm).

Comment	—Work in multiple parts cataloged together. These individual parts could also have been cataloged separately.
Main Entry	—Entry was given under title because of diverse responsibility for the work.
Area 1	—Title recorded appears on all the disk labels. Thus title on the unifying element, the container, was not used.
	—Programmers were listed for both the Apple II version and the TRS-80 version. Only the programmer for the item in hand was recorded.
Area 5	—Multiple accompanying materials. Individual physical descriptions were considered unnecessary.
Area 6	—Series title indicated.
Area 7	—System requirements listed as they were given in the documentation.
	—Variant title indicated. The container title was not chosen as the title proper even though it was on the

(Explanation continues on page 224.)

unifying element, because another title appeared on all the disk labels.

— Size of the container is given.

— No mention is made of the TRS 80 version because it is not in the library's collection.

— Contents note gives the titles on the individual disks. An audience note is combined with the contents note in order to make the relationship of the audience with the title of the part clear in the most concise manner.

— ISBNs are recorded qualified by a statement identifying the part. The ISBNs of the accompanying material are recorded last as instructed in the LC Rule Interpretation to Rule 1.8B. In libraries where the ISBN is not an access point, the use of a statement such as "The 7 disks, guide and chart each have individual ISBNs" is probably preferable to listing each of them.

Added Entries — "(Firm)" was added to the name of this corporate body to show its corporate nature.

— No access points are provided for the individual titles for two reasons: the number involved was considered excessive, and it was felt that these titles are not distinctive enough so that users would likely search for the works by those titles. These additional title access points could be provided at the discretion of the cataloger.

— No access point was provided for the title of the series because of the general nature of the series title. If one had been provided the access point would have been in the form: II. Series: Mathematics (Random House).

Chandler, James R.
　　　Nutrition—a balanced diet [computer file] —
computer program by James R. Chandler. — Computer
program. — Pelham, N.Y. : Educational Materials
and Equipment Co., c1982.
　　　1 computer disk : single sided, single density ; 5¼ in.
+ 1 study guide + 25 student lab booklets.

　　　System requirements: Apple II or II Plus; 16K RAM;
DOS 3.2 or 3.3.
　　　Title from title screen.
　　　Study guide by Pasqualina E. Maffucci.
　　　In envelope designed for 3-ring binder (29 cm.).
　　　"Grade levels 8-12"—Advertisement.
　　　Summary: Allows students to evaluate the quality of
their diets and to explore the nutritional value of food
to correct dietary imbalances.
　　　Includes bibliography in study guide.

　　　I. Educational Materials and Equipment Company.
　　　II. Title.

Area 7　　　—Author of the study guide is given in a note rather
　　　　　　than in the statement of responsibility.
　　　　　—Quotation from the advertisement is used to provide
　　　　　　the audience statement because none is given in or
　　　　　　on the item or its accompanying material.
　　　　　—Bibliography included in the accompanying material
　　　　　　mentioned in an informal contents note.

8
Description of Three-Dimensional Artefacts and Realia

10.0 GENERAL RULES

10.0A SCOPE
The rules in this chapter enable the cataloger to provide a standard description for a variety of materials which have the common feature of being three-dimensional in form. These objects can be either naturally occurring, artistic, or manufactured. The rules cover both individual objects and multipart items made up of several types of three-dimensional objects. Included in the scope of this chapter are dioramas, games which contain three-dimensional items, models, three-dimensional art works, naturally occurring objects, microscope slides, and objects requiring a microscope for viewing. The term "artefact" is used to designate objects made or modified by man. Excluded from this chapter are other three-dimensional objects which are covered in Chapters 2 through 9 of *AACR 2* (e.g., globes, books, sound recordings, etc.).

There has been some confusion in the past as to which of the chapters for description covered "video games," that is, whether they were to be treated as games or as machine-readable data files. This issue was clarified in *Guidelines for Using AACR 2 Chapter 9 for Cataloging Microcomputer Software*. There, Rule 9.0A indicates that "caluclators, electronic toys, etc.," issued as "self-contained units," with integral program encoded microchips, are covered by Chapter 10, not Chapter 9, and should thus be treated as games.

10.0B SOURCES OF INFORMATION

10.0B1 Chief Sources of Information
Reflecting the fact that little, if any, information appears on the objects themselves, the chief sources of information for materials covered by this chapter are the item itself, accompanying text, and a container issued by the publisher or manufacturer. This container does not have to be integral to the object. When information appears on more than one of these sources, information found on the object, including information on permanently affixed labels, is preferred over that from other sources (for multipart works which lack a unifying element, see also Rule 10.0H).

10.0B2   Prescribed Sources of Information

For each area of the description there are different prescribed source(s) from which information can be taken without having to enclose it in square brackets. For materials covered by this chapter, the use of prescribed sources of information is simpler than with other types of materials because only either the chief source or "any source" is used. Information for the Title and Statement of Responsibility, Edition, Publication, Distribution, Etc., and Series Areas must come from the chief source of information. All other information in the description can be taken from any source.

**10.0H   ITEMS WITH SEVERAL CHIEF SOURCES
OF INFORMATION**

Multipart items with a container that is a unifying element

For items composed of two or more parts, the container which serves as the unifying element is the preferred source of information for the package. This is different from the general instruction for multipart items given in Rule 1.0H which relegates the container to a lesser status as a prescribed source of information.

Multipart items without a container that is a unifying element

Multipart packages which lack a unifying container relating to all of the parts are described, however, according to Rule 1.0H. This rule requires that a part which functions as the first part should be used as the chief source of information. If no part serves as a first part, any part that gives the most information should be used as the chief source of information. Often, a part which bears the latest publication date will provide the most complete information for the package. Information from various parts can also be combined with information from either the first part or the unifying element of the item. When information given in several chief sources varies, these differences can be indicated in the Notes Area.

Teacher's manual as the chief source of information

The metric center [kit] / written by Ada Booth. — Rev. [ed.] / reviewed and edited by Bryne Bessie Frank. — Palo Alto, Calif. : Enrich, 1974.
[The kit contains realia, models, and written teaching material. The title page of the teacher's guide provides the information for much of the description, i.e., the collective title, statement of responsibility, and the date.]

Single Part Items

Although Rule 10.0B1 indicates that the object itself should be preferred over other chief sources of information, Rule 10.0H, through its reference to Rule 1.0H, indicates that for single part items with several chief sources of information, the chief source of information bearing the latest publication date should be preferred over the one indicated as first chief source of information in the rules (see Rule 10.0B1 above).

10.1 TITLE AND STATEMENT OF RESPONSIBILITY AREA

10.1B TITLE PROPER

The title proper is recorded as instructed in Rule 1.1B. Many objects covered by this chapter do not have a title on the object, its accompanying materials, or its container. For these items, the cataloger must supply a title. This supplied title should be a word or phrase describing the item and might come from a publisher's catalog or a reference source. Whenever a title is supplied by a cataloger, a note must be made indicating the source of that title (Rule 10.7B3).

Supplied titles single items

[Conestoga wagon] [model]

[Clock face] [model]

Supplied titles multipart items

[Metric measuring devices] [kit]

[Union soldier's costume] [realia]

10.1C OPTIONAL ADDITION. GENERAL MATERIAL DESIGNATION

Even though the generic term "object" used by British cataloging agencies is perhaps a better choice as a GMD for some items cataloged in this chapter, North American libraries are limited in their assignment of GMDs to those appearing in List 2 of Rule 1.1C1. For materials covered by Chapter 10, these GMD terms are:

diorama   model
game   realia
microscope slide

Although the definition of the term "game" limits its scope to materials whose play follows prescribed "rules," the scope of what constitutes the "rules" can be rather broad. Thus, jigsaw puzzles, a type of material not generally considered to have rules, are assigned the GMD "game." The term "realia" is used to designate real objects while "model" is assigned to three-dimensional representations of an object. Because "realia" is the most general of the terms from which one can choose, material which does not fit into any of the other categories will be assigned this as their GMD.

10.1C2 [Kits]

A multipart item consisting of two or more distinctive material types should be assigned the GMD "kit" if none of the items is predominant. British libraries would assign the GMD "multimedia" in this situation. The different material types which comprise a kit are not limited to items covered by Chapter 10. Thus, a kit could consist of a filmstrip, a sound recording which is not accompanying material to the filmstrip, and a model. Catalogers should be cautious, however, to ensure that the two or more items that make up the kit are not accompanying materials to a predominant item.

Although the term "kits" is most often associated with materials covered in Chapter 10, its use is not limited to this chapter. Any combinations of multiple types of material can be treated as kits (see Rules 6.1C2, 7.1C2, 8.1C2, etc.). Because of this, the specific instructions for the description of a kit are covered under General Rule 1.10 rather than in the rules in Chapter 10. Due to the frequent combination of three-dimensional artefacts and realia into one unit, kits will receive greater treatment in this chapter of this text than in others.

> [Spain] [kit]
> *[A collection of realia, models, and printed materials. The title does not appear on the item, its container, or accompanying material.]*

> You discover Saudi Arabia [kit]
> *[A collection of naturally occurring objects and artefacts.]*

10.1E1 Other Title Information

Objects covered by this chapter often have other title information located on their containers. Because the container and accompanying materials are prescribed sources of information for titles in addition to the item itself, the "other title information" is recorded without square brackets. According to Rule 1.1F12, a phrase related to the statement of responsibility that is indicative of the nature of the work should be recorded as "other title information" rather than as a part of the statement of responsibility.

> Peabody language development kits [kit] : level 2 / authored and edited by Lloyd M. Dunn, James O. Smith. —

> Wff'n proof [game] : the game of modern logic / Layman E. Allen. —

> Battle cry [game] : American Heritage game of the Civil War. —
> *[The name of the company contributing to the contents of the game is recorded as other title information as found on the item. The title varies on different parts of the item. This title is taken from the game board.]*

In many cases, the nature of subtitles associated with published three-dimensional artefacts and realia, particularly games, is such that they serve to define more clearly the nature of the material than does the title proper. Because of this, catalogers may wish to record this "other title information" in a quoted note (Rule 10.7B5) rather than in the Title and Statement of Responsibility Area. Catalogers should be aware, however, that the practice of placing short subtitles in a note is technically only possible when using a level one description. Levels two and three require that "other title information" appear in Area 1, unless that information is "lengthy" (Rule 1.1E3).

Subtitles recorded as notes

"Parker Bros. real estate trading game."
[Subtitle to the game Monopoly.]

"The triangle domino game."
[Subtitle to the game Tri-Ominos.]

"Gaming together with 288 possible futures."
[Subtitle to the game Futuribles.]

"A 'make it fun' game of library research skills."
[Subtitle to the game Cool chicken.]

10.1F STATEMENTS OF RESPONSIBILITY

Statements of responsibility should be recorded as instructed by Rule 1.1F. The term "responsibility" in this chapter refers not only to creation of the content, but also to assembly for display, selection of items to be included, and the preparation of the materials assembled. Statements of responsibility should include phrases found in the chief sources of information which explain the relationship of the person(s) or corporate bodies to the item. When multiple titles are present, each statement should be related to its appropriate individual title. If the relationship of a statement to a title is unclear, the cataloger should add, in brackets, a word or short phrase which explains the relationship.

Configurations [game] : number puzzles and patterns for all ages / by Harold L. Dorwart. —

Motorcycle moto cross [game] / by the Radlauers. —

Indian jewelry [realia] : a display / by Joanna Wentworth. —

10.1G ITEMS WITHOUT A COLLECTIVE TITLE

If an item lacks a collective title, the titles of the individual works should be recorded as instructed in Rule 1.1G. If the items lacking a collective title are related, a collective title can be supplied by the cataloger. When such a collective title is given, details about the individual works can be given in the physical description and the notes.

Supplied individual item titles

[Metric ruler ; litre container ; metric measuring tape ; metric grid] [kit]

Supplied collective title

[Metric measuring devices] [kit]

10.2   EDITION AREA

Statements about issues of artefacts which contain differences from other issues, or which are named reissues, should be recorded as instructed in Rule 1.2B.

Rev. ed. —

RPM ed. —

1935 commemorative ed. —

Edición Espanola. —

If an item with multiple individual parts lacks a collective title and is cataloged as a unit, edition statements which apply only to individual parts should be recorded following the title and statement of responsibility of the part with which it is associated (Rule 10.2B5). These edition statements are separated from the title and statement of responsibility by a full stop. If the item has a collective title and the individual parts have differing edition statements, these statements can be indicated in the Note Area.

10.4   PUBLICATION, DISTRIBUTION, ETC., AREA

Instructions for recording information about published items in this area are given in Rule 1.4. For items not actually published, i.e., naturally occurring items not "mounted for viewing or packaged for presentation" and artefacts whose primary purpose is not communication, no place or publisher, distributor, etc., are recorded (Rules 10.4C2 and 10.4D2).

The intent of the statement "not intended primarily for communication" is not explained anywhere in *AACR 2*. Essentially, the phrase addresses whether an item has been prepared or packaged in multiple copies to serve an informational purpose rather than the role for which it was originally intended. A cannonball can provide an example of the evaluation of the intent of an item. A cannonball, manufactured as ammunition for a cannon, but now a part of a library's collection, serves as a representation of cannonballs. Because the original intent of the manufacturer of the item was not to create cannonballs to serve the information needs of library users, but rather to serve as ammunition, this item would be considered as one "not intended primarily for communication." If on the other hand, this same cannonball were to be packaged by a commercial firm to serve an informational role in libraries, perhaps issued with a guide and a history of cannonballs, then this cannonball would be considered to be "intended primarily for communication."

Frog metamorphosis [realia]. — New York : Creative Playthings, [197-?]
[Naturally occurring object intended for viewing.]

Petrified wood [realia]. —
[Naturally occurring object not "mounted for viewing or packaged for presentation."]

10.4F   DATE OF PUBLICATION, DISTRIBUTION, ETC.

For published materials, the publication date is recorded as instructed in Rule 1.4F. Dates are also recorded for naturally occurring objects prepared for presentation or viewing; however, no dates are recorded for naturally occurring objects if these conditions do not exist. Artefacts not intended primarily for communication would have only their date of manufacture recorded in Area 4.

Publication date

A Bit of U.S.A. [realia]. — Phoenix, Ariz. : A Bit of U.S.A., [1969]
[Naturally occurring objects "mounted for viewing."]

No date

[Coral] [realia].
[Naturally occurring object, lacking a title, not "mounted for viewing or packaged for presentation."]

Date of manufacture

[Dentures] [model]. — [1978]
[Artefact intended primarily for communication.]

10.4G   PLACE OF MANUFACTURE, NAME OF MANUFACTURER, DATE OF MANUFACTURE

When a place and publisher are not recorded because they are unknown, or because of instructions given in the rules above, the place and name of the manufacturer can be recorded according to the provisions of Rule 1.4G. In recording the name of the manufacturer, include phrases taken from prescribed sources of information which indicate the manufacturer's role in the production of the item (Rule 1.4D3).

10.4G2

If the manufacturer or assembler of the material has been named previously in the statement of responsibility, it should not be repeated in this area, even if no place or publisher has been recorded.

10.4G3   *Optional Addition*

Optionally, a cataloger can record the place, name, and/or date of manufacture if they appear on a prescribed source of information and if they differ from the place, name, and date of publication. For some materials which have been manufactured by several agencies at different times, this option can provide useful information and should be used. The Library of Congress will apply this option on a case-by-case basis.

10.5   PHYSICAL DESCRIPTION AREA

10.5B   EXTENT OF ITEM (INCLUDING SPECIFIC MATERIAL DESIGNATION)

The number of physical items, accompanied by a term which describes the item, is the first element recorded in the Physical Description Area. This rule lists terms which may be used. These terms are:

diorama	microscope slide
exhibit	mock-up
game	model

Because of the diverse nature of the materials covered by this chapter, the terms which may be used are not restricted to this standardized list. Thus, if none of the terms given in the rule is appropriate to the item being cataloged, another term may be supplied by the cataloger. Supplied terms should be the name of the item, stated in a concise form (e.g., hand puppet, musket, seashells, etc.). Again, because of their diverse nature, this addition of terms by the cataloger is a rather common occurrence when cataloging three-dimensional realia and artefacts.

48 specimens

1 vase

As an option to this rule, a cataloger may drop the name of the item from the statement and give only the number of items, provided the item's name is identical with the GMD used in Area 1. As was true for a similar option in another chapter, the Library of Congress will not apply this option. It is also probably better for other multimedia libraries to follow this LC policy in that relatively little space is saved on the record in return for creating a statement which may mislead catalog users.

10.5B2

When appropriate, the cataloger should add to the designation of the item the number and names of the pieces.

1 game (18 capital letter cubes, 18 small letter cubes, 3 mats, 1 timer, 1 instructional manual)

1 jigsaw puzzle (2,500 pieces)

1 vertebrae set (atlas, axis, cervical, thoracic, lumbar)

If a group of objects cannot be adequately described due to the number of different types of objects involved, or because the number of some or all is difficult to determine, the physical description may be limited to the use of a single specific material designation and the phrase "(various pieces)." As an option, additional information about the pieces can be given in a note (Rule 10.7B10). Although this is not a particularly desirable alternative because of the limited amount of information given, it can meet the information needs of the catalog user when combined with the use of a note. The Library of Congress has indicated that they will apply this option on a case-by-case basis.

    1 vertebrae set (various pieces)

    Five natural bone vertebrae on nylon filament.
    [This is a note made for the vertebrae set.]

10.5C OTHER PHYSICAL DETAILS

10.5C1 Material
The material of which an item or items is made is given when this information can be stated concisely. If this information cannot be given in a concise form, the cataloger is instructed either to omit the statement of material or to give the information in a note. This rule specifically instructs that the material of which a microscope slide is made should only be indicated if the material is other than glass.

10.5C2 Colour
For multicolored items, color indication is limited to the abbreviation "col."; if the item is in one or two colors, the cataloger can indicate the specific colors or record "b&w." As was the case with the rule dealing with the material of microscope slides, the indication of their color also is given special consideration in this rule. Here, the cataloger is instructed to indicate microscope slides which have been stained.

10.5D DIMENSIONS
The dimensions of an object can be important to users in determining the appropriateness of an object to their needs. Similarly, the dimensions of its container, if its size differs drastically from that of the object, can be important in locating the item.

10.5D1 [Object]
Information about the dimensions of an object should be given whenever this information is appropriate. One determination of appropriateness would be the ability to measure or express the size of an object in a meaningful way. Dimensions are to be given in centimeters, rounded to the next whole centimeter. If it is not clear which dimension is being recorded, the cataloger should also indicate this. Most often, the dimensions of height, width, and depth are recorded in that order. An exception to this is the dimensions of a microscope slide, which are given as length by width.

10.5D2 [Container]
Whenever an object is housed in a container issued by the publisher, both the name of the container and its dimensions should be recorded. These dimensions are recorded following those of the object itself. If the dimensions of the object are not given, the dimensions of the container are given after the indication of color. Generally, information about a container used to ship an item to a library would not be recorded. Similarly, the dimensions of a container not issued by the publisher but supplied by the library would not be given in this location. This

information would be more appropriately recorded in a note along with an indication that this was not the original container.

1 stethoscope : metal and plastic ; 58 cm. long in box, 21x11x3 cm.

1 clock face : plastic, b&w ; 18 cm. in diam.

2 puppets, 440 cards, 700 chips, 10 posters, 2 sound cassettes, 1 timer, 2 lesson manuals, 1 teacher's guide ; in container, 36x50x26 cm.

1 microscope slide : stained ; 8x3 cm.

10.5E   ACCOMPANYING MATERIAL
The name of accompanying textual or sound material should be indicated using one of the provisions of Rule 1.5E. Of the four methods described in that rule for recording this information, method c., recording the details in a note, and method d., recording the name of the material at the end of the physical description, are preferable. The use of the "optional addition" to method d. of providing further physical description for the accompanying material is also recommended, particularly when the accompanying material requires equipment for its use.

Multipart items or kits described according to the rules in both this chapter and Chapter 1 will often have accompanying guides and instructions. These materials can be listed as part of the extent of the item element of the Physical Description Area, at the end of that area or in a note (Rule 10.7B11). Care should be exercised to differentiate between materials which accompany an object in the kit and materials which are additional parts of the kit.

Accompanying material at the end of the Physical Description Area

1 human skeleton : plastic, col. ; 66 cm. long in case, 84x23x17 cm. + 1 illustrated key sheet.

Accompanying material as part of the extent of element statement

1 game (32 letter cubes, 1 playing mat, 1 timer, 1 guide) : in container, 22x15x3 cm.

10.6   SERIES AREA
Series information for three-dimensional artefacts and realia is recorded as instructed in Rule 1.6. Although the use frequency of the occurrence of series is not as high for materials covered by this chapter, some published items are issued as part of a series.

(Games for thinkers)

(Community decisions)

(Tutor-aid)

(A Game for a change)

10.7 NOTE AREA

10.7B1 Nature of the Item

A note indicating the nature of the item should be provided unless another part of the description indicates its nature. With the types of objects covered in this chapter often lacking descriptive or distinctive titles, the provision of information about the nature of the item in this first note is preferable to placing some or all of it in a summary note which appears later in the description. If the succinct indicator of the nature of the item given in this note is sufficiently informative, a summary note may be unnecessary.

> Adult and pupa mounted on wool. Wingless form.

> "Subsidiary card set for use with masters game."

> Ventral ganglions with double nerve cord.

> Simulation game of the Japanese attack on Pearl Harbor in 1941.

10.7B3 Source of Title Proper

A note indicating the source of the title proper is required when no title information is available from a prescribed source. The nature of the material covered in this chapter frequently requires that the cataloger supply a title proper.

> Title supplied by cataloger.

> Title supplied from teacher's guide.

> Title supplied from supplier's catalog.

10.7B4 Variations in Title;
10.7B5 Parallel Titles and Other Title Information

Frequently, titles appearing on the different prescribed sources of information of artefacts and realia will vary from the one chosen as the title proper. These variant titles can be useful in the identification of a unique item, particularly if an access point is provided for the variant title. Title information omitted from Area 1, that is, lengthy subtitles for reasons of brevity, should be recorded in a note. See the discussion of the use of this note for subtitles under Rule 10.1E1.

> Title on container: American Heritage battle cry.

10.7B6 Statements of Responsibility

This note is used to record variant names of persons and corporate bodies already named in the statement of responsibility and also to record statements of responsibility for individuals and corporate bodies not indicated previously in the statement of responsibility. These notes can supply useful information, particularly for multipart items with collective titles where little or no information has been recorded in the statement of responsibility. These indications of responsibility can relate to either all or selected parts of the work.

Devised by Marion Kingsbury.

Developed by Harrison Keller ; drawings by Rebecca Campbell.

"Erase-a-game" idea developed by Dr. Marvin Farbstein and Ronald I. Caplan.

A system developed by the National Fire Protection Association as a result of research in association with the National Bureau of Standards.

10.7B7. Edition and History
If an object or group of objects is derivative of other creations, that information should be recorded in this note. This note can also be used to record information about the history of the item. When recording an element of information which has prescribed ISBD punctuation in another part of the description, that punctuation should be retained in this note, except that the space, dash, space between areas of the description is not used.

Activities adapted from: The metric lab [kit] / Ada Booth.

Puzzles originally designed to accompany the author's text: The geometry of incidence.

"Revision of the 1969 edition."

"The original version of this simulation was prepared for the Navy Personnel Research and Development Center."

10.7B9 Publication, Distribution, Etc.
Details about the publication, distribution, manufacture, or date of an item, not recorded in Area 4, can be given in this note.

Dates differ: Container, c1977, guide, c1976.

Manufacturer information obtained from shipping container.

10.7B10 Physical Description
The note provides information about the physical description of the item not given previously in the Physical Description Area. Any object that requires equipment or special conditions for its use should be described in sufficient detail to guide its use. This physical description information may be combined into one note or given in several. The issue of clarity should guide the cataloger in providing the description over that of brevity. Even in those instances where a contents note names the individual parts, a description of the characteristics of the parts may prove necessary or useful. Additionally, if the option to Rule 10.5B2 to give only the specific material designation and the term "various pieces" is exercised, a note should be provided which identifies the component parts of the item, if this information is considered "useful."

Physical description indicated with "(various pieces)"

Contains 6 interior boxes for student teams with 36 crisis manuals, 36 information file books, 36 badges, 6 Decision-choice wheels, 6 identification easels, 12 checksheet pads, 6 report pads, various group unit cards and bills.

Contains 1 teacher's box with control manual (160 p.), 1 Consequences calculator, and 1 filmstrip (62 fr.) + 1 sound disc (10 min. : analog, 33⅓ rpm, mono. ; 7 in.).

> *[This physical description information has been placed into two notes to improve readability. The "+" is used to indicate that the sound disc is an accompanying material to the filmstrip rather than a separate item.]*

Contains 18 red letter cubes, 18 blue letter cubes, 1 timer, and 1 instruction book (168 p.)

Rectangular, decorated, heavily chased.

Coupe shape with gold rim.

Specimens are mounted.

10.7B11   Accompanying Material
When insufficient information about accompanying material is given in the Physical Description Area, the use of this note may be essential. This is especially true when equipment is needed for the material's use. This note is also used to record information about the location of the accompanying material if this is not evident.

Booklets : Idea book for Cuisenaire rods at the primary level / by Patricia S. Davidson. Primary math coloring book : puzzles for Cuisenaire rods / by Evelyne M. Graham.

Guides mounted on specimens.

Instructions for play on inside of container.

Text entitled: Getting to know Saudi Arabia / by Theodore O. Phillips.

Manual includes modeling directions.

10.7B14   Audience
As previously recommended in other chapters, a note preceded by the introductory term "Audience:" is most easily located on the catalog record by the user. For materials covered in this chapter, different types of audience information can be useful depending upon the nature of the item in hand. This information can address the intellectual or grade level of the item, specialized users, or the number of people for whom an item is intended (e.g., the number of players for a game). As is the case with audience notes in other chapters, this information can only be recorded if it is taken from the item.

In most cases, it is best to record the audience information in the way it was given on the item rather than rephrasing the statement and risking the possibility of changing its meaning or scope. Care should be taken though to ensure that what appears to be an audience statement is in fact one. Statements such as "for kids ages 7-77," while defining a potential audience level at the earliest age, certainly do not truly define a maximum age for play. In a situation such as this one, the cataloger should consider either not recording the audience level at all or stating only the useful age information.

Some information, such as the number of players, normally recorded in the audience note, may, at the discretion of the cataloger, be included as part of the summary note. This is most commonly done when the item requires both an audience indication and a summary.

Audience: Grades 6 and up.

Audience: Blind and physically handicapped people.

Audience: Nurses.

Audience: Secondary students, for 36 players and teacher.

For 2-6 players.

For 2-4 students.

10.7B17 Summary
The use of a summary note is recommended when the combination of information in the title and other parts of the description, particularly the nature of the item and contents notes, does not clearly indicate the nature of the item.

Summary: Flannel board designed to develop skills in classification, determine relationships between objects, and promote skills in using judgment and discrimination.

Summary: Includes specimen of worker, soldier, and winged form for low power microscopy, macrophotography, and field identification.

Summary: Complete set of upper and lower teeth of an adult human demonstrating good occlusion.

Summary: 10 whole mounts commonly used in protozoan studies.

Summary: Board game for 2 to 5 players. Designed to instruct players about the operation and development of a coal mine.

10.7B18 Contents
A contents note should be provided whenever parts of a multipart item have individual titles. Although not stated in this rule, a contents note can also be used if the items can be specifically names, even though they do not possess individual titles.

Contents: Ameba proteus — Difflugia — Radiolaria — Euglena — Chilomonas — Paramecium caudatum — Stentor — Tetrahymena — Voticella — Plasmodium vivax.

Contents: Double convex — Plano convex — Concavo convex — Double concave — Plano concave — Convexo concave.

Contents: Merry-go-round — Ferris wheels — Roller coaster — Octopus.

Contents: drawer 1. 1 teacher's guide, 1 SDM set, 1 activity card set, 38 planter cups, 36 planter bases, 4 seed packs, 3 sprinklers, 16 trays, 1 wax marker — drawer 2. 5 containers — drawer 3. 4 containers, 1 light source — drawer 4. 2 nets, 32 magnifiers, fish food, 5 eyedroppers, 32 tumblers, 10 lids, 1 thermometer — drawer 5. 1 baster, 6 funnels, 20 filter discs — drawer 6. 16 vials, 16 caps — Sand and soil box.

10.7B9 Numbers

Numbers, exclusive of ISBNs and ISSNs, relating to a single object, or to a package of items, should be recorded. In some cases, packages of material will consist of items produced or published by another publisher. These items may carry numbers which are related to their original publication rather than with the package developed by the current publisher. These numbers should also be recorded in this note. Numbers recorded in this note, while not particularly important to most users, do provide a unique identifier for an item.

Although no specific guidelines exist in the rule or from the Library of Congress for recording numbers in this note, in some cases catalogers may wish to "borrow" the guidelines in Rule 6.7B19 for sound recordings. This rule requires that both the "label name," that is, the name of the publisher, and the number appear in the note.

If previously published items have ISBNs or ISSNs associated with them, these numbers are best recorded in Area 8, where the relationship of the ISBN or ISSN to the specific item with which it is associated can be clearly shown by the use of a qualifier.

Kit no. 1002 ; filmstrip no. FS 1002.

N. 502.

"CX 2646."

10.7B20 Copy Being Described and Library's Holdings

The note is used to record information on "peculiarities or imperfections" in the copy held by the individual library and also to record other aspects of the library's copy that are not common to all copies of the item. Particularly for naturally occurring items, a description of the condition of the item may provide information which could affect its potential use. If this information is not described in the physical description notes, it can be given here.

Kit contains an order form for some perishable materials.

Teacher's manual missing.

Container autographed by the game's creator.

10.8 STANDARD NUMBER AND TERMS OF AVAILABILITY AREA

10.8D *Optional Addition.* **Terms of Availability**
   This rule employs the instructions of Rule 1.8D for recording the terms under which an item is available. That rule calls for recording the price of an item if it is for sale, or a brief statement of other terms under which it is available, if not for sale. In its Interpretation to Rule 1.8D, the Library of Congress instructs its catalogers to give the price of an item only for monographs which are cataloged under Chapters 2 ("Books, Pamphlets and Printed Sheets"), 5 ("Music"), 6 ("Sound Recordings"), 7 ("Motion Pictures and Videorecordings"), and 8 ("Graphic Materials") and which were issued during the past three years. If these LC guidelines are followed by multimedia libraries, no price would be recorded for materials covered by this chapter. In all likelihood, the indication of the price serves no useful purpose for catalog users and should probably not be recorded anyway, regardless of LC policy on the matter.
   Some types of library materials, particularly three-dimensional objects, may require some restriction in their use and circulation. Some are commonly restricted in their circulation to instructional staff for classroom use while others may not circulate outside the library or are unavailable for interlibrary loan. This information, of key importance to the potential user, should be indicated here.

Available on a rental basis only.

For use in media center only.

For teacher instruction only.

For medical personnel only.

Consumable materials must be duplicated for use.

Live animal components must be ordered from the company.

EXAMPLES: Descriptive Cataloging for Three-Dimensional Artefacts and Realia

Diorama

> A Village in India [diorama]. — Philadelphia : DCA
> Educational Products, c1969.
> 1 diorama (various pieces) : plastic, paper, and
> cardboard, col. ; in envelope, 32x23 cm. + 1 guide. —
> (DCA daily diorama. Series 3, Peoples of the world ;
> DD-30)
>
> Contains 5 foreground transparencies, 2 backgrounds,
> 5 story sheets, and 1 easel.
> Summary: Illustrations of rural and city life in India
> which can be rearranged to create different scenes.
>
> I. DCA Educational Products. II. Series.

Area 5   — Due to the nature of the item, an indication of its size
                would be inappropriate.
Area 6   — Series and subseries.
Added Entries — Series proper traced. A reference would be made
                from the subseries title to the series title proper.

Game

> Clue [game] : Parker Brothers detective game. — Salem,
> Mass. : Parker Bros., c1972.
> 1 game (various pieces) ; in box, 25x51x4 cm.
>
> Contains 1 game board, 6 tokens, 6 miniature
> weapons, 1 die, 21 clue cards, 1 note pad, 1 case file
> envelope, 1 instruction sheet.
> For 3 to 6 players.
>
> I. Parker Brothers Incorporated.

Area 1   — Other title information indicates the nature of the
                game.
Area 5   — More general indication of the game's contents given
                when the pieces cannot be stated concisely.
Area 7   — Use of the option to Rule 10.5B2 to give the details of
                the pieces not mentioned in Area 5 in a note. Instruc-
                tion sheet is mentioned here although it could have
                been given instead in the accompanying materials
                statement.
                — Note to indicate number of players.
Added Entries — Provided at the option of the cataloger.

Battle cry [game] : American Heritage game of the Civil
War. — Springfield, Mass. : Milton Bradley, c1962.
1 game (22 blue soldiers, 22 grey soldiers, 1 board,
1 die) ; in container, 50x35x5 cm. + 1 booklet.

Instructions on inside of container lid.
Booklet entitled: The Civil War : an outline history /
prepared by the editors of American Heritage.
Audience: Ages 9 to adult.
Summary: Game for 2 or 4 players allows students to
simulate battles described in booklet and recreate the
Civil War.

I. American Heritage Publishing Company.

Area 1	—Title from game board as chief source of information.
Area 5	—Accompanying material covers the entire game and is thus placed at the end of the physical description.
Area 7	—Title on booklet differs from game board.
	—For games, the summary can indicate number of players.
Added Entries	—Cataloger chose not to trace the separately titled booklet.

Allen, Robert W., 1931-
The propaganda game [game] / by Robert W. Allen,
Lorne Greene. — 1972 ed. — New Haven, Conn. :
Autotelic Instructional Materials, 1972, c1966.
1 game (40 example cards, 4 technique cards, 4
tokens, 1 clear thinking chart) ; in container, 15x13x3
cm. + 1 instruction manual.

Based on the book: Thinking straighter / by George
Henry Moulds.
Audience: For teenagers and adults.
Summary: Designed for 2 to 4 players to introduce
techniques used to distort thinking.

I. Greene, Lorne. II. Moulds, George Henry.
Thinking straighter. III. Title.

Main Entry	—Entry under the person responsible for the intellectual content of the game.
Area 1	—Statement of responsibility appears prominently on the item.
Area 2	—Edition statement recorded as it appears on the item.

(Explanation continues on page 244.)

Area 4　　　　—Applying the "optional addition," both the publica-
　　　　　　　tion date and the copyright date are recorded because
　　　　　　　they differ.
Area 7　　　　—Edition and history note. Note indicates that the item
　　　　　　　upon which this work is based was a book because
　　　　　　　some nonprint materials are based upon works in
　　　　　　　other than book format.
　　　　　　　—Audience indicated on the item.
　　　　　　　—Summary note includes the number of players.
Added Entries—Access point for the second named author.
　　　　　　　—Access point provided for the book upon which the
　　　　　　　work is based. Users of the book will thus be led to
　　　　　　　its related game.

　　Chess challenger "7" [game]. — Miami, Fla. : Fidelity
　　Electronics, [197-]
　　　　1 game (1 gameboard, 36 chess pieces, 1 gameboard
　　overlay) : brown and tan ; 31x21x3 cm. in box 41x24x7
　　cm. + 1 owner's manual/instruction booklet + 1 rule
　　booklet + 1 AC adapter.

　　　　Rule booklet: Let's play chess : official rules of chess
　　from the U.S. Chess Federation.
　　　　Summary: Seven levels of play. Special features
　　include random computer responses, position verifica-
　　tion, opening defenses from chess books and change-
　　ability of sides in mid-game.
　　　　Model BCC.

　　　　I. Fidelity Electronics, Incorporated.

Comments　　—Electronic game as a self-contained unit. The micro-
　　　　　　　chip that controls the game is an integral part of the
　　　　　　　game unit.
Area 1　　　　—The "7" in the title proper was contained within quo-
　　　　　　　tation marks on the item. The cataloger chose to
　　　　　　　retain the quotation marks used on the item.
Area 7　　　　—Indication of the booklet's title provided at the
　　　　　　　option of the cataloger.
　　　　　　　—Summary note used to indicate special features of the
　　　　　　　item. This information could also have been placed
　　　　　　　in an informal contents note.
　　　　　　　—The model number could have been treated as an
　　　　　　　edition statement if different versions of the game,
　　　　　　　that is, those with sensory movement detection or
　　　　　　　audio input, had different model numbers but shared
　　　　　　　a common title. In this case, the different models
　　　　　　　also possess different titles proper.

Added Entries—Added entry provided for the "publisher" because this could serve as an access point for users desiring a similar form of electronic game produced by this firm who have no knowledge of the titles of these games.

Monticello [game]. — Racine, Wis. : Western Pub. Co., [198-?]
　　1 jigsaw puzzle (1000 pieces) ; cardboard, col. ; 55x70 cm., in box 26x32x7 cm. — (Whitman guild 1000 jigsaw puzzle ; series 4)

　　Whitman: 4710-4.

　　I. Western Publishing Company. II. Series.

Area 5　　　—Dimensions are of the completed puzzle and its container.
Area 7　　　—Providing the name of the publisher before the numbers associated with the item follows a pattern used in *AACR 2* for sound recordings. This pattern is neither required nor prohibited.
Added Entries—Series added entry allows for a retrieval of puzzles from this firm by the indicator of their difficulty, that is, the number of pieces. This added entry is at the option of the cataloger.

Kit

Metric survival kit [kit] / Mathematics Education Task Force, California State Department of Education. — Sunnyvale, Calif. : Enrich, 1975.
　　1 grid, 1 cube, 1 ruler, 1 thermometer, 1 measuring tape, 1 spring scale, 1 mesh bag, 7 mass pieces ; in container, 30x16x16 cm. + 1 activities booklet + 1 inservice guide.

　　Activities adapted from: The Metric lab [kit] / Ada Booth.
　　Audience: Teachers.
　　Summary: Manipulatives for use in teacher training with activities for use in classroom.
　　EN40100.

　　I. Booth, Ada. The metric lab. II. California. Mathematics Education Task Force.

(Explanation is on page 246.)

Comment   —Kit of objects described according to Rule 1.10C2a (Revised 1985).

Area 1   —Title and statement of responsibility found on several parts including the guide and container which are unifying elements.

Area 5   —Physical description gives the extent and name of each object. No further description was considered necessary for them.

—Dimensions of the container given as an option to Rule 1.10C2a (Revised 1985). If there were a large number of pieces the statement "16 various pieces" could have been used rather than the individual pieces (Rule 1.10C2c).

Area 7   —First note is an edition and history note. Although no rule requires the use of the GMD with the title, it is included to show the type of material upon which this work was based. This could also have been indicated by stating "Activities adapted from the kit:".

—Audience indication given in the guide.

—Summary note indicates the purpose of the kit.

Added Entries—Added entry for the group responsible for content.

—Added entry also provided for the item from which the kit was adapted. This previous work is entered under the heading which would serve as the main entry for that work. Although the use of the GMD "kit" would be informative as a part of this added entry, LC does not use GMDs in added entries. This added entry was made at the option of the cataloger.

Booth, Ada.

    The metric center [kit] / written by Ada Booth. — Rev. [ed.] / reviewed and edited by Bryne Bessie Frank. — Palo Alto, Calif. : Enrich, 1974.

    1 tape measure, 1 thermometer, 2 rulers, 1 container of stacking masses, 1 cube, 10 rods, 20 activity masters, 6 performance tests, 10 cartridges, 1 Telor device ; in container, 35x21x13 cm. + 1 teacher's manual.

    Interchangeable programmed learning cartridges to be used with Telor device.

    Audience: Grade 6 and up.

    Summary: Laboratory oriented approach to the metric system and measurement.

    No. S02.

    I. Title.

Comment	—Materials gathered and manufactured to use with these activities.
Main Entry	—Main entry for the author of the activities.
Area 2	—Edition statement taken from the teacher's guide, the unifying element.
	—Abbreviation "ed." is in square brackets because it was added by the cataloger.
Area 4	—Although some parts have the date "c1973," the item was published in 1974.
Area 5	—Physical description developed according to Rule 1.10C2a (Revised 1985).
	—Teacher's manual applies to the entire kit and is thus treated as accompanying material rather than as a part of the kit.
Area 7	—First note relates to the nature of the item and equipment required for its use.
	—Audience information from the teacher's guide.

Microscope slide

A Termite [microscope slide] = Isoptera. — Skokie, Ill. : Sargent-Welch, [197-?]
1 microscope slide : dry mount, col. ; 5x5 cm.

Summary: Includes specimen of worker, soldier, and winged form for low power microscopy, macro-photography, and field identification.
57095.

I. Sargent-Welch Scientific Company. II. Title: Isoptera.

Area 1	—Title proper taken from item. Second word is capitalized because the first word of the title main entry is an article.
	—Parallel title, also taken from the item, follows the GMD.
Area 5	—Dimensions are length by height.
Area 7	—Number borne by the item which is not an ISBN or ISSN.
Added Entries	—Entry for the publisher is at the option of the cataloger. It was provided because it provides another nonsubject access point beyond the title that might likely be known by users and because it identifies a corporate body which produces a specific type of item.
	—LC policy is to trace parallel titles.

Blood of animal [microscope slide]. — Japan : Tasco, [197-?]
12 microscope slides ; 7x3 cm., in box, 12x7x3 cm.

Contents: Chicken blood — Cow blood — Dog blood — Fish blood — Frog blood — Guinea pig blood — Horse blood — Human blood — Mouse blood — Pig blood — Rabbit blood — Snake blood. 1560-B.

I. Tasco (Firm)

Area 4	—City of publication unknown, country of publication is known.
Area 7	—Contents have no established order within the set. Cataloger listed the contents in alphabetical order.
Added Entries—	"Firm" added to the name of the heading to indicate its corporate nature.

Model

[Dentures] [model]. — [1978]
1 pair dentures : plastic ; in box, 13x10x18 cm.

Summary: Complete set of upper and lower teeth of an adult human demonstrating good occlusion. Hinged to show jaw action.

Area 1	—Supplied title.
Area 4	—Place and publication information unknown.
	—Name of manufacturer unknown, date of manufacture known.
Area 5	—Size of the item is not given because it was not possible to indicate its size in a meaningful way.
Area 7	—Use for the item described in a summary note.

Miniature skeleton [model]. — Skokie, Ill. : Sargent-Welch, [197-?]
1 human skeleton : synthetic, bone col. ; 66 cm. long in case, 84x23x17 cm. + 1 illustrated key sheet + 2 illustration cards.

Articulation at main joints, hands and feet molded in 1 piece. Movable mandible.

I. Sargent-Welch Scientific Company.

Area 1   —Title from the item.
Area 5   —Material of which the item is made is identified.
              —"Bone" is the color of the item not the material. "Col." was added to this word to indicate this.
              —Length of the item and its container are given.
              —Accompanying material described with terms used by the item.

The Human eye [model]. — Wheeling, IL : Linberg, [197-?]
    1 model : plastic, red and white ; in box, 11x26x5 cm. + 1 stand + 1 instruction sheet. — (Human science)

Unassembled.
Instructions in English, French, German and Spanish.
Summary: Parts of the eye can be numbered to indicate individual muscles and parts of the eye.
Kit no. 1336.

    I. Series.

Comment   —Unassembled model kit.
Area 4   —"IL" is used for the abbreviation of Illinois rather than "Ill." which appears in appendix B because "IL" is the way the abbreviation appears on the container.
Area 5   —Specific colors indicated because there were fewer than 3 colors.
              —When model is assembled, place and name of publisher would not be recorded but rather the place and name of the person who assembled the model would be named in the manufacturer's area. Place and name of original publisher could be given in a note.
              —Model being unassembled, recording its dimensions would be inappropriate. Dimensions of the container are given.
Area 7   —Notes indicate language of the accompanying material not evident from other elements of the description. Languages are recorded in the order in which they would appear in the *Library of Congress Subject Headings* because none is indicated as predominant (LCRI to Rule 1.7B2).

Napoleon 12-pounder [model]. — Halesite, N.Y. : Marine
    Model Co., [196-?]
      1 model : metal, col. ; 21x12x9 cm. — (Guns of
history)

    Scale: 1:16. ¾ in. to 1 ft.
    Assembled and painted.
    No. 1126.

    I. Marine Model Company. II. Series.

Comment	— Assembled model kit.
Area 4	— Some catalogers will maintain that a publisher should not be recorded in this area when an unassembled model kit haas subsequently been assembled, rather that the person who assembled the model and his or her location should be listed as the manufacturer following the date. While the listing of the person performing this function would be valid for a model built from "scratch," it is not felt to be appropriate for a preformed scale model where all the person did was glue the parts together and paint them. Therefore, in this example the publisher is still listed in its normal position. No mention was made of who assembled the model because this information is considered useless to any potential user.
Area 7	— Scale recorded using the conventions given in *AACR 2*, Chapter 3 for cartographic materials.

Realia

Frog metamorphosis [realia]. — New York : Creative
    Playthings, [197-?]
      4 frogs : col. ; 10x12x3 cm.

    Specimens imbedded in a plastic block.
    Summary: Frogs in 4 stages of development from
tadpole to frog.

    I. Creative Playthings.

Area 1	— Title from the object.
Area 5	— Specific material designation supplied by the cataloger rather than a SMD from Rule 10.5B1.
Area 7	— More detailed identification of the specimens given in a note. This note could have been combined with the summary note.

> —Summary note is needed to indicate the scope of the item.

Added Entries—Provided for the same reason Sargent-Welch was traced in the previous examples.

[Stethoscope] [realia]. — [196-?]
  1 stethoscope : metal and plastic ; 58 cm. long in
box, 21x11x3 cm.

Area 4   —Artefact, not intended for communication, is described without publication information.
           —Date indicates probable date of manufacture, decade uncertain.
Area 5   —Materials of which the object is made are indicated.
           —Word "long" is added to the dimensions to indicate the dimensions being reported.
           —Dimensions of the container recorded in addition to those of the item.

[Bicentennial of the United States Navy commemorative medal] [realia]. — 1975. ([Philadelphia, Pa. : U.S. Mint])
  1 medal : brass ; 8 cm. in diam. + 1 stand

Title supplied by cataloger.

I. United States. Mint (Philadelphia, Pa.)

Area 1   —No title on the item.
Area 4   —Date of manufacture recorded.
           —Place and name of manufacturer are also given. They were placed in square brackets because this information is not derived from a prescribed source of information (the item, its accompanying material, or its container).
Area 5   —Size given in terms of the diameter as the most appropriate measurement. "Diameter" must be abbreviated (appendix B).
           —Stand considered accompanying material.
Area 7   —Source of title note.
Added Entries—Entry provided for the manufacturer in order to supplement access to the item beyond that of the supplied title.

[Sun dial] [realia]
    1 seashell ; 4 cm. in diam.

    Title supplied by cataloger.

Comment	—Naturally occurring object not mounted for display or presentation.
Area 1	—Cataloger supplied a title, using reference source, which specifically identified the type of seashell being described.
Area 4	—All publication, distribution, manufacture information, including date, is inappropriate for this type of item.
Area 7	—Source of title note.

    Texas Instruments electronic slide rule calculator
[realia] : TI-30. — [1976?]. (Dallas, Tex. : Texas Instruments)
    1 calculator : plastic, col. ; 8x15x4 cm. + 1 owner's manual + 1 AC adapter.

    LED display.
    Special functions include powers and roots, reciprocals, logarithms, trigonometric functions, degrees, radians, grad conversions, hyperbolic and inverse hyperbolic functions.

    I. Title: Electronic slide rule calculator.

Comment	—This item is treated like an electronic game because it is a single unit with an integral micro-chip.
Area 1	—Assuming that some other calculators issued by this firm have the same title proper with a different model number, the model number was treated as a form of "other title information," that is, the nondate element which varies among similarly titled works from the same publisher. This number could also have been recorded as a note.
Area 4	—Because this is an artefact not primarily intended for communication, no place or publisher is given.
	—Place and manufacturer recorded. Although it has been named in the title, Rule 10.4G2 indicates that this information should not be recorded if the information has appeared previously in the "statement of responsibility."
	—Date of manufacture inferred from copyright date of owner's manual.
Area 7	—First note used to indicate the nature of the character display.

Added Entries—Additional title access point provided for the part of
the title following the name of the manufacturer.

—For a dictionary catalog it is probably unnecessary to
provide an access point for Texas Instruments
because its name is the lead element in the title
proper. In a library with a three-way divided catalog,
an online or microfiche catalog with separate title
indexes, or a library which may change its catalog to
any of these forms, a separate access point would
have been made for this corporate body.

9
Description of Microforms

11.0 GENERAL RULES

Rules in this chapter cover all types of publications in microform, whether opaque or transparent. This includes microforms on film (in reels, cassettes, and cartridges), on fiche, and microopaque cards. It also includes microfilm secured in aperture cards.

Aperture cards are data cards which may or may not contain eye-readable information on the card. The cards are usually keypunched for automated retrieval. When cataloged, the information on the microform insert in the card is used for the description. Microfiche are sheets of base material containing frames of microimages. Microfilm is contained on reels, in cartridges, or on cassettes and is composed of frames of microimages running parallel to either the width or the length of the film. All microformats except microopaques are filmed on a transparent base. Microopaques contain microimages on an opaque background. Microforms are covered in this text since equipment is required to read or view these works.

Microforms covered in this chapter include both original works published in microformat and reproductions in microform of previously existing works. From the outset, the treatment accorded microreproductions of previously published works by *AACR 2* did not achieve general acceptance. The reason for this was that *AACR 2*'s approach was radically different from previous microform cataloging practices under earlier cataloging codes. These codes had used information relevant to the original work for bibliographic description. Under *AACR 2*, information relevant to the microform is used. A note is used to provide information about the original. Thus, title, publisher, date of publication, etc., information describe the microform rather than the original item. Many catalogers of microform materials have indicated that this approach was unsatisfactory. They preferred that the description emphasize the original source rather than its reproduction in the micro format.

The failure to achieve a change in this approach from the bodies responsible for the revision of the rule resulted in the Library of Congress issuing a set of Rule Interpretations to Chapter 11. These Rule Interpretations in effect established policies which reinstated previous cataloging practices for the cataloging of microreproductions. This LC policy statement was issued in the Fall 1981 issue of *Cataloging Service Bulletin*. This policy applies to all microreproductions, including books, pamphlets, printed sheets, cartographic materials, manuscripts, music, and serials. The Library of Congress continues to implement *AACR 2* when determining the access points and their form of heading.

Most libraries that catalog this type of microform have chosen to follow LC's policy in the creation of bibliographic descriptions for these items. LC does apply Chapter 11 when cataloging original microforms. Although microreproductions of previously existing works are the most common form of microform found in multimedia libraries, this text will address the rules for both original microforms and microreproductions in separate sections. Because original microforms are relatively rare in most libraries, the rules for microform reproductions of previously existing works will be considered first.

MICROFORM REPRODUCTIONS OF PREVIOUSLY EXISTING WORKS

11.0A SCOPE

The Library of Congress Rule Interpretations for Chapter 11 apply to microform reproductions of previously existing works. Works covered by these Interpretations are items covered by the following *AACR 2* chapters for description: Chapter 2 ("Books, Pamphlets and Printed Sheets"), Chapter 3 ("Cartographic Materials"), Chapter 4 ("Manuscripts"), Chapter 5 ("Music"), Chapter 8 ("Graphic Materials"), and Chapter 12 ("Serials"). The Interpretations also apply to microform copies of dissertations produced by University Microfilms International.

In implementing these Interpretations it should be remembered that their purpose is to emphasize the information appearing on the original item in the creation of the bibliographic description rather than the information related to the reproduction. Thus, Rule 1.11 and the rules in Chapter 11 will be used only to assist in the development of a note which describes the characteristics of the microform reproduction. These Interpretations do not affect the *AACR 2* rules for choice of access points and form of headings.

11.0B SOURCES OF INFORMATION

11.0B1 Chief Sources of Information

The chief sources of information to be used are those identified in the appropriate chapter for the original form of the item. These reproduced chief sources of information should be treated as though they are the original.

11.0B2 Prescribed Sources of Information

As was the case with the chief source of information, the prescribed sources of information are those identified in the appropriate chapter for the original form of the item.

11.1 to 11.6   TITLE AND STATEMENT OF RESPONSIBILITY AREA TO SERIES AREA

For each of these areas, the information called for by the appropriate chapter for description for the original item should be used in developing the description. Thus, for a microreproduction of a map, Rules 3.1 to 3.6 would be used. In addition, the option to Rule 1.1C2 to include the GMD "microform" in the description is applied by the Library of Congress. Catalogers should also implement any other LC Rule Interpretations used by their library for these chapters.

In some cases, particularly for physical description information, it may not be possible to fully describe all of the characteristics of the original because of a lack of information. Whenever this occurs, these elements are excluded from the description. Catalogers can use catalog records for the original work to assist them in developing these descriptions. Care must be exercised, however, to ensure that the catalog record being used describes the edition in question.

11.7   NOTE AREA

Notes related to the original item should be developed from the appropriate chapter for description, as was done for Areas 1 through 6.

Additionally, a note should be made which gives details about the reproduction of the item, its publication, and its availability. This note is normally given as the last note. It should begin with the term which is the specific material designator for the form of the reproduction, either "aperture card," "microfiche," "microfilm," or "microopaque."

Following this term, details called for in Area 4 of Chapter 11 (i.e., publication, distribution, etc., information) should be recorded in both the order and form called for by the rules for that area. Other details specific to the reproduction that come under the coverage of Areas 5, 6, or 7 should be recorded following the publication, distribution, etc., information. The order and form used for these elements should also be the same as those used in these areas. If information related to Rule 11.7B10 (Physical Description Note) needs to be recorded here, it should precede any series information also being recorded. This means that information about reduction ratios, readers, or film should be given before any series information. In all cases, however, a full stop and two spaces precede the next area rather than a space, long dash, space.

Microfilm. Ann Arbor, Mich. : University Microfilms International, 1985. 1 microfilm reel : negative ; 35 mm.

Microfilm. Woodbridge, Conn. : Research Publications, 1979. 1 microfilm reel ; 35 mm. (Fowler collection of early architectural books ; reel 26, no. 141)

Microfiche. Honolulu : Law Library Microform Consortium, 1979.   microfiches : negative
[A serial. Size is 11x16 cm]

Microfiche. Westport, Conn. : Greenwood, 1976. 18 microfiches. (PA-47)

Microfiche. Chicago : Library Resources, c1970. 1 microfiche ; 8x13 cm. (The Library of American civilization ; LAC 20001). Very high reduction.

Microopaque. New York : University of Rochester Press for the Association of College and Research Libraries, 1953. 1 microopaque ; 8x13 cm. (ACRL microcard series ; no. 2)

ORIGINAL MICROFORMS

11.0 GENERAL RULES

11.0A SCOPE
The following discussion of the rules is predicated upon the assumption that a library has adopted the Library of Congress's Rule Interpretations for this chapter. Thus, the discussion will only address application of the rules to original microforms. Libraries which have not adopted the LC Rule Interpretations can apply these rules to both microform originals and to microreproductions of previously existing works. When this is done, the provisions of Rule 11.7B22 must be implemented.

11.0B SOURCES OF INFORMATION

11.0B1 Chief Sources of Information
The original text of this rule was revised in 1982. The chief source of information for an original microfilm is the title frame. This frame is usually located near the beginning of the item and contains the full title. Sometimes it may also contain information about the publication of the microfilm. This same source is used as the chief source of information for original microfiche and microopaques. For these two microformats, when no title frame exists, or when the information given there is insufficient, the eye-readable header data at the top of the fiche or opaque serve as the chief source of information. This header title should not be used, however, if a more complete title appears on accompanying eye-readable material or a container. These sources would be used instead as the chief source of information. For aperture cards, the chief source of information is the title card for the set of aperture cards or the card itself if a single aperture card is being cataloged. Whenever information normally present on a title frame or card is dispersed over successive frames or cards, these multiple sources should be treated as a single chief source of information.

11.0B2 Prescribed Sources of Information
In each area of the description there are different prescribed source(s) from which information can be taken without having to enclose it in square brackets. For the Title and Statement of Responsibility Area, the chief source of information serves as the prescribed source of information. For some other areas (Edition, Special Data for Cartographic Materials and Serials, Publication, Distribution, etc; and series) the chief source of information, the rest of the item, and the container are prescribed sources, although the chief source of information is the preferred source. Other areas of the description (Physical

Description, Notes, Standard Number) allow the information to be derived from any source.

In all but a few cases, information required by the chosen level of description can be taken from any source provided that the information is placed within square brackets. Additionally, catalogers are always free to record information in a note without the need of brackets.

11.1 TITLE AND STATEMENT OF RESPONSIBILITY AREA

The title proper of an original microform should be transcribed under the provisions of Rule 1.1B.

11.1C *OPTIONAL ADDITION.* GENERAL MATERIAL DESIGNATION

The general material designation follows the title proper. For all types of microforms, the GMD "microform" is used. Parallel titles, "other title information," and their associated punctuation follow the GMD.

11.1D PARALLEL TITLES

Parallel titles are recorded following the title proper and the GMD according to the instructions given in Rule 1.1D. A parallel title is preceded by a space, equals sign, space. For level two descriptions, the cataloger is instructed to record the first parallel title. If a subsequent parallel title is in English, it is also recorded.

11.1E OTHER TITLE INFORMATION

Other title information should be recorded according to the provisions of Rule 1.1E. For microfiche and microopaques, it is the presence of this information which may determine whether an eye-readable title on accompanying material or a container is used as the chief source of information over the title on an eye-readable header title. The header title, due to a lack of space, may lack other title information included on one or more of the other sources. Lengthy other title information can be abridged (Rule 1.1E3) or given in a note (Rule 11.7B5). In addition, a word or words explaining the title proper can be added in square brackets as other title information according to Rule 1.1E6. These words should be in the language of the title proper. Information of this nature is best recorded, however, in a summary of contents note.

11.1G ITEMS WITHOUT A COLLECTIVE TITLE

As was the case with other types of nonprint materials, several items may be published together without a collective title on one or more physical units. This is more common, however, for microform reproductions of previously existing works than it is for original microforms. When this situation occurs the individual works can be described as a unit or as separate items. Although either method is adequate, providing separate catalog records may be preferable. Separate records can provide more detailed information in a less complex structure and are therefore more easily understood by users. When cataloged as separate records, a "with" note is used to link the related records (Rule 11.7B21). The Library of Congress uses the unit description style for nonprint materials.

11.2 EDITION AREA

Information concerning the edition of a microform should be recorded as instructed in Rule 1.2B. The Library of Congress does not apply the option of providing an edition statement for an item which does not have an edition statement, although it contains significant changes from a previous edition. It is strongly suggested that multimedia libraries follow LC's policy. If this edition information is considered important, it can be given in a note (Rule 11.7B7).

11.3 SPECIAL DATA FOR CARTOGRAPHIC MATERIALS AND SERIALS

11.3A CARTOGRAPHIC MATERIALS

Mathematical data for an original cartographic item in microform should be recorded following the provisions of Rule 3.3.

11.3B SERIALS

The numeric and/or alphabetic, chronological, or other designation for an original serial on microform should be recorded as instructed in Rule 12.3. This information should be for the first issue of a serial. If the cataloging record is developed from other than the first issue, the issue used should be identified in a note (Rule 12.7B22, Item Described) and no information recorded in this area.

11.4 PUBLICATION, PRODUCTION, DISTRIBUTION, ETC., AREA

Determining the information to be recorded in this area does not pose difficult problems if Rule 1.1 and its subrules are followed. The place of publication, name of the publisher, distributor, etc., and the publication date of the microform are recorded following the provisions of Rules 1.4C, 1.4D, and 1.4F, respectively. A 1985 Revision to *AACR 2* added Rule 11.4F2, which instructs that the date of an unpublished microform should be given if that information is "readily available" and should be omitted when it is not.

The Library of Congress applies, on a case-by-case basis, optional Rule 1.4E, which allows for adding a statement of function to the name of the publisher, distributor, etc., to clarify the information. It is recommended that libraries also apply this option on an "as needed" basis.

11.5 PHYSICAL DESCRIPTION AREA

11.5B1 EXTENT OF ITEM (INCLUDING SPECIFIC MATERIAL DESIGNATION)

The total number of physical units being described, followed by a specific material designation, are the first two elements in this area. The specific material designations for microforms are limited to the following terms:

aperture card	microfilm
microfiche	microopaque

For microfilm, catalogers must add to the term "microfilm" the appropriate term which describes its container. The terms which may be used are "cartridge," "cassette," and "reel." For microfiche, the term "cassette" can be added when appropriate. For microfiche, the number of frames can also be given, within parentheses, if this number can be easily obtained.

As an option, catalogers may drop the designation "micro" from the specific material designation if the GMD "microform" has been used. The Library of Congress is not following this option and, for the benefit of its users, most multimedia libraries will probably want to follow LC's policy.

11.5C OTHER PHYSICAL DETAILS

11.5C1 [Negative Image]
Images on a microform can be either positive or negative. A positive image appears to be the same as most printed material: dark letters on a light opaque background. Negative images reverse this pattern, with light letters on a dark background. Whenever the image on a microform is a negative image, this should be indicated. However, no indication is made if the image is positive.

11.5C2 [Illustrations]
When a microform consists wholly or in part of illustrations, this should be indicated here following the provisions of Rule 1.5C. If the illustrations are in color, the instructions in Rule 11.5C3 must also be followed.

11.5C3 [Color]
If some or all of a microform is colored, this should be indicated. If the colored microform contains no illustrations the indication should be given as "col." Colored microforms with illustrations are indicated by "col. & ill." or "col. ill." The latter statement indicates that only the illustrations are colored while the former statement indicates that the microform is in color and contains illustrations.

11.5D DIMENSIONS

11.5D2 Aperture Cards
Both the height and width of aperture cards (in centimeters) must be recorded.

11.5D3 Microfiches
The dimensions of microfiche (height x width) must be recorded whenever those dimensions are other than 10.5x14.8 cm, i.e., ca. 4x6 in. These dimensions should be in centimeters. This rule is a revision from the one originally published in *AACR 2*, which required that the dimensions of microfiche always be recorded.

11.5D4 Microfilms
The width of a microfilm should be recorded in millimeters. This rule, like the previous one, is also a revision of the rule originally published in *AACR 2*. That rule required, in addition to the width dimension, that the diameter of the microfilm reel be given in inches if its size was other than three inches.

11.5D5   Microopaques
Like aperture cards, the height and width of microopaques should be recorded in centimeters.

11.5E   ACCOMPANYING MATERIAL
The name of material accompanying a microform should be recorded and, optionally, the material's physical description. This option should generally be applied if the size of the material is considered significant. The provisions of Rule 1.5E should be used to record the information about the accompanying material. If it is considered necessary to indicate the location of the accompanying material, a note (Rule 11.7B11) should be used. Because of the relatively small size of microforms, it is generally useful to know the size of material accompanying the work as well as its location, unless both the accompanying material and the microform are stored in a common container. If the location of the accompanying material is specific to a particular library, that information should be given in a terms of availability statement.

11.6   SERIES AREA
Series information relating to an original microform is recorded according to the provisions of Rule 1.6.

11.7   NOTE AREA

11.7B1   Nature, Scope, or Artistic or Other Form of the Item
This note is used to record information about the nature, scope, etc., of the item if it is not apparent from the rest of the description. Some of this information may already have been given in the Title and Statement of Responsibility Area or in a summary or contents note. When this occurs, this note should not be made.

11.7B3   Source of Title Proper
A statement indicating the source of the title proper must be made if that title was derived from other than the chief source of information. Because several different sources can serve as the chief source depending upon the fullness of the title, it is recommended that this note always be made whenever the title's source is other than the title frame.

11.7B4   Variations in Title
Frequently, titles appear in variant forms on different prescribed sources of information and, less frequently, in variant forms within the same prescribed source. It is particularly important to record a title in eye-readable form that varies from the title recorded as the title proper.

The Library of Congress's Interpretation for the variation in title rule in other chapters for the description of nonprint materials established a policy which formalized the decision-making process for a variation in title note. This same policy could be applied to microforms. LC indicates that the first step is to determine whether an additional access point is desired for that title variation. This determination should be based upon the conditions given in Rule 21.2 (Changes in Titles Proper). These conditions follow:

- a change occurs in the first five words of the title (exclusive of initial articles in the nominative case)

- the addition, deletion, or change of important words in the title

- a change occurs in word order

If, based on the rule, a decision is made that an additional access point is necessary, then a variation in title note should be made to justify the use of the added entry.

11.7B6 Statements of Responsibility

A note should be made for the names of persons and corporate bodies important to a work who were not named in the statement of responsibility, either because they were not named on the chief source of information or because their contribution was not considered significant enough to justify its location there. This note is particularly important when several groups have sponsored or endorsed a publication but were not named in the statement of responsibility. The names of these groups often become closely associated with the work.

11.7B9 Publication, Distribution, etc.

Information about the publication, distribution, etc., of a work that was not given in Area 4 can be given here if that information is considered important.

11.7B10 Physical Description

This note is used to record three elements of information for microforms: reduction ratio, readers, and film used.

Reduction ratio

A reduction ratio is an indication of the number of times a linear dimension of the original has been reduced in size. This ratio is usually expressed in terms of "x" (e.g., 16x, 25x, 32x, etc.). A 16x reduction ratio indicates that a work is 1/16th the size of the original.

The reduction ratio can vary for all types of microforms. This information is important because the material should be viewed on a reader equipped with a lens appropriate to the reduction ratio of the film. Reduction ratios between 16x and 30x are frequently used. Two very commonly used reduction ratios are 19x and 21x. This rule requires that the reduction ratio be given only if it is outside the 16x to 30x range. When given, a term describing the ratio must be used rather than the ratio itself. Those terms and their associated reduction ratios are:

Low reduction	Less than 16x
High reduction	31x to 60x
Very high reduction	61x to 90x
Ultra high reduction	greater than 90x

For ultra high reduction, the recording requirements differ in that both the term describing the reduction and the reduction ratio are given. This is done because in this high reduction range, a more exact match between the characteristics of the equipment and the film is necessary. When the reduction ratio varies within the item, the phrase "reduction varies" should be given rather than attempting to describe the range of different reductions used.

Reader

The name of the reader designed for use with microfilm in cassettes or cartridges should be given if it has a bearing upon use of the film. In some instances, microfilm in a specific type of cartridge or cassette can only be used with a particular type of reader.

Film *[Optionally]*

As an option, catalogers may also record in this note the type of film used. This information can be useful because of the varying archival qualities and durability of different types of film. This information is generally of more use to the library, however, than it is to the user of the microform. Thus, it is recommended that libraries establish a consistent policy on whether to record this information based upon its usefulness in the management of library operations.

11.7B11 Accompanying Material
There are occasions when original microforms are issued with accompanying material, usually in eye-readable form. This note is used to record the location of the accompanying material when appropriate. It can also be used to provide details about the accompanying material not mentioned in the Physical Description Area or given in a separate description. This is the place where a cataloger may record the title, statement of responsibility, and other details about an accompanying text.

11.7B13 Dissertations
Although many dissertations are available on microform, few (if any) are issued originally in a microformat. Thus, this note will seldom (if ever) be used for original microforms. When cataloging microform reproductions of dissertations, the use of LC's Rule Interpretation would result in using the equivalent of this note in the chapter which deals with the original form of the dissertation.

11.7B14 Audience
As was the case with other materials, the intended audience or intellectual level of a microform may be given if that information was stated on the item, its container, or its accompanying material.

If no audience information is available from these sources, the cataloger is prohibited from writing his or her own audience statement. There are some cases, however, in which the audience level is known, although it is not actually stated on the required sources. In these situations, the information can be given in a summary note (Rule 11.7B17) or a cataloger can sidestep the restrictions of this rule without using a summary note by simply quoting the statement and giving its source. Whether the quotation or summary note is used, the cataloger should base his or her statement upon information from another source rather than upon the cataloger's determination of audience based upon an examination of the work.

11.7B16   Other Formats Available
If an original microform is also available in hard copy, this should be indicated in this note. It is recommended that this note only be made, however, if the hardcopy is part of the library's collection.

11.7B17   Summary
Microforms, like some other types of nonprint materials, cannot be scanned without the use of some type of hardware. As was the case with these other types of nonprint materials, the summary note for microforms becomes significant if the title or other parts of the description do not sufficiently explain the type of material, scope, or point of view of the work. If information about a work can be expressed through the use of the titles of its parts, this information should be given in a formal contents note (Rule 11.7B18) rather than here.

The summary note should be both brief and objective. Information in the summary note can be taken from other sources without attribution. Traditionally, when using a summary note for all forms of materials, the Library of Congress begins the note with the word "Summary:".

11.7B18   Contents
A contents note is used to indicate, either fully or selectively, the presence of material in the work that is not stated or implied in other parts of the description. It can also be used to stress the importance of particular items within the work. This information can be recorded in either a formal or an informal note. Formal contents notes begin with either the word "Contents:" or the phrase "Partial Contents:".

11.7B19   Numbers
Microforms are frequently assigned numbers by their publishers. These numbers should be given in this note if they are considered important. ISBNs and ISSNs, however, should be given in Area 8 rather than in this note.

11.7B20   Copy Being Described and Library's Holdings
Any peculiarities or imperfections in a library's copy of an original microform should be recorded in this note. If the work is a multipart work and the library does not hold the complete set, this should also be indicated here. If the library does intend to complete the set, the rule instructs that a "temporary:" note be made to this effect.

11.7B21   "With" Notes
When multiple-part works without collective titles are cataloged separately, this note is used to link the parts. The parts should be listed in the order in which they occur on the work. This note must begin with the word "With:".

11.7B22   Notes Relating to Original
This note, added by the 1982 Revisions to *AACR 2*, provides a place to record information about the original work not being issued as a microreproduction. If the Library of Congress policy on the cataloging of microforms is adopted, libraries will have no use for this note. Instead, microreproductions of previously existing works will have the information about the original work

distributed throughout the description, while original microforms have no "original" work upon which to comment.

11.8   STANDARD NUMBER AND TERMS OF AVAILABILITY AREA

International Standard Book Numbers and International Standard Serial Numbers should be recorded in this location following the provisions of Rule 1.8.

EXAMPLES: Descriptive Cataloging for Microforms

Microform Reproductions of Previously Existing Works

> Hickey, Thomas Butler, 1947-
> Research report on field, subfield and indicator statistics in OCLC bibliographic records [microform] / by Thomas B. Hickey. — Dublin, OH : OCLC, Office of Planning and Research, Research Dept., 1981.
> 147 p. — (Research report series ; report no. OCLC/OPR/RR-81/1)
>
> Principally tables.
> Microfiche. Alexandria, Va. : ERIC Document Reproduction Service, 1981. 2 microfiches : negative. (ERIC reports). ED 202 484. IR 009 363.
>
> I. OCLC. II. Title. III. Title: Field, subfield and indicator statistics in OCLC bibliographic records.

Main Entry	— Entry under the person responsible for the intellectual content of the work.
	— Heading is in *AACR 2* form.
Area 1	— GMD "microform" recorded after the title proper.
Area 5	— Size of the original could not be determined.
Area 7	— Summary unnecessary because of the content detail provided in the title.
	— Date in the microfiche note is the date of the publication of the microfiche.
	— Negative image is indicated.
	— No size is recorded because it is 10.5x14.8 cm.
	— Numbers given by the publisher are noted. In this case, the ED number is very useful in identifying and locating the work in the library.
Area 8	— No standard number assigned.
Added Entries	— Entry provided under the name of the original publisher whose name is closely associated with this work.

(Explanation continues on page 266.)

—Entry for the publisher is in the *AACR 2* form established by LC policy.
—Entry provided for a variant of the title.

Coulson, John E.
    System analysis in education [microform] / John E. Coulson and John F. Cogswell. — Santa Monica : Systems Development Corp., 1965.
    14 leaves : ill. ; 28 cm. — (SDC Professional Report ; SP 1863)

    Cover title.
    Presented at the Conference on Development and Use of Data Banks for Educational Research, Boston, Dec. 4, 1964.
    Microfiche. Springfield, Va. : Clearinghouse for Federal Scientific and Technical Information, 1965. 1 microfiche (19 fr.) : negative. AD 611865.

    I. Cogswell, John. II. System Development Corporation. III. Conference on Development and Use of Data Banks for Educational Research (1964 : Boston, Mass.) IV. Title.

Area 6   —Series information related to the original publication not the microfiche version. If related to the microfiche it would have been recorded in the reproduction note.

Area 7   —Source of title proper indicated.
    —Conference information is given in a note to allow for the creation of an access point for the conference with which this work is associated.
    —Number of frames was readily established.
    —Negative images indicated.
    —Microfiche publisher's numbering recorded.

Added Entries —Access point provided for the second named author and the corporate body responsible for the work.
    —Access to the work also provided through the name of the conference at which the work was presented.

Moran, Barbara Burns.
　　Career progression of male and female academic
library administrators [microform] / by Barbara Burns
Moran. — [1981]
　　170 leaves ; 28 cm.

　　Typescript.
　　Thesis (Ph.D.)—State University of New York at
Buffalo, 1982.
　　Also available in hardcopy.
　　Bibliography: leaves 167-170.
　　Microfilm. Ann Arbor, Mich. : University Microfilms
International, 1984. 1 microfilm reel ; 35 mm.

　　I. Title.

Area 5　　　　—Place and name of publisher inappropriate for an
　　　　　　　　unpublished dissertation.
　　　　　　　—Date reflects the date of the submission of the disser-
　　　　　　　　tation.
Area 7　　　　—Dissertation status indicated in a formal note.
　　　　　　　—Date reflects the date of the degree.
　　　　　　　—Library has this work in a hardcopy format also. A
　　　　　　　　preferable way to indicate this would be to make a
　　　　　　　　separate entry for the hardcopy version.

Gross, Charles, 1857-1909.
　　The sources and literature of English history from the
earliest times to about 1485 [microform] / by Charles
Gross. — 2nd ed. — New York : A.M. Kelley, 1970.
　　xxiii, 820 p. ; 24 cm.

　　More than 3234 titles in a classified arrangement.
　　Reprint. Originally published: 2nd ed., rev. and enl.
London ; New York : Longmans, Green, 1915.
　　Includes index.
　　Appendices: A. Records of the Deputy-Keeper of the
Public Records — B. The Historical Mss. Commission.
— Rolls series — Chronological tables of the principal
sources.
　　Microfiche. Littleton, Colo. : Rothman, [1986]. 10
microfiches : negative. (Law books recommended for
libraries : Legal history ; no. 68)
　　ISBN 0-678-00636-9

　　I. Title. II. Series.

(Explanation is on page 268.)

Comment	—One work in a microform reprint series. The work is a microfiche of a 1970 reprint edition of a 1915 work.
Area 2	—Edition statement from the original work.
Area 4	—Place, publisher, and date of the reprint edition.
Area 7	—Note listing the appendices set up like a formal contents note.
	—Reprint note gives the publication information for the original work. The edition statement is given because it differs in wording from that on the reprint edition.
	—Series statement in the microfiche note gives a main series, a subseries, and the numbering for the subseries.
Area 8	—ISBN on the 1970 reprint edition.

Original Microforms

Bio-base [microform] : 1984 master cumulation. —
[Detroit] : Gale Research Co., c1984.
211 microfiches : negative + 1 guide (111 p. ; 15 cm.)

Title from header.
Subtitle: A periodic cumulative master index on microfiche to sketches found in over 500 current and historical biographical dictionaries.
"Compiled by the staff of Biography and genealogy master index."—t.p. verso of guide.
Guide has title: Bio-base : 1984 master cumulation : introduction and bibliographic key.
Kept up-to-date by supplements accompanied by a guide.
ISBN 0-8103-1621-8. — ISSN 0742-2318

I. Gale Research Company.

Area 5	—Negative image indicated.
	—User's guide recorded as accompanying material.
	—Physical description given for the accompanying material because the guide is substantial in size.
Area 7	—Source of title note.
	—Second subtitle given in a note because of its length.
	—Title of guide given because its subtitle indicates its scope.
	—Supplements indicated.
	—Both an ISBN and an ISSN are given in the guide.

GPO sales publications reference file [microform]. —
Washington, D.C. : U.S. G.P.O., [Supt. of Docs.,
distributor], 1979-
   microfiches : negative + 1 user's manual

   Bimonthly.
   Title from header.
   Continues: Publications reference file.
   Supplement: GPO new sales publications.
   User's manual (on separate microfiche) has title: PRF
user's manual : a guide to using GPO sales publications
reference file. 1981.
   Contains three arrangements: stock number, Supt. of
Docs. classification number, and alphabetical sequence
which includes titles, series, key words, key phrases,
subjects and personal authors.
   Item 552-B (microfiche).
   S/N 721-002-00000-4.
   Supt. of Docs. no.: GP 3.22/3:
   Description based on: May 1979.

   I. United States. Superintendent of Documents. II.
United States. Government Printing Office. II. Title:
Publications reference file. III. Title: PRF. IV. Title:
P.R.F.

Comment	— Serial issued only in microformat.
Area 3	— Information not available about the first issue.
Area 4	— Date given as an open entry.
Area 5	— Three blank spaces are left before the word "micro-fiches" to indicate that the work is incomplete.
	— Negative image indicated.
	— User's manual is listed as accompanying material.
Area 7	— Frequency note.
	— Source of title given because it was not taken from the text on the fiche.
	— Relationship to other serials given in two notes. The earlier work and the supplement would be cataloged separately.
	— Location is given for the user's manual in fiche format.
	— Existence and location of the index given.
	— Three different numbers given on the item. Each is recorded in a separate note.
	— Issue that was the source of the description is given because this was not the first issue.

(Explanation continues on page 270.)

Added Entries—Access points provided for both governmental bodies associated with this work.
—Access points also provided for the title of the work this serial continued and variants of that title that affect filing.

Alternative catalog newsletter [microform]. — No. 2 (June 1978)-no. 26 (Dec. 1980). — Baltimore : Milton S. Eisenhower Library, Johns Hopkins University, 1978-1980.
   27 microfiches : negative.

   Bimonthly.
   No. 1 issued in hardcopy only.
   ISSN 0161-7192.

   I. Milton S. Eisenhower Library.

Comment	—Serial issued only in microformat after the first issue.
Area 3	—Beginning and ending numerical and chronological designations recorded.
Area 5	—Total number of fiches indicated. Some issues of the journal were contained on more than one fiche.
Area 7	—Editors are not normally identified for a serial unless their names are considered important in identifying the serial. This was not considered to be the case here.
Area 8	—International Standard Serial Number.
Added Entries	—Access point provided for the corporate body issuing the serial because its name is closely associated with the serial.

National newspaper index [microform]. — Apr.
   1979-   . — Belmont, Calif. : Information Access
   Co., c1979-
      microfilm reels ; 16 mm. + 1 user's guide.

    Monthly (cumulative).
    For use on an IAC Index microfilm reader.
    Information in the user's guide also present at the
beginning of the microfilm.
    Also available online through DIALOG and in an
annual microfiche cumulation.
    Index to: New York times, Wall Street journal,
Christian science monitor, Los Angeles times and
Washington post.
    ISSN 0273-3676

    I. Information Access Company. II. Title: IAC
national newspaper index. III. Title: I.A.C. national
newspaper index.

Area 5   —Size of microfilm is always given.
Area 7   —Note indicates that a specific type of reader must be
      used.
      —Other forms of availability indicated.
      —"Index to" note is used in place of a summary note
      for serials.
Added Entries—Access points provided for the name of the publisher
      and two variants of the title that include an acronym
      and an initialism for the publisher.

10
Access Points for Nonprint Materials

21.0 INTRODUCTORY RULES

After the cataloger has determined the content of the bibliographic description for a nonprint item, access points (i.e., headings) must be chosen to enable the user to locate the bibliographic record in the catalog. These access points relate to persons, corporate bodies, and titles associated with the item. This chapter addresses the selection of both main access points (main entries) and additional access points (added entries).

21.0B SOURCES FOR DETERMINING ACCESS POINTS

The preferred sources of information for choosing access points are closely related to the chief source(s) of information discussed in Rules 1.0A, 1.1A2, and the specific rules for chief sources of information given in each specific chapter for description. These rules are found under the mnemonic rule numbering structure .0B. "Sources of Information," which follows the chapter number (e.g., 6.0B, 8.0B, etc.). It has been indicated in previous chapters that the chief source of information and its acceptable substitutes differ from one descriptive chapter to another and may also vary for different formats within a chapter. Rule 21.0B strongly suggests that, generally, only statements appearing prominently in the chief source of information or its substitutes should be used in determining access points. Information in the content of the item or from outside the item is to be considered as access points only when statements appearing in the chief source are considered "ambiguous or insufficient."

At first, it may seem that these general directions are very restrictive and possibly eliminate access points which are necessary or useful in the retrieval of bibliographic records for nonprint materials in a library catalog, whether this catalog is manual or online. Just as the knowledge of the cataloger comes into play when determining the information to be recorded in the bibliographic description, this knowledge is also a critical factor in selecting appropriate and useful access points for the item. It should be remembered, however, that this general rule does not prohibit the use of information derived from virtually any source as an access point, but merely attempts to provide some structure to its selection. The rule does not state that the access point must be derived from information in the Title or Statement of Responsibility Area or from any other specific area of the description, but rather that it must come from the prescribed sources of information used to develop Area 1 statements. If the information is not recorded in Area 1, the relationship of the access points to the nonprint item should be made clear in the bibliographic description.

21.0D *OPTIONAL ADDITION.* DESIGNATION OF FUNCTION

This rule allows the cataloger to add to a heading an indication of the function an individual performed for a work. These indications of function are limited to four functions: compiler, editor, illustrator, and translator. These functions are only given using abbreviations (i.e., comp., ed., ill., and tr.). Generally, except for illustrators, these functions do not apply to most nonprint materials. The Library of Congress has indicated that it will not apply this option for nonprint materials.

21.1 BASIC RULE

21.1A. WORKS OF PERSONAL AUTHORSHIP

21.1A1 Definition

A person who is chiefly responsible for the intellectual or artistic content of a nonprint item is considered to be a "personal author." Individuals fulfilling this function may include artists, photographers, cartographers, composers, and in some cases, producers, directors, animators, or other individuals responsible for an original concept and general production of nonprint materials. In some cases, performers on films, videorecordings, and sound recordings are considered the personal authors of a work.

21.1A2 General rule

If one or more individuals are responsible for the intellectual or artistic content of a nonprint item, the main entry should be under the heading for the person responsible or the person principally responsible if more than one person is named. In some cases of "shared" or "mixed" personal authorship the first person named will be the main entry. Added entries can be made for other individuals according to the provisions of Rules 21.29-21.30.

The use of a personal author as the main entry varies considerably with different types of nonprint material. While the entry for many sound recordings and art works will be under the heading for a personal author, this type of heading is relatively rare for most nonprint materials, including motion pictures, videorecordings, filmstrips, slides, and three-dimensional artefacts and realia.

21.1B ENTRY UNDER A CORPORATE BODY

21.1B1 Definition

Corporate bodies most often responsible for the content of a nonprint item are associations, institutions, particularly educational institutions, nonprint publishers, government agencies, and conferences.

21.1B2 General rule

Entry under a corporate body requires that the work "emanate" from the corporate body and that it comes under one or more of the following categories:

a. works of an administrative nature related to the body itself,

b. some legal, governmental, or religious works,

c. works which record the collective thought of the body,

d. reports of the collective activity of a conference, expedition, or event provided it is prominently named,

e. activities of a performing group as a whole on a sound recording, video-recording, or film which extend beyond mere performance,

f. cartographic materials provided that the body functions as more than just the publisher or distributor.

It should be noted that category b. was revised slightly to include religious works by the 1983 Revisions to *AACR 2*, while category f. was added to the rules by the 1982 Revisions.

Under this rule, the requirements to be met for entry under corporate body are much more restrictive than those of previous cataloging codes. In general, for most nonprint materials, the usual involvement of a corporate body does not justify the entry of the work under that body. This is particularly true for publishers, whether they are commercial or nonprofit. There are, however, some exceptions to this generalization. Cartographic materials, sound recordings, videorecordings and films do come under categories e. and f. Thus the performance by a group on a sound recording which included the performance of only its own material would qualify for entry under the corporate body (the group). Additionally, a sound recording or videotape of a corporate meeting would qualify for entry under corporate body. Whenever doubt exists as to whether a work is included in one or more of the categories, the rule instructs the cataloger to conclude that it does not.

The Rule Interpretation of the Library of Congress to this rule provides additional background discussion and guidelines for its implementation. Specifically, as it affects nonprint materials, LC cautions that a performing group's contribution must exceed "mere" performance (category f.). LC indicates that this means that the group must be responsible "to a major degree" for the work's artistic content. For cartographic works (category e.), the cataloger is advised to consider the nature of the corporate body and its cartographic output, in addition to information about the cartography of the work, when deciding whether the body is the producer of the work.

21.1B3

Whenever a corporate body does not come under at least one of the categor-ies in Rule 21.1B2, the main entry should be chosen as though no corporate body were involved. It must be remembered that although Rule 21.1B2 might not allow a corporate body to be the main entry, it does not prohibit that body from being used as an added entry provided that the corporate body is prominently named and meets the conditions of Rule 21.30E (Added Entries — Corporate Bodies).

21.1C ENTRY UNDER TITLE

The title is used as the main entry under several circumstances which are common to nonprint materials:

1. When personal responsibility is unknown or diffuse and the work does not emanate from a corporate body.

Diffuse responsibility is defined in Rule 21.6C2 as responsibility "shared between more than three persons or corporate bodies where principal responsibility has not been attributed to any one, two, or three of them." This rule also calls for the provision of an added entry under the heading for the first named person or corporate body. For nonprint materials, additional added entries may also be needed for other persons or corporate bodies associated with the item, although the rule does not specifically prescribe their use.

2. Works which are collections or the result of editorial direction.

Edited works are not common to nonprint materials. Collections are more common, but their existence is most often confined to the sound recording format. Entry for collections and works produced under editorial direction are covered under Rule 21.7. These collections include independent works by different persons or corporate bodies, complete or extracted works, contributions to a work produced under editorial direction, or works which consist partially of independent works of personal authors or corporate bodies and partially of items produced under editorial direction. When these works possess a collective title, entry is made under the collective title (Rule 21.7B). Works which lack a collective title are entered under the heading appropriate for the entry of the first work in the collection (Rule 21.7C). The entry of collective sound recordings is covered by Rule 21.23 (Entry of Sound Recordings). This rule is discussed in greater detail later in this chapter.

3. Works which emanate from a corporate body but which do not come under the provisions of Rule 21.1B2.

When an item cannot be entered under a corporate body, the work is entered under the heading which would have been the main entry had the corporate body not been present. The first consideration would be entry under personal authorship or the heading for the person considered chiefly responsible as prescribed by the rule for entry of works of shared responsibility. When neither of these two situations applies, entry for the work is made under title. This latter situation is very common for most nonprint materials except sound recordings and microforms. Thus, although most nonprint materials are entered under title, it is not an automatic process as it was under earlier cataloging codes. In *AACR 2*, the cataloger must first consider entry under corporate body or personal author. Only when this type of entry is not possible is entry made under the title.

4. A work which has been accepted as sacred scripture.

This condition seldom applies to nonprint materials.

In a Rule Interpretation to Rule 21.1C, the Library of Congress has introduced a fifth circumstance for entry under title.

5. The work has contributions of more than one type and the statements of
    responsibility for each are given in the chief source of information in
    such a way as to "diminish the importance of the persons named in
    relation to the title."

This "interpretation" addresses a situation particularly common to nonprint
materials, especially motion pictures, videorecordings, filmstrips, and slides. It
requires entry under title whenever the contributions of the individuals, as stated
in their relation to the title, indicate that they are being given only "technical
credit" rather than artistic or intellectual credit for the content of the item.

21.4 WORKS FOR WHICH A SINGLE PERSON OR CORPORATE BODY IS RESPONSIBLE

Works for which one person or corporate body is responsible are entered
under the heading appropriate for that person or body.

21.8 WORKS OF MIXED RESPONSIBILITY. MODIFICATIONS OF OTHER WORKS

This rule addresses two different categories of modifications: (1) works
which are modifications of previously existing works and (2) works in which
different persons or corporate bodies have made differing contributions. Many
nonprint items are modifications of works previously published and thus come
under category 1. Their treatment is given in Rule 21.9.

21.9 WORKS THAT ARE MODIFICATIONS OF OTHER WORKS. GENERAL RULE

Works which "substantially" modify an original work's "nature," "content,"
or change its "medium of expression" should be entered under the heading
appropriate to the new work. For nonprint materials, this modification most
frequently involves a change from a print format to a nonprint one. Thus, for a
film version of a novel, entry would be under the heading appropriate for the film
rather than the heading for the original novel. Specific rules for the application of
this general rule are given in Rules 21.10 through 21.23.

21.16 ADAPTATIONS OF ART WORKS

Some materials which would be described using Chapter 8 or Chapter 10 will
come under this rule. An adaptation from one graphic medium to another would
be entered under the heading for the adapter (Rule 21.16A), while a reproduction of an art work would be entered under the heading appropriate for the
original work (Rule 21.16B). In each case, an added entry would be made for the
heading which was not chosen as the main entry.

Collections of reproductions of one artist are entered differently depending
upon whether the collection has accompanying text. If the collection has no
accompanying text, main entry is under the heading for the author with an added
entry for the artist (Rule 21.17A). If, however, the collection is accompanied by

text, the entry is made under the heading for the author of the text, if that person is named prominently in the chief source of information, with an added entry for the artist (Rule 21.17B). If this condition is not met, main entry is made under the heading for the artist. In cases of doubt, the cataloger should prefer main entry under the artist.

21.23 ENTRY OF SOUND RECORDINGS

21.23A One Work

A sound recording of one work, whether music or spoken word, should be entered under the heading for the work. The most common use of this rule would be the entry of a musical work under the heading for its composer. Added entries should be made for "principal" performers if there are fewer than four. (A footnote to this rule indicates that only performers stated prominently in the chief source of information should be considered to be "principal performers.") When there are four or more principal performers, an added entry for only the first named principal performer is called for. Some libraries may wish to deviate from this rule by making added entries for all principal performers rather than for three or fewer, if these performers are considered to be important access points for catalog users.

21.23B Two or More Works by the Same Person(s) or Body (Bodies)

A sound recording of two or more works by the same person(s) or corporate body (bodies) should be entered under the heading for these works. This usually results in entry under the personal author. Added entries should be made for three or fewer principal performers. As indicated in Rule 21.23A, if there are more than three principal performers, an added entry should be made only for the first named.

21.23C Works by Different Persons or Bodies. Collective Title

Sound recordings and music videos that contain works by different persons or corporate bodies should be entered under the heading for the person or body which is the principal performer if the work has a collective title. When there are two or three persons who are considered to be principal performers, main entry should be made under the heading for the first named with added entries made for the others. If there are four or more principal performers, main entry should be under title. The text of this rule was revised by the 1983 Revisions to *AACR 2*.

The intent of this rule is to provide the entry for the sound recording under the principal performer(s) who are considered the unifying element of the work. Ever since it was first used in *AACR 2* the feature of "principal performer" has caused problems in cataloging sound recordings. In recognition of these problems the Library of Congress eventually provided additional guidance to its catalogers in dealing with the principal performer issue. In an Interpretation to this rule, which also applies to Rule 21.23D, LC first discussed some of the problems inherent in the literal application of the rules. Several of these LC guidelines are given below:

- Persons who perform as members of a corporate body should not be considered as separate performers unless the name of the performer appears in conjunction with the name of the corporate body, for example, Frankie Valli and the Four Seasons, Huey Lewis and the News, etc. Related to this, LC also indicates that conductors and accompanists are not considered to be members of the corporate body with which they perform. Thus, they could be considered as principal performers.

- If there is only one performer named in the chief source of information, that performer should be treated as the principal performer. Where there are several performers named in the chief source of information, the principal performers are those given prominence. If all performers are given equal prominence, all are to be considered principal performers. If no performer is named on the chief source, the work should be treated as lacking a principal performer.

- Relative prominence should be based on the "wording, layout, and typography." Names printed in association with each other in the same size and style of writing are to be considered as having equal prominence. When the same size and style of writing are used, but the names appear in different places on the chief source of information, those in a superior position, that is, a higher position on the chief source, should be considered to have greater prominence. This principle of superior position is not applied to names appearing in a list.

21.23D Works by Different Persons or Bodies.
No Collective Title

This rule addresses sound recordings and music videos which lack a collective title, contain works by different persons or bodies, and are cataloged as a unit (Rule 6.1G2). The text was revised by the 1983 Revisions to *AACR 2*.

The rule divides these works into two categories. The first category consists of sound recordings where the participation of the performer(s) extends beyond mere performance or interpretation. This type of performer participation is common for jazz, rock, and popular music. The second category involves sound recordings where performance does not extend beyond mere performance or interpretation. This is commonly the case with classical and other forms of "serious" music.

For works covered by the first category, entry should be made under principal performer. If there are two or three principal performers, main entry is made under the first named with added entries for the others. Where there are either no principal performers or four or more principal performers, main entry should be made under the heading appropriate to the first named work.

A LC Rule Interpretation to Rule 21.7B is related to this rule. This Interpretation deals with sound recording collections which have twenty-five or fewer musical works entered under two or more headings requiring analytical added entries for up to fifteen analytical works. This interpretation presents a series of conditions which will determine the number of analytical entries appropriate in a variety of conditions. It excludes the provision of these analytical entries for: (1) works requiring more than fifteen analytical added entries; (2) "pop, folk, ethnic, or jazz" music; (3) recitals with a performer orientation rather than musical repertoires; or (4) incomplete multipart items.

Works in the second category, those where performance does not extend beyond mere performance or interpretation, should have their entry made under the heading appropriate to the first work, with added entries made for the other works (Rule 21.7C). This latter rule, as interpreted by the Library of Congress, calls for analytical added entries for the other works provided that there are fifteen or fewer works entered under two or more different headings. The situations under which analytical added entries would not be made under Rule 21.7B, mentioned above, also apply to Rule 21.7C.

21.29 GENERAL RULE FOR ADDED ENTRIES

Access points provided by added entries are extremely important for non-print materials. The frequent use of the title as the main entry for nonprint items will often necessitate the provision of additional entries which might be of use to the library patron in retrieving a catalog record. These added entries could include all or some of the persons and corporate bodies having responsibility for the item. Although some of the rules for the determination of main entry instruct the cataloger to make added entries for specific types of individuals or groups, the provision of added entries is not restricted to those individuals or groups. Other added entries could be provided if they are necessary or useful access points for the catalog user. Some of these entries are provided for under Rule 21.30.

Conceivably, any heading, whether person or corporate body or title, under which a catalog user might assume a nonprint item is entered, is a candidate to be an added entry. In support of this principle, Rule 21.29B allows for the use of an added entry for any person, corporate body, or title if "some catalogue users" might think that the item has been entered under a heading or title other than the one used as the main entry. Additionally, added entries beyond those called for by this rule which seem appropriate "in the context of a given catalogue" are allowed under the provisions of Rule 21.29D.

Added entries should be justified by information provided somewhere in the description although this information does not need to appear in the body of the entry. Thus, notes are a prime source for information upon which to base added entries. This is particularly important to cataloging agencies which use level one description or in other ways limit their use of notes.

AACR 2 does not specify any particular order for the arrangement of tracings. In an Interpretation to Rule 21.29 the Library of Congress has prescribed the following order of tracings for its catalogers:

1. Personal Name

2. Personal Name. Title

3. Corporate Name

4. Corporate Name. Title

5. Uniform Title

6. Title traced as "Title-period"

7. Title traced as "Title-colon"

Within these categories, LC indicates that the order of the entries should reflect the order in which the related data appear in the bibliographic description.

21.30 SPECIFIC RULES FOR ADDED ENTRIES

These rules describe specific instances or relationships in which individuals or corporate bodies might be considered as additional access points for a work. Those instances or relationships which are particularly important for handling nonprint materials include collaborators, writers, corporate bodies, and related works.

Generally, when one, two, or three persons or corporate bodies are associated in a given capacity with an item, added entries are made for those name headings which are not the main entry. If four or more persons or bodies are similarly associated, an added entry is made only for the heading for the first named. However, if the library finds it to be important that the other headings also serve as access points, Rule 21.29D gives license to do so.

Rules 21.29 and 21.30 are primarily oriented toward functions performed by persons and corporate bodies associated with print materials. Because of this, the Library of Congress has issued Interpretations to these rules which provide additional guidance for the creation of added entries for nonprint materials. LC indicates first that added entries should be made for all "openly named" persons and corporate bodies who have made contributions to the creation of the work.

In addition to this broad guideline, LC provides more detailed guidance. It indicates that added entries should be provided for directors, producers, and writers, as well as for other individuals if their contribution is considered "significant." Excluded from this are works for which an added entry has been made for a production unit or company. In this situation, added entries would be provided for persons only if their contributions are considered to be "significant."

LC further indicates that, in those situations in which a person is the main entry, added entries should not be made for other persons who have contributed to the creation of the item unless the work is known to be a work of "joint responsibility or collaboration" or if the contributions of the persons are determined to be "significant." Added entries should also be made for individuals who interview others, are interviewed, or deliver addresses, lectures, etc. Similarly, added entries should be provided for persons who discuss their lives, work, etc.

According to LC, added entries generally should be made for "featured players, performers, and narrators." If there are many players, added entries should only be made for those players prominently given in the chief source of information. When this cannot be used as a criterion, added entries are provided for each player unless there are more than three.

An exception to this instruction is made for motion pictures and videorecordings where main entry is under the heading for a performing group. In these situations, no added entry should be made for individual members of the performing group. If the name of one of the members of the group precedes or follows the group's name, that person should not be considered to be a member of the group. This then allows an access point to be made for the heading for that person. This Interpretation by LC for motion pictures and videorecordings is similar to their Interpretation for sound recordings, discussed earlier.

Guidance in the provision of added entries for performers named on sound recordings was issued by LC in a Rule Interpretation to Rule 21.29D. Here, LC instructed that added entries should not be made for persons who functioned primarily as members of a corporate body for which an added entry has been provided. Some additional LC guidelines for sound recordings follow:

- Conductors and accompanists should not be considered to be members of the bodies they conduct or accompany; thus added entries could be provided for them. Similarly, an individual whose name precedes the name of a group is not to be considered a member of the group and, thus, could be traced.

- Added entries for members of unnamed jazz ensembles should generally be made even if one or more of the members are given greater prominence than the others. Added entries should not be made for members of an unnamed group which accompanies a featured performer. Added entries are also not made for persons who participate in only a small number of works in a collection or for persons whose role is considered minor.

- When many persons are performing the same function, added entries should only be made for those persons given the "greatest prominence" in the chief source of information. If all are treated identically in the chief source, prominence should be established from information found on other places on the sound recording. If this does not solve the problem, added entries should be provided only for those persons performing the "most important" functions.

- When both the chorus and the orchestra of an opera company perform on a sound recording, an added entry should be given only for the heading of the parent body. An additional Interpretation to Rule 21.30E indicates, however, that if an added entry is also needed for either the chorus or orchestra, that added entry could also be made.

- If a performer's role is minor, or if the performer only participates in a few works in a collection, no added entry would be made for the performer.

- If the heading for a performer is made an access point, and that performer is also the composer of one or more works on the sound recording, added entries (name. title) should also be made for those works.

21.30B COLLABORATORS

For collaborators, whether personal or corporate, added entries should be made for up to three collaborators. If the main entry is made under the heading for one or two or three collaborators, added entries should be made for the other collaborator(s). When the main entry is under a corporate body or under the title, added entries should be made for up to three collaborators. If there are four or more collaborators, an added entry should be made only for the first named.

21.30E CORPORATE BODIES

Any prominently named corporate body can be represented by an added entry. Excluded from this general provision are corporate bodies functioning exclusively as distributors and manufacturers. Publishers are also excluded unless their responsibility extends beyond that of mere publishing.

The contributions of many publishers of nonprint materials do extend beyond the business function of publishing to the point where some publishers are named in the statement of responsibility. In most instances, however, the publisher will be named only in the Publication, Distribution, etc., Area. Regardless of where the publisher's name appears in the description, if its function is sufficiently broad, an added entry can be made for it. Publishers of many nonprint items are often more prominently represented on the item than are other persons associated with the work. Likewise, many catalog users often consider the publisher of a nonprint item as its author. Because of these factors, catalogers should seriously consider making added entries for publishers of nonprint materials under the provisions of Rule 21.29B. The Library of Congress has standardized this approach for its catalogers by instructing in a Rule Interpretation that added entries should be made for all corporate bodies of audiovisual materials mentioned in the Publication, Distribution, etc., Area.

21.30G RELATED WORKS

Nonprint materials based on other print or nonprint items, or associated with other published works in any way, may need to have their relationship to those items expressed in the description of the record. It should be emphasized that the mere provision of a note to express a relationship of a related or associated work does nothing to enhance retrieval of the new item based on the user's knowledge of the relationship. Thus, access to the related or associated record needs to be further established through the provision of an access point for it. Remakes, sequels, reissues with different titles, or the names of authors and titles related to the item may provide valuable access to nonprint media.

In an Interpretation to this rule, LC indicates that, when establishing these added entries for related works, the form of the entry should conform with the main entry, form of heading, and form of title appropriate for the related work. This means that when making an added entry for a related monograph, a cataloger should begin the entry with the main entry element for that related work, written in its proper form, followed by the title, when appropriate.

21.30J TITLES

Although many types of nonprint materials, such as motion pictures, filmstrips, artefacts, realia, etc., frequently have main entry under title, other nonprint materials, such as sound recordings, cartographic materials, etc., often have their main entry under a person or corporate body. Whenever the main entry is made under an entry other than title, a decision must also be made as to whether to provide access to the work through its title. *AACR 2* indicates that an added entry should be made for the title proper of works where the main entry is under a personal, corporate or uniform title heading unless one of four conditions exists. These four conditions are:

1. the title proper and the main entry, or its reference, are "essentially" identical.

2. the title proper has been supplied by the cataloger.

3. the title proper and a subject heading, or its reference, are identical and the catalog records are to be filed in a dictionary catalog.

4. a "conventional" uniform title has been used as the main entry for a musical work.

The conditions covered under 2, 3, and 4 are relatively common occurrences when dealing with nonprint materials, particularly the use of supplied titles for three-dimensional artefacts and realia and some graphic materials and the use of uniform titles for sound recordings.

In its Interpretation to this rule, the Library of Congress indicates that it does not intend to apply the restrictions stated in 1 and 3 above, and will provide title added entries for these works. Furthermore, although LC does not provide title added entries for uniform titles, it will provide an added entry for a title proper that is the same as the uniform title.

In addition to these exceptions to the *AACR 2* rule, LC provides further guidance to its catalogers in the assignment of additional title added entries beyond the added entry for the title proper. Some of these instructions are the result of the effects of computer-assisted filing and its resultant filing rules and computer indexes created for records in an online catalog. The situations LC covers in its Interpretation are many and varied and too lengthy to be given in their entirety in this text. Catalogers should consult the LC Rule Interpretations to Rule 21.30J for more detailed information. Listed below are some of the major situations in which additional title added entries would be provided by LC.

- Alternative titles.

- Titles stated in Area 1 in a work which lack a collective title.

- Cover titles, parallel titles, and added title page titles when they differ "significantly" from the title proper.

- Caption titles, half titles, running titles, and other title information. These are provided as title access points only if the work was also published under that title, or is cited in reference sources by that title, or in some way receives "prominence" that would influence users to search under that title rather than the main entry.

- Titles with abbreviations in the first five words. The added entry is made for the title with the word for which the abbreviation stands spelled out.

- Portions of a title within a title, if this part of the title is considered to be a likely access point for users of the catalog.

- Titles where an ampersand is used in the first five words. The additional title would replace the ampersand with the word "and."

- Corrected titles.

- Titles with letters, acronyms, or initialisms in the first five words. If the title proper includes spacing or punctuation between the letters, an additional added entry is made for the title without spacing or punctuation between the letters. However, if the title proper has no spaces or punctuation between the letters, no additional access point would generally be made for the title with spaces or punctuation between the letters.

- Titles where numbers, including nondate Roman numerals, occur in the first five words. This practice would also be followed if an access point were made for "other title information" and the number occurred in its first five words.

- Titles where a sign or symbol occurs in the first five words. The additional title added entry is made for the title with the sign or symbol replaced by its name, or written form. This added entry is only provided if the word or name can be stated concisely and the additional title is considered to be a likely access point for users.

- Titles where a statement of responsibility precedes the title in the title proper and its uniform title excludes the statement of responsibility. The additional title access point is made for the part of the title which follows the statement of responsibility.

- Situations where data in the first five words of the title might likely be sought by users of the catalog under another form. In these cases, an additional added title added entry would be provided for that form.

As a final point of guidance, LC indicates that in situations in which the title of a work comes under several of the situations listed above, additional title added entries need not be made for each situation. Instead, LC instructs its catalogers to make title access points for only the "most useful" title elements.

21.30L SERIES

The general instruction given by this rule calls for an added entry for each separately cataloged work in a series. As an option to the rule, a cataloger can also provide the numeric or other designation given to the work. The Library of Congress is applying this option.

The rule also indicates that added entries should not be made for a series where (a) the items in the series share only common physical characteristics or (b) where the numbering of the series implies that the series information is used "primarily for stock control or to benefit from lower postage rates." A third restriction not to make series added entries for author series was cancelled by the 1982 Revisions to *AACR 2*. When the cataloger is in doubt as to whether a series should be traced or not, the rules instruct the cataloger to make the series added entry.

In an Interpretation to this rule, the Library of Congress has indicated that it intends to continue to follow its previous practice under *AACR 1* by restricting, to some degree, the use of series access points for some series beyond that called for by *AACR 2*. Specifically, LC traces the following types of series:

a. those published before the twentieth century. This also includes reprints of these works.

b. works entered under a personal author. The type of publisher of the item is not a factor in making this access point decision nor is the fact that the item is a multipart item a consideration.

c. publications of a noncommercial corporate body. University presses are treated as noncommercial publishers.

d. publications of small or "alternative" presses even though these may be commercial publishers.

Not all of these categories affect nonprint materials equally. Categories a. and b. will probably require the generation of more series added entries for nonprint materials than will categories c. and d.

In addition to listing conditions under which it will provide series access points, the Library of Congress also has issued a series of conditions, in addition to those already given in the existing rule, under which no series added entry should be made by its catalogers. These extra conditions include:

a. series issued by commercial publishers in which the series title indicates "primarily" a literary genre. This condition applies regardless of whether the publisher's name is part of the series title or not. LC does caution that, in cases where the series title narrows the literary form or addresses the form to a particular audience, the series title should not be considered to be one that is "primarily" a literary genre.

b. series issued by commercial publishers in which the series title indicates little about the "content, genre, audience, or purpose" of the items within the series.

c. unnumbered subseries within a numbered main series where that subseries title contributes nothing to the subject matter of the title of the main series.

LC further indicates that, if a series falls into those situations in which LC has instructed both to provide a series added entry and not to provide a series added entry, the entry should be made. LC also advises that in cases of doubt series added entries should be made, as well as in cases in which the cataloger feels that the series would serve a "useful colocation" purpose regardless of the lack of informative words in the series title.

As was the case with LC policies dealing with which series should be provided access points, some of the conditions in which LC will not make series added entries are more pertinent to nonprint materials than others. Conditions b. and c. are situations commonly encountered with nonprint series. Considering the relatively high frequency of the use of series for some types of nonprint materials, and the need to limit the catalog to only useful access points because of the negative retrieval factors introduced by unnecessary size, the use of the LC restrictions on the assignment of series added entries is advisable for most, if not all, multimedia libraries.

GENERAL MATERIAL DESIGNATORS

Prior to 1981, the Library of Congress added medium designators, the fore-runners of *AACR 2*'s GMDs, to all entries, including added entries, for nonprint materials in all but a few instances. In *AACR 2*, the use of GMDs in added entries for nonprint materials is not directly addressed. In *Cataloging Service Bulletin* (no. 10, Fall 1980, p. 14), LC changed this policy. In its statement LC noted that different international cataloging agencies have differing policies regarding the use of GMDs. Because of this, LC adopted a policy of ignoring the GMD when filing upon the Title and Statement of Responsibility Area. As an adjunct to this policy, LC indicated that it was not adopting the option of providing a GMD in a uniform title (Rule 25.5E). In a further clarification of this policy (*CSB* no. 15, Winter 1982, p. 32), LC indicated that exclusion of GMDs from titles applied to all title added entries, whether uniform titles or any other type. Thus, catalog records issued by LC for nonprint materials will not include GMDs as part of title or series added entries.

Some multimedia librarians may consider this practice by the Library of Congress as one which deprives users of useful information in selecting appropriate documents. One case in point is the situation in which a filmstrip is based upon a motion picture. If an added entry is provided for the motion picture, it will only indicate the title of the work rather than follow it with a GMD. Previously, the added entry would have consisted of the title of the motion picture followed by the media designator "motion picture" in brackets. Thus, unless users read the edition and history note on the catalog record, they will not know whether the added entry represents a book, a sound recording, etc. Multimedia librarians may wish to reexamine the effects of LC's decision in light of their own users' needs before adopting this LC policy. This is particularly true if the library currently uses the GMD as a filing element. Any library deviating from the LC policy should consider the implications of this decision in terms of the work involved of modifying all LC cataloging to conform to the library's local decision.

Appendix A
Aids for Cataloging Nonprint Materials

CATALOGING RULES

AACR 2 AND REVISIONS

Anglo-American Cataloguing Rules, 2d ed. Edited by Michael Gorman and Paul W. Winkler. Chicago: American Library Association, 1978.

Anglo-American Cataloguing Rules. Second Edition. Revisions. Chicago: American Library Association, 1982.

Anglo-American Cataloguing Rules. Second Edition. Revisions 1983. Chicago: American Library Association, 1984.

Anglo-American Cataloguing Rules. Second Edition. Revisions 1985. Chicago: American Library Association, 1986.

American Library Association. Committee on Cataloging. Description and Access. Guidelines for Using AACR2 Chapter 9 for Cataloging Microcomputer Software. Chicago: American Library Association, 1984. (Superseded by the 1987 draft revision of Chapter 9.)

Anglo-American Cataloguing Rules. Second Edition. Chapter 9, Computer Files. Edited for the Joint Steering Committee for Revision of AACR by Michael Gorman. Draft Revision. Chicago: American Library Association, 1987.

AACR 1 AND REVISIONS

Anglo-American Cataloging Rules, North American text. Chicago: American Library Association, 1967.

Anglo-American Cataloging Rules. North American Text. Chapter 6, Separately Published Monographs. Chicago: American Library Association, 1974.

Anglo-American Cataloging Rules. North American Text. Chapter 12 Revised, Audiovisual Media and Special Instructional Materials. Chicago: American Library Association, 1975.

Anglo-American Cataloging Rules. North American Text. Chapter 14 Revised, Sound Recordings. Chicago: American Library Association, 1976.

INTERNATIONAL STANDARD BIBLIOGRAPHIC DESCRIPTIONS

International Federation of Library Associations and Institutions. *ISBD(M), International Standard Bibliographic Description for Monographic Publications,* 1st standard ed. rev. London: IFLA International Office for UBC, 1978.

International Federation of Library Associations and Institutions. Joint Working Group on the International Standard Bibliographic Description for Cartographic Materials. *ISBD(CM), International Standard Bibliographic Description for Cartographic Materials.* London: IFLA International Office for UBC, 1977.

International Federation of Library Associations and Institutions. Joint Working Group on the International Standard Bibliographic Description for Printed Music. *ISBD(PM), International Standard Bibliographic Description for Printed Music.* London: IFLA International Office for UBC, 1980.

International Federation of Library Associations and Institutions. Working Group on the General International Standard Bibliographic Description. *ISBD(G), General International Standard Bibliographic Description,* annotated text. London: IFLA International Office for UBC, 1977.

International Federation of Library Associations and Institutions. Working Group on the International Standard Bibliographic Description for Non-Book Materials. *ISBD(NBM), International Standard Bibliographic Description for Non-Book Materials.* London: IFLA International Office for UBC, 1977.

LIBRARY OF CONGRESS CATALOGS

Selected LC catalogs containing cataloging information for nonprint materials. For distribution information consult the most recent issue of *Catalogs and Technical Publications* of the Cataloging Distribution Service of the Library of Congress. This publication also contains information on reprint editions available for Library of Congress publications which are out-of-print.

CATALOGS OF AUDIOVISUAL MATERIALS

Audiovisual Materials. [microform]. 1983- .
Contains Library of Congress catalog records for "motion pictures, filmstrips, transparency and slide sets and videorecordings and kits." These data

were previously available in the book format of *Audiovisual Materials*. Microfiche. Issued quarterly with cumulative indexes.

Audiovisual Materials. 1979-1982.
Contains Library of Congress catalog records for "motion pictures, filmstrips, transparency and slide sets, videorecordings and kits."

Films and Other Materials for Projection. 1973-1978.
Contains Library of Congress catalog records for "motion pictures, filmstrips, sets of transparencies, slide sets and videorecordings."

Library of Congress Catalog: Motion Pictures and Filmstrips. 1953-1972.
Contains Library of Congress catalog records for "motion pictures and filmstrips."

Library of Congress Author Catalog. 1951-1952.
Contains Library of Congress catalog records for "motion pictures and filmstrips."

CATALOGS OF CARTOGRAPHIC MATERIALS

National Union Catalog. Cartographic Materials [microform]. 1983- .
Contains catalog records of "single sheet maps, map sets, atlases and maps treated as serials" cataloged by the Library of Congress and contributing libraries. Microfiche. Issued quarterly with cumulative indexes.

Library of Congress Catalog: Maps and Atlases. 1953-1955.
Contains Library of Congress catalog records for "maps, relief models, globes and geographical atlases."

Library of Congress Author Catalog. 1950-1952.
Includes Library of Congress catalog records for maps and atlases.

Cumulative Catalog of Library of Congress Printed Cards. 1947-1949.
Includes Library of Congress catalog records for maps and atlases.

CATALOGS OF MICROFORMS

National Register of Microform Masters. 1965-1983.
Lists microfilmed materials for which master negatives exist. It includes monographs, dissertations, pamphlets, and serials. Microform masters are now reported in *NUC Books* and *New Serial Titles*.

CATALOGS OF MUSIC MATERIALS

Music, Books on Music and Sound Recordings. 1973- .
Contains catalog records from the Library of Congress and other contributing North American libraries for "music scores, sheet music, libretti, books about music and musicians and sound recordings."

Library of Congress Catalog: Music and Phonorecords. 1953-1972.
Contains catalog records from the Library of Congress and other contributing North American libraries for "music scores, sheet music, libretti, books about music and musicians and sound recordings."

NATIONAL LIBRARY OF MEDICINE CATALOGS

Health Science Audiovisuals [microform]. 1984- .
Cumulates all catalog records for audiovisuals cataloged by NLM from 1975 to date. Microfiche. Quarterly.

National Library of Medicine Audiovisuals Catalog. 1978- .
Contains National Library of Medicine catalog records for all audiovisual materials cataloged since 1978. Beginning in 1984, indexed citations for audiovisual serials are included in an appendix. This information was previously published in the *Index to Audiovisual Serials in the Health Sciences.* Issued quarterly. The fourth quarterly issue is an annual cumulation.

National Library of Medicine Audiovisuals Catalog, Annual Cumulation 1977.
Contains the citations which appeared in the AVLINE section of the 1977 issues of NLM's *Current Catalog.*

National Library of Medicine AVLINE Catalog, 1975-1976.
Contains entries for works added to AVLINE during 1975 and 1976. Arranged by subject with bibliographic data. No access provided by name or title.

NICEM CATALOGS

Audiovisual cataloging records developed by the National Information Center for Educational Media. These publications are issued in new editions independent of each other. Publication began in 1968. Place and publisher varies. Available in print format, microfiche, CD-ROM, and online from DIALOG. The DIALOG file (File 46) is titled *A-V Online.*

Audiocassette Finder. 1st ed. 1987.
Replaces *Index to Educational Audio Tapes.*

Film and Video Finder. 1st ed. 1987.
Replaces *Index to 16mm Educational Films* and *Index to Educational Videotapes.*

Index to 8mm Motion Cartridges. 6th ed. 1980.
Discontinued with this edition.

Index to 16mm Educational Films. 8th ed. 1984.
Discontinued with this edition. Replaced by *Film and Video Finder.*

Index to 35mm Educational Filmstrips. 8th ed. 1985.
Discontinued with this edition. Replaced by *Audiocassette Finder.*

Index to Educational Audio Tapes. 5th ed. 1980.

Index to Educational Overhead Transparencies. 6th ed. 1980.
Discontinued with this edition.

Index to Educational Records. 5th ed. 1980.
Discontinued with this edition.

Index to Educational Slides. 4th ed. 1980.
Discontinued with this edition.

Index to Educational Videotapes. 6th ed. 1985.
Discontinued with this edition. Replaced by *Film and Video Finder.*

Index to Producers and Distributors. 6th ed. 1985.

ONLINE BIBLIOGRAPHIC UTILITIES

National Library of Medicine. AVLINE.
Contains all NLM cataloging of audiovisual materials since 1975.

OCLC Online Computer Library Center. *Online Union Catalog.*

Research Libraries Group. Research Libraries Information Network.

OTHER CATALOGING AIDS

GENERAL

Library of Congress. *Cataloging Service Bulletin.* 1978- . ISSN 0160-8029.
Provides current information on Library of Congress practices in the areas of descriptive cataloging, classification, subject cataloging, and publications. Quarterly.

Library of Congress. *Library of Congress Information Bulletin.* 1941- . ISSN 0041-7904.
Provides current information on Library of Congress projects, internal activities, publications, and summaries of meetings of national library associations. Weekly.

On-Line Audiovisual Catalogers Newsletter. Vol. 1- , 1981- . ISSN 0739-1153.
Provides information related to problems associated with cataloging non-print materials online, particularly with OCLC. The cataloging information provided is generally of value to libraries who are not cataloging their audiovisual materials online. Bimonthly.

SPECIFIC NONPRINT MATERIAL FORMATS

Cartographic Materials

Anglo-American Cataloguing Committee for Cartographic Materials. *Cartographic Materials: A Manual of Interpretation for AACR2*. Chicago: American Library Association, 1982.

Maps Online Users Group. *Map Online Users Group Newsletter*. No. 1- , 1982- . ISSN 0749-338X.
Quarterly.

Sound Recordings

Music Library Association. *Music Cataloging Bulletin*. Vol. 1- . Ann Arbor, Mich.: Music Library Association, 1970- .
Monthly.

Motion Pictures and Videorecordings

White-Hensen, Wendy. *Archival Moving Image Materials: A Cataloging Manual*. Washington, D.C.: Library of Congress, 1984.

Graphic Materials

Betz, Elizabeth W. *Graphic Materials: Rules for Describing Original Items and Historical Collections*. Washington, D.C.: Library of Congress, 1982.

Zinkham, Helena, and Elizabeth Betz Parker. *Descriptive Terms for Graphic Materials: Genre and Physical Characteristic Headings*. Washington, D.C.: Library of Congress, 1986.

Computer Files

Dodd, Sue A. *Cataloging Machine-Readable Data Files: An Interpretive Manual*. Chicago: American Library Association, 1982.

Dodd, Sue A., and Ann M. Sandberg-Fox. *Cataloging Microcomputer Files: A Manual of Interpretation for AACR2*. Chicago: American Library Association, 1985.

Index

National Information Center for Educational Media, 4, 17, 290-91
National Library of Medicine catalogs, 290
Nature, scope, or artistic forms of item,
notes on
cartographic materials, 50
microforms, 261
motion pictures and videorecordings,
125. *See also* Note area
sound recordings, 82
three-dimensional artefacts and realia,
236
Negatives
microforms, 260
Networks, 1, 3, 6-7, 9
NICEM. *See* National Information Center
for Educational Media
Nonprint media material collections, 5-7
in academic libraries, 6
in public libraries, 6, 9
in school libraries, 5-6
in special collections, 5-6
in special libraries, 6-7
user needs, x, 7-8
Nonprint media materials, 1-4
cataloging of, prior to *AACR 2*, ix, 8-9
collections, 5-7
definition, 27-35
standardization of terminology, 2-3, 7,
20-21, 26
Nonprocessed sound recordings, 92. *See
also* Sound recordings
Note area, 14-15
cartographic materials, 49-54
computer files, 195-206
general rules, 40-41
graphic materials, 161-71
microforms, 256-57, 261-65
motion pictures and videorecordings,
125-34
sound recordings, 82-92
three-dimensional artefacts and realia,
236-41
Notes
optional nature of, 14-15
Numbers
borne by items, notes on, 18
cartographic materials, 54
computer files, 204-5
graphic materials, 170
microforms, 264
sound recordings, 82, 91
three-dimensional artefacts and realia,
240

Online catalogs, 5
Open Systems Interconnection, 6. *See also*
Levels of description; Users' needs
Other formats available. *See* Alternative
formats

Paintings. *See* Art originals; Art works;
Graphic materials
"Partial generality," 14
Performers
motion pictures and videorecordings
notes on, 126-28. *See also* Access
points
sound recordings, 69
notes on, 85-86. *See also* Access
points: sound recordings
statement of responsibility, 85-86
Personal authors
entry under general rule, 273. *See also*
Access points
Photographs. *See* Graphic materials
Physical description area
accompanying materials (general rules),
39
cartographic materials, 48-49
computer files, 192-94. *See also* File
characteristics area
general rules, 38-39
graphic materials, 155-60
notes on, 165-66
items available in different format, 39,
89-90
microforms, 256, 259-61
notes on, 262-63
motion pictures and videorecordings,
117-24
notes on, 122, 130-31
sound recordings, 75-81
notes on, 87-89
three-dimensional artefacts and realia,
233-35
notes on, 237-38
Pictures. *See also* Graphic materials
definition, 32
Playing speed
sound recordings, 78-79
videorecordings, 123
Playing time
motion pictures and videorecordings, 118
sound recordings, 75-76
Prescribed sources of information. *See*
Sources of information